SCIENCE OF PSI
ESP AND PK

SCIENCE OF PSI

ESP AND PK

By

CARROLL B. NASH, Ph.D.

Professor of Biology
Director of the Parapsychology Laboratory
St. Joseph's University
Philadelphia, Pennsylvania

CHARLES C THOMAS • **PUBLISHER**
Springfield • Illinois • U.S.A.

Published and Distributed Throughout the World by
CHARLES C THOMAS • PUBLISHER
BANNERSTONE HOUSE
301-327 East Lawrence Avenue, Springfield, Illinois, U.S.A.

© *1978, by* CHARLES C THOMAS • PUBLISHER
ISBN 0-398-03803-1
Library of Congress Catalog Card Number: 78-2689

Printed in the United States of America
N-1

Library of Congress Cataloging in Publication Data

Nash, Carroll B., 1914-
    Science of psi.

    Bibliography: p. 250
    Includes index.
    1. Psychical research. I. Title.
BF1031.N36   133.8   78-2689
ISBN 0-398-03803-1

PREFACE

THE PURPOSE of this book is to make a systematic and orderly presentation of the chaotic accumulation of experiences, experiments, and hypotheses pertaining to the paranormal, with the desire of furthering the establishment of the study of psi as a science. Grateful recognition is given to those who have preceded me in this task and to the individuals who will follow in the endeavor. Important findings may have been overlooked, and appreciation will be given to readers of this treatise who call them to my attention. Some reports were omitted because they were confirmations of previous discoveries, and others were left out because they were questionable. To some readers the judgment in the latter case will seem to have been overdemanding, while to others it will appear to have been too credulous. In the latter case, the reader is referred to the original article for forming his own judgment concerning it.

In addition to surveying and coordinating the field of parapsychology both for the nonspecialist and for the psi researcher, this work is designed to be used as a text or as a reference book for courses in psychical science or for courses which include paranormal phenomena within their province. For the student, the study of parapsychology affords a better introduction to the scientific method than is offered by most sciences. Instead of being taught against a background of established facts and explanations, psychic science provides the students with the opportunity of applying the scientific method to unsolved problems.

Indebtedness is expressed to the Rand Corporation for allowing use in Table I of the Appendix a portion from *A Million Random Digits with 100,000 Normal Deviates;* to F. E. Croxton for permission to reprint in Tables II and V of the Appendix portions of *Tables of Areas in Two Tails and in One Tail of the Normal Curve* and *Values of F* copyright 1949 by Prentice-Hall,

v

Inc.; to R. A. Fisher and to Oliver and Boyd, Ltd., of Edinburgh for permission to reprint, in Tables III and IV of the Appendix, portions of Tables III and IV from *Statistical Tables for Biological, Agricultural, and Medical Research.* I am grateful to Rex Stanford, Vincent Ryan, Catherine Nash and John Kearney for their invaluable criticisms of portions of the manuscript.

CONTENTS

SCIENCE OF PSI
ESP AND PK

Chapter 1

INTRODUCTION

*P*si,* represented by the Greek letter ψ, is action not mediated by presently known physical means between objects at least one of which is living or possesses mind. How far mind extends down the scale of living organisms and, perhaps, inanimate objects, and whether it exists after death are questions yet to be answered. Evidence of psi is provided by spontaneous and induced experiences and by experimental studies. *Psychical research* and *parapsychology* are terms commonly used for the science of psi, which may come to be also called *psiology*. Eventually, parapsychology and psychology may be combined into a single science of *psychics* treating of mind and complementing physics, which deals with matter and energy.

Although psychical research has made use of the scientific method at least since the middle of the nineteenth century, it was not officially recognized as a science until 1969 when the American Association for the Advancement of Science accepted the Parapsychological Association as an affiliated organization. Like other sciences, parapsychology has laws and principles which are unique to it and are not simply extrapolations of those belonging to other fields.

Psi is divisible into *psi gamma* (psi γ) or *extrasensory perception (ESP)* and *psi kappa* (psi κ) or *psychokinesis (PK)*. Psi gamma is the incoming or perceptive branch of psi. It is analagous to sensory function but is extrasensory, i.e. without the use of sense organs. Psi kappa is the outgoing or active branch of psi. It is analagous to motor activity but is extramotor, i.e. without the use of motor organs such as muscles and glands. These two *modalities* or manners of occurrence of psi have been traditionally studied with the use of cards and dice, respectively. ESP is

---

*Key terms or their derivatives appear in italics when first used and are defined in the glossary.

3

measurable by identifying the hidden faces of cards, while PK may be indicated by causing the selected faces of randomly moving dice to land uppermost.

ESP is the mental response of a perceiving entity to an external event without the use of sense organs. The response may be at an unconscious level. ESP has three principal modalities: *telepathy*, *clairvoyance*, and *precognition*. Telepathy is extrasensory response to the mental state of another entity, while clairvoyance is extrasensory response to a physical state. Precognition is extrasensory response to a future state. Distinction between these three modalities of ESP can be illustrated on the basis of the method by which each is tested with a deck of cards. In telepathy, commonly called thought transference, the *subject* or *percipient* attempts to identify each card after the *agent* looks at it. In clairvoyance, the subject calls each card before the *experimenter* or anyone else sees it. Because no one else knows the *target* face when the percipient attempts to identify it, clairvoyance is not mind reading but is direct perception of the target object. In precognition, which may be utilized in prophecy, the subject calls the cards before their future order is determined. After his calls have been recorded, the cards are placed in a new arrangement, which is compared with the order predicted by the subject.

PK (psychokinesis), another modality of psi, is mental influence on a physical state without the use of motor organs. In PK the affected physical state may be a material object already in motion, such as a randomly rolling die that is caused to land with a selected face uppermost, or it may be a stationary object such as a compass needle that is paranormally set in motion.

Psychic phenomena may take place spontaneously or they may be induced to occur. While *spontaneous psi phenomena* are studied in natural settings, *induced psi phenomena* can be tested under experimental conditions. *Paranormal* events, whether spontaneous or induced, may be manifested either by mental response shown by the subject's behavior, as in ESP, or by an object's physical response, as in PK.

The subject's mental response in ESP may appear either as

perception or as action. If the response takes the form of perception, it may be registered as an *impression*, a *dream*, or an *hallucination*, although these three mediating vehicles of psi gamma may not be all inclusive. When the response is expressed as an action without the doer's conscious effort, such as *automatic writing*, it is called an *automatism*. If the impression, dream, or hallucination is described by the subject, a report concerning it may be placed in a case collection for analysis. Descriptions of thousands of spontaneous psychic experiences have been collected and categorized into the various forms in which these phenomena occur.

In experimental situations, in contrast to spontaneous cases, the response of the subject to the target object or his effect on it is induced. The target object's reaction in PK may be one of landing in a desired position if it is randomly moving; it may consist of changing its speed or direction of movement if it is in non-random motion, e.g. a moving pendulum; or it may take the form of moving if it is initially stationary. The physical target may be a *molar* object as in the case of a die, a molecular object as in the case of enzyme activity or temperature alteration, or a subatomic object as in the case of the alteration of radioactivity or electrical flow. The PK effect may occur spontaneously but with evidence of purpose as in *poltergeist* phenomena. Although unconsciously caused, poltergeist manifestations may consist of controlled activity such as the movement of objects in guided directions, e.g. stones paranormally thrown at a house.

The love of the mysterious is strong in many persons and, in them, it gives rise to wishful belief in some seemingly psychical phenomena that are incredible to others. It is necessary to critically examine the evidence offered by addicts of the marvelous. On the other hand, the skeptic's allegation of fraud, malobservation, or misinterpretation must also be closely and critically scrutinized. Many ostensibly paranormal phenomena are the product of chance, self-deception, and fraud. Unfortunately for the rapid progress of psychical research, it is human nature to deceive and to be deceived. Many *psychics* have been discovered cheating even though at other times they have produced paranormal phenomena. A psychic may resort to fraud when, because of the uncertain nature of psi, paranormal phenomena fail to appear after a long period of successful demonstrations. Deceit is particularly likely to occur in the *trance* state. In a *dissociated* condition the psychic may resort to deception, which he would not consciously practice. If uncontrolled, the psychic may cheat because within his fantasy there may be no borderline between what is done by his own hand and what he achieves paranormally. Unfortunately, fraud is made easier by the apparent need for partial or complete darkness to produce some paranormal phenomena.

Because of the complicated nature of many psychical phenomena and the resulting difficulty of assessing their reality, simple measures of demonstrating psi are necessary. Methods such as card calling and dice rolling may be boring and unimaginative, but they have the virtue of being controllable in order to preclude self-deception and fraud. Such simple events as successful card-calls and dice-rolls, however, may be due to chance and must be accumulated in large quantities that are subjected to statistical analysis to decrease this possibility.

Not all of the experimental findings reported in this treatise have been successfully repeated. In some attempted repetitions insignificant results were obtained, and in others psi was expressed negatively with respect to a factor with which it was previously found to be positively associated. In evaluating these findings, it should be kept in mind that psi does not always appear and, when it does occur, it may be expressed in an opposite direction to that expected. This may be because of the action of uncontrolled factors. In experiments in which psi was expressed in opposite directions, as when psi was associated positively with a given factor in one experiment and negatively associated with that variable in another, the finding in the majority of the experiments is reported. It is manifestly impossible in a work of this size to include the results of all psi experiments. When no majority finding was evident, the correct association between psi and the particular variable was judged on the basis of relevant characteristics of psi indicated by other experiments. The degree of success of this method in revealing the characteristics of psi will be determined by the results of future experiments.

REVIEW QUESTIONS

1. If any of the following terms fail to strike a chord in your memory, ascertain its meaning with the aid of the index and the glossary: agent, automatic writing, automatism, clairvoyance, dissociation, dream, experimenter, extrasensory perception, hallucination, induced psi phenomenon, impression, modality of psi, molar, paranormal, parapsychology, percipient, poltergeist, precognition, psi, psi gamma, psi kappa, psiology, psychic, psychical research, psychokinesis, spontaneous psi phenomenon, subject, target, telepathy, trance.

2. In what year was the Parapsychological Association accepted as an affiliated organization by the American Association for the Advancement of Science?

3. The subject's response in ESP may take any of what four principal forms?

4. What may be the target object's response in PK?

5. Distinguish between molar, molecular, and subatomic target objects.

6. What are the drawbacks and the virtues of simple methods of studying psi such as card calling and dice rolling?

7. Why is it important to question ostensibly psychic phenomena?

8. Why may psi be expressed in opposite directions in attempted repetitions of experiments?

Chapter 2

DEVELOPMENT OF PARAPSYCHOLOGY

SOME ACQUAINTANCE with the historical development of a science is essential for savoring its full flavor, comprehending its nature, and predicting its future. This is no less true of parapsychology than of any of the other disciplines into which man's knowledge of the universe is conveniently compartmentalized.

Primitive Man*

Psychical phenomena are a part of the human makeup and, as such, predate the origin of the written word. Even without written records to acquaint anthropologists with the characteristics of prehistorical paranormal phenomena, they are discernible through the study of present day, primitive societies. Primitive man is *animistic* and believes that an object behaving in an unusual way is alive and possesses a soul or *spirit*. Paranormal action is taken for granted by primitive man, and to him it may take the form of either of two types of magic. One kind of magic is imitative and involves the principle that like produces like. An example is the attempt to injure a person by inserting pins into a likeness of the intended victim. Imitative magic can also be used to produce positive benefits, such as securing game through dances that mimic activities of the desired animal and of the successful hunter. The other type of magic is contagious and is based on the belief that things once joined together possess a linkage after they are separated. A sorcerer may work his will upon a person by obtaining some of his hair or nail clippings, and footprints may be used to lame a man by placing sharp pieces of stone or bone in them.

---

*For further reading see R.L. Van de Castle. "Psi Abilities in Primitive Groups," *Proceedings of the Parapsychological Association*, 7:97-122, 1970; and M. Eliade, *Shamanism: Archaic Techniques of Ecstasy* (Princeton, Princeton University Press, 1972).

By autosuggestion or by *hypnotic* spells cast by priests, primitive man may enter a trance state in which he exhibits psychic phenomena.   Trance dances are widely produced and involve possibly paranormal feats such as firewalking, handling red-hot coals, or stabbing daggers into one's flesh without apparent harm. The trance state may be facilitated by drugs.   Its uses include location of lost objects, determination of the welfare of absent members of the tribe, and prediction of future events.

Certain individuals within the tribe may function as *shaman,* medicine man, or witch doctor and exercise paranormal power for practical purposes.   The South African psychiatrist-anthropologist Laubscher (1938) reported the case of a native witch doctor who repeatedly demonstrated ESP powers.   The story is told in Laubscher's words:

> I explained to Solomon Daba that I could not accept the numerous claims of supernormal powers made by himself and his followers unless I could verify them for myself. He agreed to submit himself to any test I might wish to carry out. I therefore decided to buy an article on my next visit and test his powers for myself.
>
> Now Solomon Daba lives about sixty miles away from Queentown. On leaving for his kraal, I buried in the ground a little cheap purse, wrapped in brown paper. Over the spot I placed a flat brown stone and on top of this a flat gray stone. Not a soul was in sight during this operation of burying the purse, nor did I, from the first moment the idea came into my mind, divulge my intention to anyone. From the moment I bought the purse it was not seen by anyone, nor had anyone but myself any knowledge of the nature of the article to be used for this test. I left my assistant in the car and went into the bush to bury the article. On leaving the spot, I traveled at an average speed of about 35 miles an hour. I mention this to obviate the possible explanation that he was informed by runners before my arrival.
>
> Shortly after my arrival I requested a seance dance and told him I had prepared a test. During the dance Solomon Daba described in minute detail the article, the nature of the locality in which it was buried, the brown paper in which it was wrapped, as well as the color of the stones. During the dance I never once gave any information to show that he was on the right track. This is only one of many experiments in which Solomon Daba acquitted himself very well.

The British anthropologist Geoffrey Gorer (1935) reported

information given to him by a West African shaman:

> Our sponsor and interpreter was the priest. After a time he came
> out and said to me, "You live in a white house on a hill surrounded
> by trees; you have a mother and two brothers who are walking under
> the trees" (a quite adequate description of my home and family, and
> it was very probable that on June 25th they would have been walking
> in the garden in the evening). Then he turned to Benga and said,
> "You have no home. In the place you think of as home there are
> many people. Your two sisters are well, but your dead mother's
> husband was taken very ill two days ago: he will recover, however,
> before you see him again." This was exact in every particular: On
> June 23rd Benga's stepfather had had a severe attack, as we verified on
> our return to Dakar, and he was quite convalescent before we re-
> turned. We were more than a thousand miles from Dakar at the
> time and had received no communications from there for the better
> part of a month.

The primitive man may believe he is *possessed* by a god or by
a spirit of a deceased person who enters and controls his body.
The possessed individual may divulge information that may be
paranormal, such as the murderer of the deceased person.   The
most important function of the shaman, medicine man, or witch
doctor is healing.   Illness is generally attributed by primitive
societies to displacement of the patient's soul by that of a spirit.
To effect a cure the shaman *exorcises* the demon or spirit who
has caused the illness by possessing the patient's body.   The
shaman may leave his body to capture the ejected soul of his
patient, or he may serve as a *medium* and become possessed by
spirits for whom he acts as a mouthpiece vocalizing curative procedures.   In carrying out his procedures the shaman may enter a
hut that shakes and from which raps and various voices proceed as
though from different locations even when the shaman is bound.
Such phenomena are forerunners of the *direct voice* and ostensibly paranormal physical effects in modern *séances*.

Ancient Civilizations*

Psychic phenomena were recognized in most of the old
cultures of the world such as in Egypt, Mesopotamia, India,

---

*For further reading see E.R. Dodds. "Supernormal Phenomena in Classical
Antiquity," *PSPR, 55*:189-237, 1971.

China, Persia, Israel, Greece, and Rome. What would have been considered at a later time to be a spirit or a *secondary personality* speaking through a *prophet* was considered in an ancient age to be divine. The Jews accepted such communications as coming straight from God, and Egyptians appointed prophets as court officials. The prophet Elisha is said to have divined the military secrets of the King of Syria and to have divulged them to the King of Israel (2 Kings 6:8), an activity worthy of the envy of the CIA. Joseph, interpreting the Pharaoh's dream, predicted the seven fat and the seven lean years (Genesis 41:1), while a dream of Nebuchadnezzar's was not only revealed to Daniel in a vision but was interpreted by him to the Babylonian king (Daniel 2:12-44). The biblical account of the witch of Endor (1 Samuel 28:8-15) describes what may have been an early forerunner of a modern *spiritualistic* séance. Saul, king of the Jews, ostensibly achieved contact through this medium with the dead Samuel, although Saul had earlier tried to suppress psychically gifted persons. Saul was correctly informed through the communication that he and his sons would die the next day in a battle with the Philistines.

There is no ancient word for extrasensory perception, but it is approximated by the term *divination*. The Greeks distinguished external divination from internal divination. External divination was made by procedures such as the casting of bones, the inspection of entrails, and the observation of the behavior of birds. On the other hand, internal divination was accomplished either in trance or in dreaming. Not only did the Greeks believe in divination, but they attempted to explain it. Democritus, founder of the atomic theory, believed that individuals emit atomistic mental images which penetrate the dreamer's body. The great philosopher-scientist Aristotle suggested that divination was accomplished by waves analogous to those propagated in water or air.

Grecian *oracles* took place in several ways, in one of which the priestess in a trance state delivered statements that were elucidated by the priests. Sometimes the oracles were delivered before the question was put, and occasionally, appropriate replies were made to unspoken questions. The Greek historian Herodotus described a test applied by King Croesus to the oracle at Delphi. A messenger sent by the king asked the oracle, "What is the King of Lydia doing today?" Although the messenger did not know the correct answer, the oracle replied correctly that King Croesus was boiling a lamb and a tortoise in a copper pot. The trance state was sometimes achieved in Greece, Babylonia, and Egypt by gazing into a translucent object such as a mirror or a vessel of water. Questions were answered and missing objects and individuals were located through the trance state, as well as through dreaming while sleeping in temples.

One of the greatest philosophers, Socrates, heard a voice in his head which foretold events and sometimes prescribed his conduct. He heard the voice only when he was on the point of doing or saying something which he ought not to do or say. Socrates believed this being to be other than himself because it revealed things unknown to him. According to Plato, Socrates said, "I have, since my childhood, been attended by a semidivine being whose voice from time to time dissuades me from some undertaking." The Greek historian Xenophon attributed to Socrates the words, "This prophetic voice has been heard by me throughout my life; it is certainly more trustworthy than omens from the flight or the entrails of birds."

According to the Greek biographer Plutarch, a *soothsayer* in Rome warned Julius Caesar to be on his guard against a great danger on the ides of March, the day upon which he was later assassinated. Plutarch also described how Calpurnia, Caesar's wife, dreamt the night before his death that she was holding his murdered body in her arms and was weeping over it.

Porphry and Iamblichus, Greek philosophers in the third and fourth centuries AD, described procedures for bringing about the control of the medium by a spirit, including the use of an enclosure for this purpose. They also described the speaking of the spirit through the medium's mouth and ostensibly paranormal effects such as the production of discordant sounds, sweet music, lights, and *levitation* of the psychic.

Christian Era

Whether Jesus was qualitatively different from other humans and had a divine aspect that they do not possess is a religious rather than a scientific question. However, it would be remiss to dismiss the possibility of a paranormal quality to some of his acts. As more is learned about the limits of psychical activity, it will become easier to determine which of Christ's acts and those of his disciples were paranormal rather than supernatural. This development is in accord with Catholic aspirations as, according to the Dominican priest Father Reginald Omez (1958), it is the desire of the Catholic church to distinguish between the paranormal and the supernatural.

As to the Christian saints, the Jesuit priest Father Herbert Thurston (1952) believed that the evidence of paranormal activity was better from the published records of their lives than any which had been produced by spiritualists. One of these saints was Augustine of Hippo (354-430 AD), who investigated or collected reports of telepathic dreams, waking visions, precognition, and paranormal healing. St. Augustine stated that Albicerius, a diviner in Carthage, had demonstrated his supernormal powers in numberless incidents extending over many years. In one of these, a pupil of Augustine's asked Albicerius to tell him what the pupil was thinking. Albicerius replied correctly that he had in mind a line of Virgil and proceeded to quote the verse.

Another of these saints was Joan of Arc of the fifteenth century, whose voices and visions guided her in delivering France from the English invaders. Charles, the dauphin, tested her by disguising himself and by having another man dressed in royal garments. Although she was an ignorant peasant girl and had not seen Charles or his likeness before, she rejected the pretender and identified the dauphin. Joan affirmed the reality of her guiding voices and visions even though she was condemned as a sorceress and burnt at the stake. However, it is not the belief of the Catholic Church that paranormal activity is confined to saints. According to Pope Benedict XIV, not only saints but "fools, idiots, melancholy persons and brute beasts" can have experiences of "knowledge of things to come, things past, present events distant in space, and the secret places of the heart" (Haynes, 1970).

Witchcraft*

In the fifteenth to the seventeenth centuries, tens of thousands of persons of both sexes, but primarily women and mostly in Europe, were burnt at the stake for *witchcraft*. Many of the phenomena of witchcraft were ostensibly paranormal, such as speaking in unknown languages, poltergiest disturbances, and levitation. A great percentage of these women were subject to *hysterical* dissociation, and their delusions, hallucinations, and secondary personalities took their form and coloring from the superstitions and beliefs of the age. Great numbers readily came to believe that they were really witches, had nocturnal rides, and were in league with the devil.

Bacon to Swedenborg

The idea of the investigation of the paranormal by scientific methods was first put forward by the English philosopher Francis Bacon (1561-1626) (Bell, 1964). This included telepathic dreams, *psychic healing,* and the influence of thought on plants, all of which are currently studied almost four centuries later. John Dee, a mathematician at Cambridge University, held seances from 1582 to 1587 with manifestations of ESP, paranormal movement of objects, *direct writing,* and direct voices. The spiritual beings purported to be participating were not human spirits, and some of them were said to be angels (French, 1972). The idea of intercourse with distinctly human spirits established itself in the popular consciousness through the teaching of Emanuel Swedenborg (1688-1772), who was a scientist, philosopher, and theologian and one of Sweden's greatest men (Toksvig, 1948). Swedenborg had dreams and hallucinations in which he entered a world of the deceased, with whom he mingled and engaged in conversation. According to the philosopher Immanuel Kant, Swedenborg had a vision of the burning of Stockholm 300 miles

---

*For further reading see M.A. Murray, *Witch-cult in Western Europe* (New York, Oxford University Press, 1921).

away, which was corroborated in detail two days later by the arrival of a messenger.

Mesmerism*

The German physician Franz Anton Mesmer (1733-1815) was the father of hypnotism, which in its early years was called *mesmerism*. Mesmer believed that a mutual influence exists between bodies both animate and inanimate by means of a universal, invisible, animal, magnetic fluid. By performing stroking movements over his patients with a magnet or with bare hands, he redirected this fluid to cure disease. His success in treating cases provoked the jealousy of physicians in Paris, where he practiced. Their clamor forced Louis XVI to appoint a commission to investigate Mesmer's claims. The commission, which included Benjamin Franklin and the French chemist Lavoisier, concluded that no magnetic fluid could be established and that its supposed effects were the product of imagination. Until hypnotism, devoid of its mesmeric trappings, was generally accepted scientifically in the twentieth century, its study was considered to fall within the province of psychical research.

Mesmer and his followers gave public demonstrations of *traveling clairvoyance* in which hypnotized subjects claimed to travel to far places and purported to describe distant contemporaneous events (Honorton & Krippner, 1969). One of Mesmer's followers, the Marquis de Puységur, observed that a hypnotized patient sometimes perceived thoughts that de Puységur had been thinking but had not expressed. Some of his patients diagnosed ailments of their own and of others and prescribed appropriate treatment. The French physician Alexandre Bertrand and other early mesmerists recognized an apparent *community of sensation*. Tastes and odors as well as tactile and visual stimuli applied to the hypnotizer were accompanied by similar sensations in the subject even when they were not in each other's presence. Furthermore, Bertrand noted that when he gave a verbal order to a subject, while he himself was thinking exactly the opposite, the

---

*For further reading see E.J. Dingwall, *Abnormal Hypnotic Phenomena: A Survey of Nineteenth-Century Cases* (New York, Barnes & Noble, 1968).

subject fell into a state of confusion, was distressed, and did not know what to do until Bertrand made his verbal suggestion agree with his mental suggestion.

Spiritualism*

Some of the earlier mesmerists attributed the paranormal phenomena that were associated with their entranced patients to the activity of spirits of the deceased. In Germany, J.H. Jung (1740-1817), a physician and professor at the Universities of Marburg and Heidelberg, believed that in the trance state the soul could leave the body, but he discouraged communication with the spirit world. The German physician and poet Justinius Kerner published in 1829 his study of raps and poltergeist phenomena associated with a female patient and of *apparitions* perceived by this woman and others nearby. The German doctor of philosophy Heinrich Werner recorded in 1839 his study of psychokinetic phenomena connected with a female clairvoyant.

In France beginning in 1821, Baron Jules du Potet studied *apports* (physical objects paranormally transported into a closed chamber), fire resistance, levitation of the human body, and spirit communication. From a correspondence beginning in 1829 between the physician G.P. Billott and the mesmerist Jean Deleuze, it appears that *phantom* forms and apports were well known. The cabinetmaker Alphonse Cahagnet (1985) reported a study of several entranced subjects with communications from many deceased identities giving descriptions of afterlife.

As a force of some magnitude, spiritualism had its beginning in 1849 in Hydesville, New York in the house of the Fox family, whose members were disturbed by continual rappings. It was soon discovered that the rappings were answers consisting of two raps for "yes" and one rap for "no" to questions supplied by members of the Fox family and visitors. The signals declared that a murdered man was buried in the cellar. Subsequently, the skeleton of a man was said to have been found buried near the cellar in a space between two walls. Rappings and other polter-

---

*For further reading see F. Podmore, *Mediums of the 19th Century* (New Hyde Park, New York, University Books, 1963).

geist phenomena followed the two Fox sisters even when they changed their residence. A system was devised based on raps in answer to the letters of the alphabet, and some of those who sat with the Fox sisters found that they had similar powers. The movement spread until in a few years hundreds of mediums were conducting thousands of séances across the United States and Europe. Even after many tests had indicated that the raps were not produced by normal means, the Fox sisters confessed to fraud and then retracted the confession. Such instability is a frequent characteristic of psychics and, although it compounds the difficulty of their evaluation, it does not in itself negate the reality of the phenomena associated with them.

Early Experimentation*

The American physician Luther Bell in 1854 described the movement of a heavy table while five people merely held their hands above its surface (Brown, 1970). In tests with a medium who communicated through raps, he found that errors or false statements were made in answering questions when Bell could not answer them himself. In 1854 the French Count Agenor de Gasparin published his experiments demonstrating the movement of heavy bodies without contact and the alteration of weights of objects due to the application of unknown forces. Successful telepathic experiments were made by means of a table which rapped out on the floor numbers thought of by the sitters. Marc Thury, Professor of Physics at the University of Geneva, described similar investigations in 1855 and suggested the existence within man of a substance which could be extended by the individual beyond the limits of his body.

Robert Hare (1855), Professor of Chemistry at the University of Pennsylvania, published the results of his experiments using apparatus so arranged that the medium could be in indirect contact with the object he was requested to move, but was prevented from producing the full movement that was observed by any muscular force of his own. One apparatus consisted of a wooden

*For further reading see F. Podmore, *Mediums of the 19th Century* (New Hyde Park, New York, University Books, 1963).

board 4 feet long, supported on a fulcrum 1 foot from one end and attached by a hook to a spring balance at the other end. A glass vessel filled with water was placed on the board near the fulcrum. A wire-gauze cage, attached to an independent support and not touching the glass at any point, was placed in the water, and the psychic had to affect the balance by simply placing his hand into the wire cage. The balance registered variations of weight amounting to several pounds. In tests to show that the movement of tables was *paraphysical,* de Gasparin and Thury in their experiments strewed the surface of the table with flour in order to prove that the participant's hands did not touch it, and Hare in his experiments separated the psychic's hands from the table by means of a board resting freely on copper balls.

The English naturalist Alfred Wallace (1896), who proposed with Darwin the theory of evolution by natural selection, had his earliest experiences with paranormal phenomena in 1844 and remained convinced until the end of his busy life in 1903 that they had a spiritualistic explanation. He observed levitation, movement of objects without contact, alteration of weight, apports, direct writing, and *psychic photography.* Wallace was a member of the London Dialectical Society formed in 1867 to investigate alleged spiritual manifestations. The society found evidence of paranormal phenomena, such as psychic raps and communications, *materialization,* resistance to red-hot coals, direct voice, and elongation of the human body.

Perhaps the most outstanding investigator of paraphysical phenomena was the Englishman Sir William Crookes (1832-1919), who was also one of the greatest chemists and physicists of his time (Medhurst, 1972). In addition to discovering the element thallium and inventing the Crookes cathode ray tube with which X-rays were discovered, he engaged in remarkable experiments with the British psychics Daniel Dunglas Home and Florence Cook from 1870 to 1874. With Home as the psychic, he performed tests in full light on the alteration of the weight of objects somewhat similar to the tests of Hare, as well as with apparatus of his own design. He reported other phenomena produced by Home, in most instances in full light, which included reading through opaque bodies, movement of heavy bodies without contact, playing of musical instruments in cages, direct writing by means of a pencil without anyone holding it, handling of red-hot coals without being burned, elongation and levitation of Home's body, and luminous apparitions in the form of clouds or human limbs. Although Home was studied by several investigators in addition to Crookes, he was never seriously charged of fraud.

In studying the medium Florence Cook, Crookes asserted that a being who materialized and called herself Katie King was seen by him at the same time the medium was in view. The materialized figure walked, talked, and allowed herself to be photographed. Precautionary measures were taken by Crookes to prevent fraud, including placing the medium in an electric circuit which was not broken during the appearance of Katie King. Although Florence Cook was later exposed in fraud, this is the frequent history of mediums when in trance or when their powers fail them and should not result in the conclusion that all of the phenomena associated with an exposed medium were fraudulently produced. However, this characteristic of some mediums greatly adds to the difficulty of the study and evaluation of the phenomena associated with them. Even after the exposure of Florence Cook, Crookes, at a scientific conference held at the height of his fame, declared that he had nothing to retract. After his death, Crookes was accused of overlooking Florence Cook's trickery in order to carry on a clandestine love affair with her (Hall, 1962). Criticisms of an individual's work leveled after his death or after he has become physically or mentally enfeebled are hard to assess. In any case, reports of phenomena as difficult to evaluate as some of those given by Crookes can be considered only to be suggestive and only to be indicative of what to look for until corroboration by similar occurrences is obtained.

The British physicist Sir William Barrett, Professor of Physics at the Royal College of Science in Dublin, made a pioneering venture when, at a meeting of the British Association for the Advancement of Science in 1876, he reported on his experiments in which a young girl under hypnosis called cards laid between the leaves of a book with relatively good success and told the tastes and smells of various substances that the hypnotizer experienced at a distance. Barrett also tested the effect of distance on telepathy and found no diminution of success between 3 and 30 feet, the latter being the greatest distance tested.

Organized Research*

Barrett and Crookes were among those taking part in the early activities of the Society for Psychical Research (SPR), which was founded in London in 1882 for organized research into psychic phenomena. Contributing most to its founding was a group of Cambridge University scholars composed of Henry Sidgwick, Edmund Gurney, and Frederic Myers. The *Journal* and the *Proceedings* of the SPR have been published continuously until this day.

Among the earlier experiments reported in the *Proceedings* were those on the drawing of telepathically transmitted pictures by Malcolm Guthrie and James Birchall and collaborated in by Sir Oliver Lodge, one of the greatest physicists of the nineteenth century (Guthrie, 1885). These were followed by the publication of the book *Phantasms of the Living* (Gurney, Myers, & Podmore, 1886), based in part on spontaneous paranormal events. This classic in psychical research was written by Gurney, Myers, and the Oxford scholar Frank Podmore, with the assistance of Mrs. Henry Sidgwick. It was followed by the *Census of Hallucinations* (Sidgwick 1894), based on an inquiry in which 17,000 answers were obtained to the question, "Have you ever, when believing yourself to be completely awake, had a vivid impression of seeing or being touched by a living or inanimate object, or of hearing a voice, which impression, so far as you can discover, was not due to any external physical cause?" Of these, 15,306 replied "no," and 1,684 replied "yes." While hallucinations per se are not indicators of psi, some of them are of interest as possible mediators of paranormal information. The monumental work, *Human Personality and Its Survival of Bodily Death* by Frederic Myers (1903), which coordinated the results

---

*For further reading see A. Gauld, *The Founders of Psychical Research* (New York, Schocken, 1968).

of his experimental findings, observations, reading, and theorizing, was published posthumously. Myers, whose theory of subliminal consciousness predated by a few years Freud's theory of the unconscious, considered that he had found support for survival after death in psychical research.

The American Society for Psychical Research (ASPR) was founded in Boston in 1885 under the leadership of William James, America's first world-famous psychologist and philosopher. Like the SPR, the ASPR publishes a *Journal* and a *Proceedings*. James and the philosophers Richard Hodgson and James Hyslop reported remarkable results with the American psychic Leonore Piper. In 1889 she paid the first of her visits to England as guest of the SPR, where she was studied by Hodgson and others, and was one of the most celebrated and productive psychics. No evidence of fraud on her part, conscious or unconscious, was ever produced. Operating in trance, she delivered communications both orally and through automatic writing. Many investigators who were initially skeptical concluded that she received information by paranormal means, although they disagreed as to whether this should be attributed to ESP or accepted as evidence of survival.

Continental Parapsychology*

France's most outstanding parapsychologist was the physiologist Charles Richet, who won the Nobel Prize in Physiology and Medicine in 1913 for his discovery of anaphylaxis, the sensitivity of the body to foreign proteins. In 1884 he was the first to apply statistical methods to analyze the results of ESP tests. The first experiment of inducing hypnosis at a distance was conducted by two Frenchmen, the psychiatrist Pièrre Janet (1886) and the physician M. Gilbert (Richet, 1886). They found it was possible by means of mental suggestion at distances up to 2 kilometers to induce in the subject a condition of hypnotic sleep. These findings, which are indicative of ESP, were repeated by Richet with the same subject. He studied many psychics and accepted *ecto-*

---

*For further reading see C. Richet, *Thirty Years of Psychical Research: Being a Treatise on Metapsychics* (New York, Arno Press, 1975).

plasm and materializations as abundantly proved, although he did not consider that they provided evidence of survival.

One of the psychics studied by Richet was the Italian Eusapia Palladino. She and D.D. Home were two of the greatest paraphysical psychics as judged by the quality and quantity both of the phenomena they produced and of the learned men who investigated them, including Myers and Lodge. The British parapsychologist Hereward Carrington, in a séance with Palladino, felt a materialized hand dissolve within his grasp (Fielding, Baggaly, & Carrington, 1909). Unlike Home, Palladino was frequently detected in fraud when the investigators slackened the rigor of their controls. The phenomena associated with her included raps, the appearance of lights, the twanging of a guitar, the production of fine prints on clay, the levitation of tables, and the materialization of limbs and figures even when the psychic was under physical control. Another investigator of Palladino was the Polish psychologist Julian Ochorowitz (1909), who succeeded also in photographing the levitation of objects such as scissors and match boxes by the psychic Stanislawa Tomczyk.

Richet published a favorable report on the séances of Marthe Beraud, also known as Eva Carrière, according to which materialized bodies developed from masses of white material extruded from her mouth, vagina, and other orifices. The German physician Baron Albert von Schrenck-Notzing (1920) published a book favorable to this psychic's genuineness, which was amply illustrated with photographs. The psychics he studied were carefully searched before séances and sometimes examined internally, given an emetic, or required to eat a colored food on the theory that this would stain the substance that issued from their bodies if it were not ectoplasm but matter such as cheesecloth compacted into a small wad and concealed in their stomach or throat. The materialization phenomena of Eva Carrière were studied also by the physician Gustave Geley (1927), the first director of the Institut Métapsychique International founded in 1918 in Paris. Prior to the materializations the psychic was completely unclothed and then redressed in a tight garment, with her hands always held in full sight. Although the genuiness of this psychic's phenomena was the subject of considerable questioning, she was never detected in fraud. Geley and Richet, in collaboration in séances with the Polish psychic Franek Kluski, obtained molds of presumably materialized hands and feet in paraffin wax, which had openings at the wrist and ankle too small for withdrawal of the member. They also studied the ability of the Polish psychic Stephan Ossowiecki to identify messages and drawings in sealed envelopes.

The French physician Eugene Osty (1933), who followed Geley as director of the Institut Métapsychique International, employed infrared and utlraviolet rays to determine the nature of the paraphysical phenomena produced by the Austrian psychic Rudi Schneider, which included phantom arms that played musical instruments. Although Schneider was studied by several other investigators including von Schrenck-Notzing, the Swiss psychiatrist Carl Jung, and the British parapsychologist and magician Harry Price, he was never detected in fraud. The French chemical engineer René Warcollier (1938) collaborated in experiments with Osty and conducted experiments in the transmission of picture targets by ESP at distances up to 6,000 km.

The French astronomer Camille Flammarion (1900), who originated the word *psychic,* sent out an inquiry as to whether the questionee had experienced a hallucination and received 4,280 replies, 1,820 of which were in the affirmative.

Theodore Flournoy (1900), Professor of Psychology at the University of Geneva, published the results of his study with the psychic Hélène Smith, whose principal phenomena took the form of automatic writing that told of her previous *reincarnations.* He uncovered obscure books inaccessible to the psychic, which confirmed place names and persons described by her. Flournoy believed that telepathy rather than reincarnation accounted for her performance.

Gerardus Heymans (1921), Professor of Psychology at the University of Groningen, Netherlands, carried out an experiment with two assistants in which they viewed through a glass-covered hole the subject in the room beneath them. The subject successfully pointed at spaces on a board before him that were randomly selected by the experimenters from 48 spaces, even though the board was shielded from the subject's sight.

The German physician Rudolf Tischner (1925) coined the term *extrasensory perception*, and he published the results of his experiments in which he distinguished between telepathy and clairvoyance in the identification of hidden words, drawings, and objects.

The Austrian psychiatrist Sigmund Freud (1925) observed that *psychoanalysis* might be helpful in unravelling apparent instances of telepathy and making their puzzling characteristics more intelligible. He believed that some dreams could be interpreted psychoanalytically if ESP were involved in their production. One of his patients dreamed that his wife gave birth to twins, and a day later he was informed that his daughter by a previous marriage had given birth a month prematurely to a pair of twins during the night of the dream. The man did not know that she would give birth that night nor that the offspring would be twins. Freud said that, assuming the man had received this information through ESP, his dream could be psychoanalytically explained by a repressed desire that his daughter from a previous marriage replace his present wife.

The Swiss psychiatrist and parapsychologist Carl Jung offered his theory of *synchronicity* or meaningful coincidence to account for paranormal events (Jung & Pauli, 1955). He postulated that, with respect to the connection between events, a third relationship exists in addition to cause-effect and in addition to chance. This relationship is acausal but significant. The coinciding events are manifestations of an archetype or primordial form of feeling or thought, the similar split sides of which emerge into consciousness or into the physical world.

Beginning in 1926, L.L. Vasiliev (1963), Professor of Physiology at the University of Leningrad, conducted parapsychological experiments including some on the induction of hypnotic sleep and awakening in the subject at distances up to 1,700 km. The percipient's state was mechanically recorded by the pressure he rhythmically exerted on a rubber bulb held in his hand. When the subject entered the hypnotic trance, the recorded pressure changes ceased and recommenced when he awakened, thus indicating when the trance began, how long it lasted, and when it ended. Enclosing the hypnotist in an iron chamber, which, acting as a *Faraday cage,* excluded penetration by electromagnetic radiation except at extremely high and extremely low frequencies, did not interfere with the success.

W.H.C. Tenhaeff (1960), Professor of Parapsychology at the University of Utrecht, Netherlands, conducted research in ESP beginning in the late 1920s. His most spectacular work was with the Dutch psychic Gerard Croiset, who on several occasions was successful in the paranormal location of lost individuals in co-operation with the police. Tenhaeff was succeeded in 1974 by Martin Johnson, who began publication of the *European Journal of Parapsychology* written in English.

Beginning in the 1930s, Hans Bender (1968), Professor of Psychology at the University of Freiburg, Germany, investigated several areas of parapsychology, including poltergeist cases, and served as editor of *Zeitschrift für Parapsychologie und Grenzgebiete der Psychologie.*

Remy Chauvin, Professor of Animal Sociology at the Sorbonne, the University of Paris, reported an apparent PK effect on the rate of radioactive decay of uranium nitrate as measured by the frequency of blips on a Geiger counter (Chauvin & Genthon, 1965). He also reported experiments which indicated the precognitive ability of mice to avoid the side of their cage that would be electrified (Duval & Montredon, 1968).

British Research

From 1901 to 1932 several English-speaking psychics in different parts of the world, some of whom had not met one another, produced statements through automatic writing or automatic speaking, each of which alone had little meaning but which complemented one another and were found to be interconnected (Salter, 1948). These *cross-correspondences* purported to emanate from some deceased psychical researchers, including Myers, Sidgwick, and Gurney, as an attempt by them to provide evidence of their survival. While the cross-correspondences might be explained by unconscious telepathy between the automatists, no parallel is known for telepathy on such a large scale or with like complexity.

F.L. Usher and F.P. Burt (1909) were 120 and 960 miles apart during portions of their successful telepathy tests with playing cards. Their results showed the *decline effect*, the scores dropping off from the first day to the last.

Gilbert Murray, Professor of Greek at Oxford University, undertook a long series of qualitative experiments from 1910 to 1929 in which he guessed topics chosen by a group while he was out of the room. Although his success was too high to be attributable to chance, it may have been due to his extreme auditory *hyperesthesia* rather than to ESP (Dodds, 1972).

W.J. Crawford (1918), Lecturer in Mechanical Engineering at Queens University, Ireland, conducted experiments with the psychic Kathleen Goligher in which he measured an increase in her weight corresponding to the weight of a levitated table. He obtained photographs of ostensible ectoplasm extruding from the psychic's body to form rods that moved exterior objects. He traced the flow of ectoplasm from the base of the psychic's spine to her ankles by a colored track of powdered carmine.

Ina Jephson (1928), a member of the Council of the SPR, performed ESP tests of 240 subjects with the use of playing cards and obtained scores *significantly* above *mean chance expectation*. She noted a decline in the scores between the first and second guesses of the *set*.

The physicist G.N.M. Tyrrell (1936), working principally with the percipient Gertrude Johnson, used an apparatus consisting of five light-tight boxes each containing an electric light. One of the boxes was lighted randomly, and the subject lifted the lid of the box she thought it to be. The opening of any box automatically drew a line upon a paper tape, and a success was automatically recorded by a double line. As the experimenter did not know which was the correct box, telepathy was ruled out. The positive results had odds against chance of about 270,000 to one. This became an experiment in precognition when the subject was required to choose the box about half a second before the experimenter pressed the key to randomly light a box. Here again the results were statistically significant.

The psychical researcher Whately Carington (1940) conducted drawing experiments beginning in 1935 by randomly opening a dictionary on successive days and making a sketch of the first drawable word. On the same day his subjects attempted to draw the target and label it with a word. The word, not the drawing, was used for the scoring. The British statistician R.A. Fisher devised a formula for evaluating the success of the subjects by comparing the number of times a particular word was used when it was the target with the number of times it was used when it was not the target. The resultant odds against chance were astronomical. Carington observed that the subjects often made a drawing of the target selected on the preceding or succeeding day and that ESP was not focused very sharply in time.

S.G. Soal, Lecturer in Mathematics at the University of London, conducted tests of ESP in 160 subjects from 1934 to 1939 without *extrachance* results (Soal & Bateman, 1954). Carington, who had found *displacement* in his own experiments, persuaded Soal to reexamine his results to see if displacement could be found. Soal discovered that two of his subjects had been scoring substantially above chance on +1 and −1 cards, i.e. the cards respectively one after and one before that at which the agent was looking. One of the two subjects, Basil Shackleton, continued to display displacement in tests performed subsequently to the discovery of his ability to do so. At a rapid rate of calling he sometimes obtained above-chance scores on both the +2 and −2 cards. In the other subject, Gloria Stewart, the displacement effect had disappeared, and she was now scoring higher than previously, but on the target card. The veracity of some of Soal's work was thrown into question although it was defended by others (Scott et al., 1974).

Robert Thouless (1951), Professor of Psychology at Cambridge University, showed that ESP and PK may operate at the same time by performing a successful hidden-target PK experiment in which dice were thrown to duplicate concealed target faces that were discernible only by ESP.

American Psychical Research

John Coover (1917), Professor of Psychology at Stanford University, reported a test of telepathy with playing cards, which included a *control series*. As the difference between the scores of the experimental and control series was not significant, he concluded that there was no evidence of ESP in his work. However, it was pointed out later by others that, because clairvoyance was not precluded in the control series and because the combined score of the two series was significantly above the chance level with odds in the order of 160 to 1, the results of the experiment are suggestive of the action of ESP.

Leonard Troland (1917), Professor of Psychology at Harvard University, invented a machine which mechanically recorded the subject's guesses. Although the results of his tests were not significant, this was probably the first machine used for testing ESP.

A series of telepathy experiments was carried out at Harvard University by the psychologist George Eastabrooks (1927) in which he acted as a sender working with 83 college students guessing ordinary playing cards. The results were overwhelmingly positive and demonstrated that it is possible for an unselected group of subjects to evidence telepathy.

From 1923 into the early 1930s, Margery Crandon, wife of a Boston surgeon, was studied by numerous psychic investigators with respect to ostensible psychical phenomena produced in her presence. The phenomena, which included direct voice, the materialization of hands, and the production of paraffin gloves, occurred even when Margery was inspected and controlled (Tietze, 1973). While there was considerable disagreement among the investigators, it appeared that genuine paranormal phenomena occurred at the séances, in addition to probable instances of fraud.

Radio tests of ESP were carried out by Gardner Murphy, Professor of Psychology at Columbia University, in 1924. Other radio experiments were performed in England (Woolley, 1928), in Germany (Herzberg, 1928), and in the United States (Goodfellow, 1938). Like the television tests later performed in the United States (Nash, 1959, 1964), these tests of a large number of subjects guessing the same few targets cannot be satisfactorily analyzed because of the *stacking effect*. This effect results from the fact that targets are not equally popular nor do they have equally popular call sequences. Because of this, the scoring rate may be distorted when the same sequence of targets is repeatedly used even though the order of targets in that sequence was randomly selected. For example, suppose that a star has been in the public's mind because of an astronomical event. This might cause more individuals to select the star symbol as their first call than would be expected by chance. If then several subjects were tested with the same sequence of target cards and the first card happened to bear the star symbol, the scores would be elevated by this stacking effect without the occurrence of ESP. In contrast, if each subject is tested with a different, randomly selected sequence of cards, the scores would not be elevated by the subjects' likelihood of calling the first card a star.

The novelist Upton Sinclair (1930) published his successful experiments in the ESP transmission of drawings to his wife. In the 290 drawings, there were 65 "total" successes, 155 partial successes and only 70 failures. In a preface to Sinclair's book, Einstein appealed for scientific consideration of the work.

The era of the systematic development of quantitative work began in 1930 through the experiments of Joseph Banks Rhine at Duke University, where he established a Parapsychology Laboratory. In 1962 he established the Foundation for Research on the Nature of Mind in Durham, North Carolina. A division of this foundation, the Institute for Parapsychology, is a continuation of the former Parapsychology Laboratory, but it is not connected with Duke University. Instead of playing cards and numbers as targets, he substituted *ESP cards* on each of which is inscribed one of five symbols—the plus or cross, the circle, the square, the five-pointed star, and the wavy lines. The pack consists of 25 cards, five of each of the symbols, so that the *probability* of success on a single trial is one out of five. In ESP, an abbreviation coined by Rhine, he distinguished experimentally in card tests between telepathy and clairvoyance and participated in the first experimental studies of precognition and of psychokinesis. It was

Rhine's enthusiasm, ingenuity, intellectual rigor, critical judgment, and dogged determination in the face of adverse criticism that led to the establishment of parapsychology as a science that, like any other, has some unique principles and characteristics of its own. Under his leadership, publication of the *Journal of Parapsychology* was begun in 1937. His wife, Louisa Rhine (1961), accumulated and analyzed the world's largest collection of spontaneously occurring, ostensibly paranormal experiences, consisting of about 11,000 cases. Her analysis of these events into the categories of intuitions, dreams, hallucinations, and PK phenomena (such as a clock stopping or a picture falling at the moment of death of a person connected with it) has elucidated the way in which psi is manifested in everyday life and has provided insights into its mechanism.

Gaither Pratt, who worked with the Rhines at the Parapsychology Laboratory, participated in three noteworthy ESP studies. In an experiment in which Hubert Pearce, a student of religion at Duke University, served as the subject, extremely significant scores were obtained at distances up to 250 yards (Rhine & Pratt, 1954). In another experiment, thirty-two unselected subjects were tested with significant results under carefully guarded conditions (Pratt & Woodruff, 1939). In this experiment, it would have been very difficult for anyone to have committed an error deliberately or unconsciously without its being detected. Pratt's extensive experiments on the Czechoslovakian psychic Pavel Stepanek, with Milan Ryzl as coexperimenter, indicated a *focusing effect* consisting of significantly greater deviations with certain cards in the deck than with others, although all of the cards were covered with envelopes (Pratt, 1973). Criticisms were made of Pratt's work (Hansel, 1966; Medhurst & Scott, 1974); however, with such an illusive phenomenon as ESP, it may be impossible to devise and carry out an experiment with which a critic at a later time cannot find fault. The answer to such criticism may ultimately consist of the control of psi to the extent of producing a reliably repeatable experiment.

In addition to several other discoveries in psi, Gertrude Schmeidler, Professor of Psychology at the City University of

New York, found that the attitude of the subject towards ESP may affect the direction in which he or she expresses it, believers scoring positively and disbelievers negatively (Schmeidler & McConnell, 1958).

Not long after the middle of the twentieth century, two organizations were founded in the United States that have had much to do with the development of parapsychology both in this and in other countries. One is the Parapsychology Foundation, which began its work in 1952 under the direction of the psychic Eileen Garrett. It has developed a large library, sponsored international conventions on parapsychology, issued publications describing psychical research including the *Parapsychology Review*, and collected and distributed funds in support of parapsychological endeavors. The other is the Parapsychological Association, which was established in 1957 as an international organization that screens its members on the basis of their research productivity in psychical science, holds an annual convention for the presentation of parapsychological papers, and incorporates these articles in the annual publication, *Research in Parapsychology*. In 1969, the Parapsychological Association became affiliated with the American Association for the Advancement of Science.

Another organization, the Psychical Research Foundation founded in 1960 in Durham, North Carolina under the directorship of William Roll, has explored the question of whether the human self extends beyond the life span of the organism. The Trinidadian psychic Lalsingh Harribance received extensive testing there, including his ability to differentiate between sealed envelopes carrying pictures of men and those of women (Klein, 1971).

The Future of Parapsychology

Although the number of institutions teaching psychical science is rapidly increasing, its total at this writing of approximately 150 is a small fraction of the aggregate of institutions offering courses in such sciences as physics, chemistry, biology, and psychology. (A list of institutions offering courses in parapsychology can be obtained from the American Society for Psychical Research, 5 West

73rd Street, New York, N.Y. 10023.) As sciences, parapsychology and its sister science, experimental psychology, both originated in the latter part of the nineteenth century. Today, however, nearly every university has a department of psychology, but the fate of parapsychology in the academic world is yet to be determined. Whether psychical research will be subsumed by psychology, be incorporated into physics, or develop into a separate discipline of the paranormal will depend upon what is disclosed by the pursuit of this science concerning the nature of reality.

Conclusions

Man's interpretation of psi events has accompanied his cultural development through the stages of animism, demonology, spiritualism, and experimentation. Application of the scientific method to the study of paranormal phenomena may lead to the establishment of the reality of mind and of its equivalent or underlying relationship to the physical universe.

REVIEW QUESTIONS

1. If you fail to remember any of the following terms, ascertain its meaning with the aid of the glossary and the index: animism, apparition, apport, archetype, community of sensation, control series, cross-correspondences, decline effect, direct voice, direct writing, displacement, dissociation, divination, ectoplasm, ESP cards, exorcise, extrachance, Faraday cage, focusing effect, hyperesthesia, hypnotism, hysteria, levitation, materialization, mean chance expectation, medium, mesmerism, oracle, paraphysical, phantom, possession, probability, prophet, psychic healing, psychic photography, psychoanalysis, reincarnation, séance, secondary personality, set, shaman, significance, spirit, spiritualism, stacking effect, subliminal, synchronicity, traveling clairvoyance, witchcraft.

2. Describe a psychic event in the Old Testament.

3. What beliefs in paranormal phenomena were held by Aristotle, Democritus, and Socrates?

4. What psychic phenomena were associated with St. Augustine and with St. Joan of Arc?

5. What relationship to paranormal phenomena did the following have: Francis Bacon, Swedenborg?

6. When and where did modern spiritualism begin?

7. What relationship did Crookes have to psi phenomena?

8. When and where were the Society for Psychical Research and the American Society for Psychical Research founded?

9. What contributions did Frederic Myers make to parapsychology?

10. What were the contributions of Richet to psychical research?

11. What is the connection with parapsychology of each of the following psychics: D.D. Home, Florence Cook, Eusapia Palladino, Rudi Schneider and Margery Crandon?

12. Why were the results of Coover's experiment at the University of Stanford first thought to disprove ESP and then later considered to support it?

13. What were the contributions to parapsychology of the Rhines?

Chapter 3

TECHNIQUES FOR MEASURING PSI

PSI TECHNIQUES IN GENERAL AND ESP TECHNIQUES IN PARTICULAR

THE STATE of development of a science is commensurate with the techniques used to pursue it. In this chapter, techniques applied to humans are considered, methods of studying psi in lower organisms being presented in Chapter 10.

Controlled Experiments

The scientific method of comparing an experimental group with a control group, with the two groups being treated exactly alike except for the variable or factor that is being examined, must be more profoundly considered in experiments on psi than in tests of normal phenomena. This is because psi may be expressed in the control group as well as in the experimental group, as was apparently the case in the experiment by Coover (1917). In psi experiments in which the results can be analyzed statistically, this is not a drawback as the results can be compared with the mean chance expectation score, the latter serving as a statistical control. Another means of obtaining a control for comparison with the experimental results is the method of *crosschecking*. In this procedure the subject's calls are compared with targets in a distant part of the experiment at which the calls were not aimed. In crosschecking, the number of *hits*, i.e. trials in which the call and the target correspond, serves as a control for comparison with the number of hits on the actual targets. If the extrachance scores resulted from nonrandomicity of the targets, they would be expected to occur in the crosschecking as well. In most psi experiments complete absence of psi in the control group is not necessary, as the experimental and control groups can be compared with respect to the degree psi is expressed in each or with respect

34

to whether psi is expressed in a positive direction in one and a negative direction in the other.

The degree of control that is necessary varies directly with the complexity of the experiment, as the more aspects the phenomenon involves, the greater is the number of factors which must be regulated. In order not to inhibit a paranormal phenomenon without giving it sufficient leeway to be expressed, the psychic may be initially permitted to demonstrate the ostensibly paranormal effect in the manner of his choice, following which the degree of control is increased as the phenomenon becomes more manageable. If the controls do not reach a level which precludes alternative explanations, the experimental results should not be considered as being more than suggestive.

Subject's Response

The technique may require the subject to respond voluntarily to the target, or it may register an involuntary response of the subject such as a physiological reaction occurring at or near the time the target is operative. In the latter case, the term "respondent" might be more accurate for the subject than the term "percipient." If a voluntary response is required, it may consist of the percipient's attempting to orally call or describe the target, to draw or write its symbol, to point to the correct card, or to match the target card to a specimen card. The verbal description of the target may be given upon his being awakened after he has attempted to dream about the target, or the verbal description may consist of events identified with the target by *psychometry*. In this procedure the psychic holds the target object, which may be concealed in a container. The technique may require the subject to identify the target rapidly, or it may encourage him to meditate upon the target before giving his response. The response may be for *low aim*, i.e. to produce a *miss*, as well as for *high aim*.

If an involuntary response of the subject is measured, it may consist of his awakening to a hidden clock face (Bleksley, 1963), or of his going to sleep or awakening through hypnosis at a distance (Vasiliev, 1963). The time of the subject's going to sleep or awakening through hypnosis may be registered by his hand pressure on a rubber bulb. Involuntary physiological responses to the target include decrease of the skin resistance of the subject—as measured by the GSR *(galvanic skin reflex)* technique —which was found to occur following auditory stimulation of the agent (Schouten, 1976). Douglas Dean (1962) of the Newark College of Engineering registered ESP response by involuntary *cutaneous vasoconstriction,* or contraction of blood vessels in the skin, measured by a finger *plethysmograph.* When cards bearing the name of persons emotionally significant to the subject were looked at by the agent, the subject responded physiologically by a decrease in finger volume. A reduction in the alpha wave output of the brain was observed to take place in the subject when the agent received intermittent electric shocks (Tart, 1963) or was exposed to a flashing light (Targ & Puthoff, 1974). Also, an *evoked potential,* or change in the electrical field, was found to occur in the subject's cerebral cortex within one-half second after the agent was stimulated by a light flash and held the thought image of a cup of coffee (Lloyd, 1973).

Restricted-Response Tasks

Techniques differ depending upon whether the tasks are *restricted response* or are *free response.* Restricted-response targets are those with a limited number of possible symbols that are known to the subject, e.g. the five symbols of the ESP deck. (These decks are purchasable from the Foundation for Research on the Nature of Man in Durham, N.C.) The deck of cards, or any other group of serially arranged restricted-choice targets, may consist of each symbol represented an equal number of times, in which case it is called a *closed deck.* In contrast, the targets in the deck may be arranged entirely at random, in which case some of the symbols may occur with greater frequency than others. This is called an *open deck.* An advantage of the latter is that the subject may be informed after each *trial* whether it was correct. This cannot be done with a closed deck without increasing the subject's chance of scoring correctly on the remaining trials.

It is possible with certain types of restricted-choice tasks to give scoring credit on the basis of how greatly the response differed from the target. This was accomplished with the use of target cards each bearing the diagram of a clock face with an hour hand pointing exactly to one of the hours from one to twelve (Fisk & Mitchell, 1953). While the chance of a direct hit was only one in twelve, a differential scoring system was used in which each call was scored according to the distance of the called hour from the actual hour on the target card. The weighted credit for near hits, i.e. calls near the target hour but not on it, resulted in extrachance scores.

Several different methods of testing for ESP have been employed using the fixed-response targets of a deck of cards. In the basic technique the subject calls each card after the experimenter takes it from the deck. The experimenter does not look at the symbol on the card until the end of the *run* through the deck. In the down-through technique, the cards are called down through the deck before any are removed or checked by the experimenter. The open-matching technique requires the subject to assort the ESP deck into five piles, one pile opposite each of five specimen cards turned face upwards. The *blind-matching* technique differs from this only in that the five specimen cards are face down or in opaque envelopes. In the *screened touch-matching* technique, the subject points to the one of the five specimen cards that matches the target card from the ESP deck held behind a screen by the experimenter; only the experimenter handles the deck of cards. Another technique, called the *psychic shuffle,* consists of the subject's shuffling the deck of cards until he feels that the cards in it are in an order resembling those in a target deck. Tests of precognition involve the subject's predicting the order of the cards as they will be arranged in the future. At the predetermined future time, the experimenter shuffles the cards several times, cuts the deck, and compares the order of the cards with the subject's predictions.

Free-Response Tasks

With free-response tasks, the targets are relatively unrestricted and are unknown to the subject. While the targets may be partially restricted, e.g. to objects that can be drawn, their number is virtually unlimited. When the technique consists of the subject's drawing the target, the target might be a picture of the first drawable word in a randomly opened dictionary. This was the method of target selection used by Carington (1940). On the other hand, Sinclair (1930) drew whatever came into his head in the experiments with his wife as the percipient. Experiments were successfully performed in which the free-response targets were remote geographical or technical targets such as roads, buildings, and laboratory apparatus, with the sender stationed at the position of the target and looking at it (Targ & Puthoff, 1974). Free-response methods have yielded consistently stronger psi effects than restricted-response experiments in terms of the number of trials required for statistical significance (Honorton, 1975a).

In experiments testing whether the subject's dream bears a resemblance to the target picture, the picture may be on a post-card, cut out of a magazine, or it may be a print of a famous painting. In dream experiments the subject is awakened following a period in which his electronically recorded brain waves or rapid eye movements indicate that he is dreaming, and his description of his dream is tape-recorded. The subject and/or independent judges rank or rate the degree of similarity between the dream and each of several potential target pictures, the evaluator having no normal knowledge of which picture was the actual target (Ullman & Krippner, 1973). In some cases the dreams were precognitively directed to targets selected at a future date. Dreams of subjects hypnotized to dream were compared with target pictures (Honorton & Stump, 1969), as also were the verbally expressed thoughts of sensory-deprived subjects (Honorton & Harper, 1974). In all of these techniques, principally performed at the Dream Laboratory of the Maimonides Medical Center in Brooklyn, significant results were obtained, indicating that the subjects were associating with the picture targets through ESP.

The British aeronautical engineer J.W. Dunne (1927) recorded his dreams over a period of several years and observed that they were composed of images of future as well as of past experiences. His technique was a qualitative rather than a quantitative approach, and this was also true of the tests conducted by Gilbert Murray, Professor of Greek at Oxford University. After Murray left the room, one of his two daughters would choose a target, speak it aloud, and write it down. Murray would reenter the room and describe his impressions with remarkable success. However, the results may have ensued from his subliminal perception of the spoken targets due to auditory hyperacuity (Dodds, 1972).

Quantitative techniques have been used in testing psychometry, which is the alleged ability of the psychic to describe a concealed object held in his hand or to describe persons or places previously related to the object. The psychic's descriptions of several objects are evaluated and analyzed by a statistical technique such as that of Pratt and Birge (1948). This technique has also been used in evaluating mediumistic material. A number of records are taken from a psychic, each intended for a different individual who, if present, is concealed from the medium. Statistically significant result were obtained in a series of such experiments by Pratt (1969) with the psychic Eileen Garrett.

Other varied free-choice tests have been performed with psychics. In book tests, the sensitive indicates a volume where a phrase can be found connected with a particular event. In these tests, the page and the line of the book are given and the exact position of the book in the experimenter's library or in a library that the experimenter had never entered. This method was employed successfully with the English medium Gladys Leonard (Mrs. Sidgwick, 1921). In the empty-chair test, the psychic describes the person who will occupy a chair in a public hall at a designated future time. When the date arrives, a number of participants not known by the sensitive occupy chairs they have randomly selected, and the psychic's statements are checked against reality. Osty (1926), in France, was the first to apply this technique with the psychic Pascal Forthuny, and it was followed successfully by Tenhaeff (1960), in Holland, with the psychic Croiset. In the sealed-message test, the experimenter seals in a container a message known only to him, with the intent of his communicating the message through a medium after his death. Such tests by Frederic Myers (Salter, 1958) and by Sir Oliver Lodge (Gay et al., 1955) were not successful. The English psychologist Robert Thouless (1972) devised a cipher test of postmortem survival. The cipher was published with the thought that, if it is broken only after his death, this will provide evidence that the keys to the cipher are being communicated by his post-mortem consciousness rather than being obtained by the medium through clairvoyance.

Schmeidler (1966) carried out tests of haunted houses, in which several psychics independently toured the house. Each sensitive indicated on floor plans the localities where he considered the ghost to be felt and indicated on checklists his impressions of the ghost's personality, its activities, and its physical appearance. The psychics' statements were in significantly closer agreement with those of the family members who had perceived the ghost than were statements made by a control group of ordinary individuals.

Methods of Randomizing Targets

With fixed-response targets (where the number of targets is set) , the order in which the targets occur may coincide with the order in which the subject characteristically calls the targets because of his psychological preferences. This could result in extra-chance hits by the subject that are not due to ESP. If in successive runs the targets continued to be in a particular arrangement coinciding with the subject's preferred order of calling, the number of hits achieved could be statistically significant without being the result of ESP. To prevent this, the targets must be in a *random order* and their randomicity ensured for each successive run.

The targets can be placed in random order, if they are cards, by shuffling the deck several times and cutting it twice. This operation should be screened from the subject so that he will not receive cues concerning the order of the cards in the pack. A more certain method of ensuring the randomicity of the targets is to determine their order on the basis of a table of random digits, which has been tested to ensure its randomness, such as Table I of the Appendix. If the ESP symbols are used as the targets, each of the ten digits in the table of random digits can be used to represent one of the five ESP symbols and translated to it. Thus, each ESP symbol is represented by either of two digits.

The digits themselves can be used as the targets without converting them into other symbols.

Methods of Determining the Length of The Experiment and of Its Divisions

The length of the experiment should be determined in advance so that the results cannot be attributed to *optional stoppage,* i.e. stopping the experiment at a point where the results happen to be favorable just by chance. The weaker the psi effect being expressed, the longer the experiment must be for the results to be statistically significant. As it is not known in advance how strong the psi effect will be, a decision must be made on the basis of (1) how strongly psi has been found to be expressed in other experiments, (2) how long it is practicable to carry on the experiment, and (3) the danger that a decline in the scoring rate may reduce the expression of psi to statistical insignificance if the experiment is too lengthy.

The probability is the relative frequency of occurrence of a given result by chance alone. In this book, the antecedent probability or the probability of an unrealized event is symbolized by P, while the probability of an observed result is indicated by p. This is in agreement with its usage in some scientific publications, while the reverse notation is employed in others. Until agreement is reached concerning these notations, consistency of either usage throughout the publication may be the most that can be expected. The P value of a hit in a trial with an ESP deck is $1/5$, as the card may be any one of five symbols which are of equal frequency. The probability of the call and the target being the same, i.e. the P value of a hit, is the same whether the trial is for high aim to produce a hit or for low aim to miscall the target.

As guidelines for determining the length of an experiment, a psi effect producing a deviation of 5 percent from mean chance expectancy, i.e. an average of either $5\frac{1}{4}$ or $4\frac{3}{4}$ hits per run, has a p value of .02 in 350 runs of the ESP deck. That is, there are only two chances out of 100 that the results are due to chance. With the same score of $5\frac{1}{4}$ or $4\frac{3}{4}$ hits per run, a p of .05 (five chances out of 100 that the results are due to chance) is obtained with

250 runs. A psi effect producing an average of $5\frac{1}{2}$ or $4\frac{1}{2}$ hits per run yields a p of .02 with 90 runs of the ESP deck, and it has a p of .05 with 60 runs. With the same deviation from mean chance expectation, tests of PK with dice require somewhat fewer trials for significance than do tests with an ESP deck. This is because the probability of a hit on a die is less than the probability of a hit on an ESP card. The trials or runs can all be performed by one subject, or they can be equally divided among several subjects. The latter technique must be utilized if it is to be determined whether the psychic effect is generally distributed rather than being peculiar to a single individual.

With respect to the length of the divisions of the experiment, the basic division with an ESP deck is a run of 25 calls. With dice, a run has traditionally consisted of 24 trials, e.g. four throws of six dice each. Other combinations of dice number per throw and number of throws per run are equally valid. Because of a possible effect of their relative positions, comparison of factors should be made by testing for them in trials or runs that are either alternate or randomly determined, rather than comparing them in large divisions of the experiment devoted solely to testing one of them alone. For the same reason, the one of two factors to be tested first in each pair of trials or runs should be alternately selected or randomly determined.

The length of the session for the individual subject, i.e. the period during which he is tested in one sitting, should not be great enough to cause him to become bored or fatigued, with a resultant decline in his scoring level. On the other hand, it should be long enough to take maximum advantage of the subject's being present and available for the test. In the absence of empirical tests to determine the optimum length of the session, my judgment is that it should consist of from two to six runs of an ESP deck per subject.

While the experimenter may be expected to engage in longer periods of testing than the individual subject, the length of his participation in one session with one or more subjects should not exceed the length of his ability to perform optimally. This is particularly important in tests of psi where the experimenter as well as the subject may have a paranormal effect upon the scoring level. In the absence of experimental evidence concerning the optimum length of the session for the experimenter, my judgment is that it should not consist of over a dozen runs of an ESP deck.

Methods of Preventing Sensory Cues

Sensory cues that must be guarded against include those which are subliminal as well as those which are consciously perceived. There must be no object from which the symbol on the card could be reflected to the subject's eyes, such as mirrors, glass windows, the agent's eyeglasses, or even his corneas. It must be ensured that the target card is sufficiently thick to prevent the symbol on its face from being perceptible from its back. A mark or a scratch on the back of even one card in the deck may be associated by the subject with the symbol on its face and lead to significant results that are not due to ESP. This possibility can be prevented by using a different deck for each run or by concealing the cards from the subject. Sensory cues gained from the agent's facial expression or body position must be prevented. Without realizing it, the agent may have a particular expression, movement, or body position for a particular symbol, and the subject may detect this. Such cues may be prevented by placing a screen between the subject and the agent. The screen must consist of more than a simple blindfolding of the subject, as *nose peeking* is possible even with the most careful attempts at covering the eyes. Even when the eyes are covered with a moldable substance such as dough, it is possible for the subject by contracting his facial muscles to produce a crevice between the dough and his nose which permits him to peek at the target object.

Muscle reading, which is the perception of muscular movements of the agent whose hand the subject may be holding, affords a means for some performers to find a hidden object. Muscle contractions of the agent who knows the location of the hidden object may differ depending upon whether the pair is approaching the target or is moving farther away from it. Some subjects are keen enough to perceive and interpret body movements of the agent unless the latter is completely covered with a box (Soal

& Bateman, 1954). Covering only the agent's head was found to be insufficient to prevent the vaudeville telepathist Fred Marion from locating the hidden object. The agent had to be completely covered with a box except for holes for his eyes before the stage performer was unable to find the hidden object.

Auditory cues may be produced by the agent's unconscious whispering, and visual screening of the agent from the subject is not sufficient to prevent them. Precautions must be taken against deliberate attempts by the agent and the percipient to transmit signals by means of supersonic whistles or by electronic devices concealed on their bodies. Both visual and auditory cues can be prevented by placing the cards in envelopes or by employing an adequate distance between subject and agent. If the cards are not in envelopes, the possibility of the subject's obtaining sensory cues from onlookers who can see the card faces must otherwise be controlled.

In séances the sitter may respond to the medium's statements in a manner permitting the psychic to draw correct conclusions and to reveal facts pertaining to the sitter that are not produced by ESP. This is preventable by using a *proxy sitter,* that is a person representing the subject but not knowing anything about the latter, so that his responses to the medium's statements do not normally reveal anything about the subject (Thomas, 1939). If a proxy sitter is not employed, an attempt may be made to prevent the medium's finding out any facts about the sitter before he meets him at the séance. When the American Medium Leonore Piper was taken to England for tests, her actions were watched by detectives to prevent her obtaining information about her possible future subjects, and no evidence suggesting such activity by her was found (Gauld, 1968).

Methods of Instructing Subjects

If the target symbols are new to the subject, it may be advisable to display a set of the symbols before him until he has thoroughly familiarized himself with them. If the directions to the subjects are complex, they should be given in written form so that they will be understandable and will be the same for all of the subjects of the experiment. The importance of instructions to the subject is illustrated by experiments in which they were successful only when the instructions were presented to them in a certain way (Kanthamani, 1965).

If the subject knows the purpose of the experiment, it may influence his expression of psi. For example, let us consider an experiment designed to test the effect of the subject's belief in ESP in which the subject knows that believers are expected to score positively and disbelievers negatively. This knowledge may cause him to score in a direction either for or against what is expected of him, which may depend upon the degree of his cooperation rather than upon his belief in ESP. For this reason, it is better not to tell the subject what variable is being measured with respect to its connection with psi. It may be better not to reveal to the subject any more than is necessary for him to carry out the requested task. On the other hand, refusal to answer the subject's questions concerning the experiment may result in his negativism in expressing psi. Furthermore, psi expression may be increased by the subject's interest in the experiment, and this may be furthered by his understanding of its purpose. Giving the optimum information to the subject for the purposes of the experiment requires a delicate balance between disclosure and concealment and must be resolved in the design of each test.

Methods of Recording Targets and Calls and of Marking Results

Specially prepared score sheets are available for use with the ESP deck. (Score sheets can be purchased in pads of 50 sheets from the FRNM in Durham, N.C.) The sheets have spaces for recording ten runs with two columns for each run. One column is for recording the calls and the other is for recording the targets. After the symbols in either of these two columns are recorded, that column should be covered while the symbols in the other column are entered. This is to prevent the recorder's being guided unconsciously to list a symbol similar to the recorded call or to the recorded target symbol as the case may be. Whatever sheets are used for recording the data, they should be uniform, neatly prepared, and with spaces at the top for entering the name of the experimenter, the name of the subject, the date, and the number of the experimental division. Numbering the score sheets is a safeguard against their being unknowingly lost. All records should be made in ink. In checking and totalling the correct calls or hits, two independent checkers should be employed. If their results do not agree, they should be compared and the errors corrected.

ESP Testing Machines

Ideally, an ESP testing machine should present randomly selected targets and should automatically record the subjects' successes. Significant results have been obtained with the use of some ESP testing machines. One of these was the previously described apparatus built by Tyrrell (1938). The electrical engineer W.C. Stewart (1959) also obtained significant results with a machine he designed that contained five lamps and was used with a random-target generator. The physicist Helmut Schmidt (1969) constructed a random-target generator in which one of four lamps is lighted as determined by a single quantum process, i.e. the arrival of an electron at a Geiger-Müller tube. The electron is the product of the decay of radioactive strontium-90. Because the radioactive substance spontaneously disintegrates, it is not possible to determine physically when the next electron will be released. The subject presses one of the four buttons corresponding to the lamp he expects to light up next. The results, which are recorded automatically on paper punch tape, gave p values of less than 10^{-10}.

Some significant results were obtained with the use of an electronic ESP tester built at the University of Edinburgh, which both randomizes the succession of targets and automatically registers the number of hits and trials (Beloff & Regan, 1969). Targ and Hurt (1972) met with some success in their use of an ESP teaching machine with which the subject, by pressing a button, indicates his guess of which of the four targets is randomly generated by the machine. The apparatus automatically records and scores both the target generated and the subject's response and informs the subject of the correct answer.

Individual versus Group Testing

In an ESP test the question arises as to whether to test the subjects one at a time or whether to test several of them simultaneously in a group. Individual testing has the advantage of permitting greater personal contact and the establishment of greater rapport between experimenter and subject. On the other hand, even though a different set of targets must be supplied each subject in a group test to prevent a possible stacking effect, less time is consumed when several subjects are tested at the same time than when they are tested separately. Since individual testing is more time-consuming, it decreases the number of subjects who are likely to be tested. With only a few subjects, the results reflect the subjects' peculiarities rather than indicating widespread or more generally prevalent characteristics of psi. Furthermore, subjects tested in a group are confronted by fewer variables than if they are tested separately. Such variables may arise from unintentional changes between tests of the individual subjects in the experimental conditions or in the experimenter. Either group or individual testing may register the peculiarities of the experimenter or agent. This can be prevented by tests in which a large number of agents as well as a large number of subjects are employed.

Methods of Evaluating Results

Most ESP experiments are no longer directed at proving extrasensory perception. This would be comparable to continuing the stockpiling of nuclear explosives when there are already enough to destroy the world's population. Most parapsychologists believe that the experimental evidence for ESP has long been sufficient for its acceptance and that perusal of the numerous experimental reports in scientific journals should convince any openminded skeptic of the existence of ESP. Experiments should continue to be carried out not to prove ESP but to determine its parameters and characteristics, which necessitates that the tests be designed for this purpose. In order for an experiment to show whether a factor is related to ESP, the experiment must indicate that ESP took place. Unfortunately in our present state of knowledge, ESP is not always demonstrable.

In evaluating the results of an experiment, the mean chance expectation *(MCE)* score of the factor under consideration must be determined. In a run with the ESP deck of 25 cards and five symbols, $MCE = 5$ hits. From the expected score the deviation of the observed score can be calculated. The deviation is the observed score minus the MCE score, and it can be plus or minus depending upon whether more or less than the MCE number of hits per run was obtained. The degree of significance of the deviation is expressed as a probability. The lower the p value, the less is the probability that the deviation is due to chance. A probability of .05 is considered in most sciences to be low enough to indicate that the deviation is not due to chance.

If *psi missing* (a below MCE score) as well as *psi hitting* (an above MCE score) is to be considered evidential in the experiment, a *two-tailed* rather than a *one-tailed* test is made to determine the probability. It is generally assumed that the test is two tailed unless otherwise stated. Tables II and III in the Appendix are for two-tailed tests, and the probabilities in them can be divided by two if the analysis calls for a one-tailed test. If either a positive or a negative direction of scoring is to be considered as evidence of psi, a two-tailed test is correct to use. However, if scoring only in a particular one of the two directions is to be considered evidential, a one-tailed test is proper.

The precise factors that the experiment is performed to measure and how they are to be evaluated should be designated in advance. This is because experimental evidence of their existence is largely statistical, and if enough variables are measured in a given experiment or enough statistical analyses are performed, one or more of them will have a probability of .05 or less attributable to chance alone. For example, if twenty factors are measured, one of them will be expected to yield a p value of .05 solely by chance. To constitute acceptable evidence, the findings of an experiment must be a priori, i.e. predicted in advance. This does not mean that a posteriori findings are worthless. Indeed it is often through unanticipated results that discoveries are made and science progresses. However, the results of *post hoc* analyses of experimental data can be considered to be no more than suggestive. In such cases, the experiment must be considered to be no more than a pilot study, and similar results must be obtained in a confirmatory study in order to be scientifically evidential.

The rate of scoring must be distinguished from the significance of the score, which is indicated by the p value. A very high rate of scoring could be insignificant if it prevailed over only a few trials. For example, in a coin toss in which heads are the target, flipping two heads consecutively provides a rate of scoring that is 100 percent above mean chance expectancy. However, the p value is 1 out of 4, which is far from being significant. On the other hand, a scoring rate differing from MCE by only 5 percent can be quite significant if it extends over a sufficient number of trials. The probability of a score differing from chance expectancy by 5 percent is less than .05 for 250 runs of an ESP deck, less than .006 for 500 runs, and less than .00007 for 1000 runs.

CRITICAL RATIO OR Z SCORE. If only one subject is engaged in the experiment, the probability of the deviation of his score from MCE can be ascertained in the following way. The *standard deviation* (σ) is determined, and it is equal to $\sqrt{\text{(number of trials}}$ $\times$ probability of success per trial $\times$ probability of failure per trial). Substituting in this formula, in one run with an open ESP deck, $\sigma = \sqrt{(25 \times 1/5 \times 4/5)} = 2$. With a closed deck, $\sigma = 1.02$ $\sqrt{(25 \times 1/5 \times 4/5)}$ (Greenwood & Stuart, 1937). Next the *critical ratio (CR)* or *z score* is determined by dividing the deviation by the σ. To illustrate, if the subject had 175 hits in 30 runs with an ESP deck, the MCE would be $(30 \times 25)/5 = 150$, and the deviation would be $175 - 150 = 25$. The σ would be $\sqrt{(750 \times}$ $1/5 \times 4/5)} = 10.95$. The CR would be equal to $25/10.95$ or 2.28. The probability is ascertained by finding the value of the CR in a table for the conversion of CR values to p values in a two-tailed test (Appendix, Table II). From the use of this table, it is seen that the p value associated with a CR of 2.28 is .0226. This means that only in about two times out of 100 would a score in such a test be expected by chance alone to have a deviation of as much as 25. Since a p value of .05 is considered to be significant, the results in this illustration may be regarded as being extrachance.

Because this evaluation is based on the amount of the deviation without regard to its sign, a deviation of −25, which would result from a score of 125 hits in 30 runs, would be equally significant. If it were predicted that the deviation would only be positive and a negative deviation would not be considered as evidential, the one-tailed test could be used by dividing the p value by 2. In that case, the above illustration would give a p value of .0113. This value is only one-half as great and, hence, is twice as significant as if the possibility of psi missing as well as the possibility of psi hitting had been considered to be an evidential result.

CRITICAL RATIO OF THE DIFFERENCE. Whether the difference between the number of hits in two groups of trials is significant is measurable by the critical ratio of the difference (CR_{diff}) between the scores of the two groups. Where the two groups are of equal size, CR_{diff} = difference between hits in the two groups/ $\sqrt{}$ (sum of trials in both groups × probability of success per trial × probability of failure per trial). As an illustration, in 25 runs of believers in ESP there were 140 hits and in 25 runs of disbelievers there were 110 hits. $CR_{diff} = (140 − 110)/\sqrt{(25 \times 50 \times 1/5 \times 4/5)} = 30/14.14 = 2.12$ which has a p value of .034 that is significant.

Where the two groups are of unequal size, CR_{diff} = difference between average hits per run in the two groups/σ of one run × $\sqrt{[(1/\text{number of runs in group 1}) + (1/\text{number of runs in group 2})]}$. To illustrate, if group 1 had 390 hits in 60 runs and group 2 had 275 hits in 50 runs, the average hits per run would be 6.5 and 5.5, respectively, with a difference between the two averages of 1.0. The σ of one run is equal to $\sqrt{(25 \times 1/5 \times 4/5)}$ or 2. The square root of [1/number of runs in group 1] + [1/number of runs in group 2] = $\sqrt{(1/60 + 1/50)]} = 1.916$. $CR_{diff} = 1.0/(2 \times 1.916) = 2.61$ which has a $p < .01$ (Appendix, Table II) that is significant.

t TEST. Often an investigator wishes to draw a conclusion from an experiment concerning whether subjects tested under a given condition perform differently from mean chance expectation. The CR discussed above will not be appropriate for this purpose because in its computation the number of subjects tested and the variability of their scores are not considered. If one is to conclude from studying a sample of subjects that individuals in general tested under this condition tend to perform in a particular way (for instance score better than *MCE*), the statistical test must consider how many subjects are tested and how widely their scores vary. The number of subjects tested must be taken into consideration because, in estimating the performance of subjects in general from a finite sample, it must be considered that the estimate is less reliable the smaller the sample (and vice versa). The statistical test must also consider how the scores vary among subjects because the reliability of the estimate will depend upon how variable the subjects' scores are under the condition studied.

A statistic which considers both the size of the sample and the variability of the subjects' scores is the *t test,* specifically the *t* test which compares a sample mean with a hypothetical mean, e.g. with mean chance expectation. The formula for this test is $t = (M_o - M_e)/(s/\sqrt{N})$ with $df = N - 1$. M_o is the mean of the subjects' ESP scores, M_e is the expected chance mean or *MCE*, N is the number of subjects, and s is the unbiased estimate of the σ. The formula for the unbiased estimate of the σ is

$$s = \sqrt{[N\Sigma X^2 - (\Sigma X)^2]/N (N - 1)},$$

where Σ = sum of, and X = the subject's score. The symbol *df* stands for *degrees of freedom,* which in such a test is generally one less than the number of subjects tested.

To illustrate, in a test of six subjects each with ten runs of an ESP deck, the scores for the ten runs of the six subjects were 63, 60, 55, 54, 49 and 55 as shown in Table 3-I.

TABLE 3-I

DETERMINATION OF *t*

Subject	X (Observed hits)	X^2
1	63	3969
2	60	3600
3	55	3025
4	54	2916
5	49	2401
6	55	3025
Total	336	18936

$M_o = 336/6 = 56$, $M_e = 50$, $N = \sqrt{[(6 \times 18936) - 336^2]/(6 \times 5)}$ $= 4.16$, and $t = (56 - 50) / (4.16/\sqrt{6}) = 6/1.698 = 3.53$. The probability associated with the value of t is ascertained by referring to the t table of values (Appendix, Table III) in the appropriate line for the degrees of freedom which, in this illustration, are one less than the number of subjects or five. With five degrees of freedom, $p < .02$, which is significant. As in determining the p value for the CR, the p value found in Table III should be divided by two if it is a one-tailed rather than a two-tailed test.

t TEST OF THE DIFFERENCE. The t test can be applied to the difference between the scores of two groups of subjects with the use of the following formula: $t = (M_1 - M_2)/s\sqrt{(1/N_1 + 1/N_2)}$ with $df = N_1 + N_2 - 2$. In this formula, $M_1 =$ mean of the subjects' ESP scores in group 1, $M_2 =$ mean of the subjects' scores in group 2, $N_1 =$ number of subjects in group 1, $N_2 =$ number of subjects in group 2, and s is the unbiased estimate of the σ, i.e. $s = \sqrt{(N_1 - 1) s_1^2 + (N_2 - 1) s_2^2/(N_1 + N_2 - 2)}$, where $s_1 =$ unbiased estimate of the σ of group 1, and $s_2 =$ unbiased estimate of the σ of group 2.

To illustrate its use, in a test of two groups each composed of six subjects with each subject tested for ten runs of an ESP deck, the observed hits for group 1 were 59, 56, 51, 52, 55 and 57, while the scores for group 2 were 49, 53, 50, 49, 44 and 43. The sum of the observed hits for group 1 is 330 and for group 2 it is 288. $M_1 = 330/6 = 55$ and $M_2 = 288/6 = 48$. Using the method illustrated in the previous section for determining the unbiased estimate of the σ, s for group 1 $= 3.03$ and s for group 2 $= 3.79$. $t = (55 - 48) /\sqrt{5(3.03)^2 + 5(3.79)^2/(6 + 6 - 2)} \sqrt{1/6 + 1/6} = 7/(3.43 \times .577) = 3.54$. With 10 df (each of the two groups of subjects has 5 df), it can be seen from Table III in the Appendix that $p < .01$, which is significant.

CHI-SQUARE TEST. When the subjects or the experimental units are divisible into two or more classes with respect to their manifestation of psi, the frequencies within the classes can be compared with each other or with their expected values by means of the *chi-square* (χ^2) test. To illustrate, suppose that in a test of 50 subjects, 26 were rated as believers in ESP and 24 as disbelievers. Suppose that each subject was further classified as to whether his ESP score was above or below MCE. Subjects scoring at MCE can either be omitted or included in the latter group. Omitting subjects scoring at MCE, suppose 18 of the believers scored above MCE and 7 below, while 8 of the disbelievers scored above MCE and 15 below. The data are tabulated in Table 3-II in two rows and two columns.

TABLE 3-II
2 × 2 TABLE OF BELIEVERS AND DISBELIEVERS

	believers	disbelievers	total
above MCE	19	28	47
below MCE	10	73	83
total	29	101	130

$\chi^2 = [\Sigma(o - e)^2/e]$ where o is the observed frequency and e is the expected or computed frequency.

Table 3-III is a worksheet for computing the e values and χ^2 in the above illustration.

TABLE 3-III
DETERMINATION OF χ^2

o	e	$o-e$	$(o-e)^2$	$(o-e)^2/e$
	(row total × column total)/total			
18	26 × 25 / 48 = 13.54	+4.46	19.89	1.47
8	26 × 23 / 48 = 12.46	−4.46	19.89	1.60
7	22 × 25 / 48 = 11.46	−4.46	19.89	1.74
15	22 × 23 / 48 = 10.54	+4.46	19.89	1.89
			$\chi^2 =$	6.70

The $df = $ (number of rows $- 1$) (number of columns $- 1$) $=$ $(2 - 1) (2 - 1) = 1$. Referring to Table IV in the Appendix, it can be seen that the corresponding p value for a χ^2 of 6.70 with 1 df is $< .01$, which is significant. Experiments in which there are more groups or attributes than in the above illustration can be analyzed with this method by the use of additional columns and/or rows.

Yate's correction for the continuity of the normal curve may be applied by subtracting the number $\frac{1}{2}$ from the number of trials. Unless the number of trials is small, the correction is likely to have little effect on the resultant p value.

A simpler procedure for computing the χ^2 value in a 2×2 table is shown in Table 3-IV.

TABLE 3-IV

2×2 TABLE FOR DETERMINATION OF χ^2

a	c	a + c
b	d	b + d
a + b	c + d	a+b+c+d

$$\chi^2 = \frac{(a+b+c+d)\ (ad-bc)^2}{(a+b)\ (c+d)\ (a+c)\ (b+d)}$$

Substituting the values given in the above illustration,

$$\chi^2 = \frac{48(18 \times 15 - 7 \times 8)^2}{25 \times 23 \times 26 \times 22} = 6.7$$

COEFFICIENT OF CORRELATION. When it is desirable to determine the relationship between ESP scores and some other attribute, such as a personality factor, which varies in expression in different subjects, the *coefficient of correlation* (r) can be determined. As an illustration, hypothetical mean ESP scores and scores on emotional stability of ten subjects are presented in Table 3-V.

TABLE 3-V

DETERMINATION OF CORRELATION COEFFICIENT

subject	X ESP score	Y emotional stability	X²	Y²	XY
1	5.0	10.1	25.00	102.01	50.50
2	5.1	10.2	26.01	104.04	52.02
3	4.8	9.9	23.04	98.01	47.52
4	4.9	10.0	24.01	100.00	49.00
5	5.1	9.9	26.01	98.01	50.49
6	5.2	10.1	27.04	102.01	52.52
7	4.9	9.8	24.01	96.04	48.02
8	5.0	10.1	25.00	102.01	50.50
9	5.1	10.2	26.01	104.04	52.02
10	5.1	9.8	26.01	96.04	49.98
total	50.2	100.1	252.14	1002.21	502.57

The formula for the correlation coefficient is

$$r = (N\Sigma XY - \Sigma X\Sigma Y)/\sqrt{[N\Sigma X^2 - (\Sigma X^2)][N\Sigma Y^2 - (\Sigma Y)^2]}$$

where N = number of subjects. By substituting in this formula, the value of r in the above illustartion is found to be $+.403$. This is one of a possible range of values from $+1.0$, a perfect positive correlation, to -1.0, a perfect negative correlation. To determine the significance of the value of the correlation coefficient, the following formula is used: $t = \sqrt{r^2 (N-2)/1-r^2}$, with $df = N - 2$. With the data in the above illustration, the value of t is 1.245 and, with 8 df, the corresponding p is $> .20$ (Appendix, Table III), which is not significant. If the same value for the correlation coefficient had been obtained with twenty subjects, t would have a value of 3.490, which with 18 df has a $p < .005$.

VARIANCE. Psi may be expressed negatively in psi missing as well as positively in psi hitting, and this may balance out in the experiment producing no significant deviation from MCE in the total score. The positive and negative expressions of psi, however, can be combined without respect to their sign so that they will reinforce rather than cancel each other. This can be accomplished by determining the *variance* between the scores of the subjects or between the runs, and determining whether it differs significantly between two groups of subjects or between two parts of the experiment. To illustrate, suppose that in a typical 25 ESP-card run the variance between the scores of the 12 subjects with a lively interest in ESP was compared with the variance between the scores of 12 subjects with a dull mood. The hypothetical data are presented in Table 3-VI.

TABLE 3-VI
DETERMINATION OF VARIANCE RATIO

Lively interest in ESP			*Dull mood*		
subject	*X (score)*	*X²*	*subject*	*X (score)*	*X²*
1	8	64	1	5	25
2	3	9	2	6	36
3	9	81	3	3	9
4	1	1	4	4	16
5	6	36	5	6	36
6	2	4	6	4	16
7	8	64	7	5	25
8	6	36	8	4	16
9	9	81	9	4	16
10	8	64	10	7	49
11	2	4	11	6	36
12	7	49	12	4	16
total	69	493	total	58	296

With the use of the following formula—variance $= [N/(N-1)]$ $[\Sigma X^2/N - (\Sigma X/N)^2]$, where $X =$ score and $N =$ number of subjects or runs—the variance of the lively subjects is found to be $(12/11)$ $[493/12 - (69/12)^2] = 8.75$ and the variance of the dull subjects is $(12/11)$ $[296/12 - (58/12)^2] = 1.42$. The F *ratio* is the ratio between the two variances, which is $8.75/1.42 = 6.16$. The degrees of freedom are one less than the numbers of subjects in each group. Referring to Table V in the Appendix, it can be seen that with $11/11$ df the associated probability for $F = 6.16$ is $< .01$. In this illustration, the variance between the lively subjects' scores is significantly greater than the variance between the scores of the dull subjects.

In some experiments in which the positive and negative scores balance each other, psi can be shown to have taken place by comparing the observed variance with the theoretical variance. The theoretical variance $=$ number of trials $\times$ probability of success per trial $\times$ probability of failure per trial, and has infinite df. For each group of 12 subjects in the above illustration, the theoretical variance $= 25 \times 1/5 \times 4/5 = 4$. The value of the F ratio between the observed and theoretical variances for the 12 lively subjects is $8.75/4 = 2.19$, which, with $11/\infty$ df, is not significant (Table V in the Appendix). For the 12 dull subjects, the value of the F ratio is $4/1.42 = 2.82$, which, with $\infty/11$ df, has a probability $<.01$, which is significant. Low variance between the runs of a single subject indicates reliability and consistency of his psi performance. High variance between the runs of a single subject or between the scores of several subjects indicates the expression of psi even though it may take place as psi missing in some runs or subjects and psi hitting in others.

PREFERENTIAL MATCHING. In experiments with free-response targets in which the subject's response takes the form of a dream, a verbal description, or a drawing, the results may be evaluated numerically by use of *preferential matching*. The subject's response, e.g. a dream of a picture target, or a verbal description or drawing of a remote geographical locality, is compared with several randomly chosen pictures or geographical localities, as the case may be. A set of responses is matched with a set of targets, each response in the set having been made by the subject to a different one of the targets. The subject or an independent judge blindly ranks each of the responses in the order of its similarity to one of the targets and repeats this process with each of the targets. The responses may be those of one or of several subjects.

The hypothetical data in Table 3-VII supply an illustration of the use of preferential matching in an experiment of six *sessions*. Each session consisted of four dreams, and each dream was directed to a different one of four pictures. As there were four dreams and four pictures in each session, there were 16 dream-picture comparisons in each session, four of which were between a dream and its own target. Therefore, in the six sessions

TABLE 3-VII

PREFERENTIAL MATCHING

Rank								
	1	*2*	*3*	*4*	*5*	*6*	*total*	*total* × *rank*
1	2	1	3	2	1	2	11	11
2	1	2	1	0	2	2	8	16
3	1	1	0	1	0	0	3	9
4	0	0	0	1	1	0	2	8
10							24	44

there were 24 dream-target pairs. Each dream-picture pair was given a rank of 1 to 4 depending upon the similarity of the dream and the picture. From Table 3-VII it can be seen that the dream was ranked closest to its target, i.e. given a rank of 1, in 11 of the 24 dream-target pairs, given a rank of 2 in 8 pairs, a rank of 3 in 3 pairs, and a rank of 4 in 2 pairs. The expected sum of the ranks for each session is 1+2+3+4 = 10, or 60 for the six sessions. As can be seen in Table 3-VII, the observed sum of the ranks is 44, thus the deviation = 60 − 44 = 16. The $\sigma = \sqrt{(5 \times \text{number of sessions})}$* = 5.48, The $CR = 16/5.48 = 2.92$, which has a $p<.004$ (Appendix, Table III), which is significant.

Some newer methods of analysis of preferentially ranked data have been recently described (Solfin, Kelly & Burdick, 1978).

ANALYSIS OF VERBAL RESPONSE. In a test of verbal responses, such as in the psychometry of an article or in the statements directed by a medium to a sitter, there may be several articles or sitters. The psychic responds verbally to each article or sitter and his responses are judged blindly with respect to their similarity to the object. The psychic's responses to each article or sitter are each divided into separate statements. The subjects, i.e. the sitters or the owners of the articles, check each statement in each of the responses that they judge to be descriptive of themselves or the article. Subjects vary in the degree to which they judge statements to be relevant. Also, the psychic's responses to the several sitters or articles may vary in the number of statements into which they are divided and in the relevance of the statements. A technique developed by Pratt and Birge (1948) compensates for these differences. Its application is illustrated in Table 3-VIII with five subjects each of whom checked the statements in each response which he judged to be descriptive of himself.

---

*For further reading see C.E. Stuart. "An ESP Test with Drawings," *JP*, 6:20-43, 1942; and J.A. Greenwood. "A Preferential Matching Problem," *Psychometrika*, 8:185-191, 1943.

TABLE 3-VIII

ANALYSIS OF VERBAL RESPONSES

Subjects	Subject's check marks					
	Brown	Hlil	Smith	Green	Jones	Total
Brown	(7)	0	0	3	9	19
Hill	0	(0)	0	12	3	15
Smith	0	3	(26)	13	10	52
Green	0	2	0	(12)	2	16
Jones	0	4	0	4	(3)	11
Total	7	9	26	44	27	113

The $CR = \text{deviation}/\sigma$, where $\sigma = \sqrt{\text{variance}}$. The observed hits (on the diagonal) = 48, the expected hits = 113/5 or 22.6, and the deviation = $48 - 22.6 = +25.4$. The variance = $[N^2 + n^2 (\Sigma a^2) - n(\Sigma r^2) - n(\Sigma c^2)]/n^2(n-1)$, where N = number of check marks, n = number of subjects, Σa^2 = sum of squares on individual calls, Σr^2 = sum of squares of separate row totals, and Σc^2 = sum of squares of separate column totals. Substituting the appropriate values in the above formula, the variance = $[113^2 + 25(1,439) - 5(3,667) - 5(3,471)]/25(5-1) = 130.54$. The $\sigma = \sqrt{\text{variance}} = 11.43$. The $CR = 25.4/11.43$ or 2.22 and, from Table II in the Appendix, $p = .013$ in a one-tailed test. A one-tailed test is used because it is predicted that the psychic's responses will be more like the targets than *MCE*—not that they will be either more or less like the targets than *MCE*. (For a further consideration of this method see Scott, 1972.)

MAJORITY-VOTE ANALYSIS. The same set of targets is repeatedly used in the *repeated-guessing technique* either with one subject or with many subjects as in radio or television tests. Experiments in which the same set of targets is used repeatedly are subject to the stacking effect. This problem can be removed by determining the number of targets that were called by their correct symbol more frequently than they were called by any of the other symbols. The *majority-vote analysis* with ten sets of calls on the same target order of an ESP deck is illustrated in Table 3-IX.

TABLE 3-IX
MAJORITY-VOTE ANALYSIS

trial	target symbol	symbol called					
		square	circle	cross	star	waves	hits
1	square	(3)*	2	1	2	2	2
2	circle	2	1	3	2	2	1
3	square	1	2	1	3	3	1
4	square	(3)	1	2	2	2	3
5	star	0	2	3	(4)	1	4
6	waves	2	3	3	2	0	0
7	circle	2	(4)	2	0	2	4
8	star	1	3	3	1	2	1
9	waves	1	3	3	2	1	1
10	cross	2	1	(4)	2	1	4
11	cross	2	2	2	2	2	2
12	waves	2	2	1	2	(3)	3
13	circle	3	0	2	3	2	0
14	waves	1	3	3	1	2	2
15	square	2	2	2	2	2	2
16	cross	2	2	(4)	1	1	4
17	waves	2	2	2	3	1	1
18	circle	2	0	3	2	3	0
19	star	1	2	1	(4)	2	4
20	cross	1	3	1	2	3	1
21	square	(5)	3	1	0	1	5
22	star	3	3	1	1	2	1
23	star	3	2	1	1	3	1
24	circle	0	(4)	2	3	1	4
25	cross	2	3	1	1	3	1

53

*Targets called most frequently by the correct symbol are in parentheses.

There are 53 successful calls, which, with a deviation of +3, is not significant. However, ten of the 25 targets were called more frequently by the correct symbol than by any of the other four symbols, as indicated by parentheses inclosing these hits in the above tabulation. As five is the expected number of targets to receive a majority vote, the observed number of ten such targets has a deviation of +5. The $CR =$ deviation $/\sigma = 5/2 = 2.5$ which has a $p < .01$ (Appendix, Table II).

The repeated-guessing technique is a means of condensing scattered acts of ESP into a few trials and, thereby, increasing the likelihood that those trials will be correct. For this reason, it has been used to send messages by ESP. The transmission of messages by ESP is important for two reasons. One is that it provides a practical use for ESP, particularly in cases where customary means of communication cannot be used. This may occur because normal lines of communication have broken down, because none were established, or because the location of the percipient is unknown to the sender. The other reason for the importance of sending messages by ESP is that it refutes the counterhypothesis that ESP is only a probability and that the similarity between calls and targets is no more than an empty and meaningless correlation (Chap. 4).

Ryzl (1966) reported the successful transmission of a message with the subject Stepanek. With the use of the repeated-guessing technique, five three-digit numbers were transmitted without a single error. Because Stepanek's psi ability was expressed by identifying whether the concealed card had its white or its green side uppermost, the target number was encoded into a certain sequence of green and white sides, and the subject was asked to ascertain by ESP the color of the uppermost sides of the target cards. After the colors of the targets were determined by majority vote analysis, the color sequence was decoded into a number sequence. More recently, the word *"peace"* was successfully transmitted by the majority-vote method (Carpenter, 1977).

Determination of Whether a Given Individual Has Psi

If an individual has discovered a set of circumstances in which he seems to express psi, he can be tested under those circumstances but with conditions controlled in order to determine whether the ostensible psi expression is truly paranormal or whether it has some normal explanation. Some psychics have been sufficiently gifted to manifest psi in ordinary ESP and PK tests that were not specially designed to measure their particular manner of psi expression. If the individual has no identified way of expressing psi, it might require prolonged testing with each of many techniques and conditions and with many experimenters or agents before a combination of variables conducive to his psi expression is discovered. Someday a battery of tests may be developed that will establish in a practicable length of time that an individual has psychic ability, but it may never be possible to determine that he could not express psi in some previously untested situation.

Use of Altered States of Consciousness of Experimenter to Study Psi

Altered states of consciousness, as produced by meditation, self-hypnosis, or psychedelic drugs, may be entered into by the experimenter in order to make observations about paranormal phenomena that occur during his altered states of consciousness. It may be possible in an altered state of consciousness to construct theories concerning that altered state with greater insight than it is possible to do in the ordinary state of consciousness (Tart, 1972a). By altering his state of consciousness, the anthropologist Carlos Castenada (1973) obtained insight into the subjective experiences of an American Indian sorcerer, including many instances of apparent psychic phenomena. Valuable insight into the nature of psi could possibly be obtainable by the psychical researcher through critically examining paranormal phenomena during or shortly after his own altered state of consciousness.

Affect on Non-psi Experiments

It is a reasonable assumption that, if psi exists, it is not confined to paranormal experiments but may affect the results of non-psi experiments as well, without conscious awareness or intent by the perpetrator. The disappearance of initial success, which sometimes occurs upon repetition of non-psi as well as psi experiments, may result from chronological decline of psi, or it may be due to later investigators not exercising psi to the extent of their predecessors. A familiar example is the disappearance of the effectiveness of some newly discovered curative products and procedures, which perplexes the world of pharmacy and medicine and in some instances has led to suspicion of fraud.

TECHNIQUES SPECIFIC TO PK

Randomly Moving Molar Objects

Molar objects, i.e. objects larger than molecules, have been set in random motion to determine if their terminal position was affected by PK. Utilized molar objects have included cubes such as dice, discs such as coins (Thouless, 1945), and spheres such as marbles (Cox, 1954). Experiments with all of these objects have yielded significant results. Initially the dice were thrown from the hand, but in order to preclude manual control this was followed successively by the use of a cup, by the use of an inclined board with a corrugated surface down which the dice were released to roll onto a horizontal plane, and by the use of an automatically rotated cage in which the dice, untouched by the participants, were allowed to come to rest following each rotation (J.B. Rhine, 1943). To prevent the effect of die bias, each of the six faces of the die was used as the target an equal number of times in the *around-the-die* technique. Robert McConnell (1955b), Professor of Biophysics at the University of Pittsburgh, conducted a PK experiment with significant results in which the throwing and recording of the dice were completely mechanized. The dice were in a mechanically rotated cage, and their fall was recorded photographically.

In some PK tests with a pair of dice, the desired effect was to produce a combination of seven, a high-face combination of over seven, or a low-face combination of under seven (J.B. Rhine, 1945a). In other tests, the goal was for both dice of a pair to land with the same face uppermost (Reeves & Rhine, 1945). In one experiment the desired effect was to produce a high score with dice of one color and a low score with simultaneously rolled dice of a different color (Humphrey, 1947b).

In hidden-target PK experiments the subject is ignorant of the target face for which he throws the dice (Thouless, 1951). Such a test ostensibly involves ESP as well as PK. In tests of *placement PK*, randomly rolling dice or marbles have been successfully willed to terminate their rolls on desired portions of the rolling surface such as to the right or to the left of a midline (Cox,

1951; Forwald, 1969). In such experiments, the dice were mechanically released to roll down an inclined board, and each side of the midline was used as the target an equal number of times. When it was the purpose to measure the distance of the terminal positions of the dice from the midline or the distance they rolled, the landing surface was marked with coordinate lines. In a multiple-ball machine, spheres were released to tumble through a random distributing arrangement and to disperse into several collecting chutes on either side of the center (Cox, 1965b). Both sides were used as the target an equal number of times with significant results. Water from a spray was also used as the target, the subject willing more droplets to collect in the experimental tube than in the control (Cox, 1962).

Molar Objects Not in Random Motion

Hare and Crookes used a scale to measure PK (Chap. 2). More recently the Russian psychic Kulagina paranormally tilted a pair of scales and was able to hold one side of the scale down even after 10 grams had been added to the opposite side (Kulagin, 1971). She also stopped a nonrandomly moving pendulum and started a new movement of the pendulum in a different plane. In PK tests the Israeli psychic Geller caused a laboratory balance to respond as though a force were applied to the pan even though it was under a bell jar (Mitchell, 1974, p. 686). The Danish psychic Anna Rasmussen was observed to cause the movement of either or both of two pendulums while the surface of the water in a glass on the same table remained calm (Winther, 1928). Deflection of a compass needle through PK was reported by the German scientist Fechner (1876) at the University of Leipzig. More recently, compass needle deflection was demonstrated by Kulagina (Herbert, 1973). Also, feathers suspended in a bell jar were apparently psychokinetically moved (Owen, 1972b). That one person can psychokinetically influence the galvanic skin response of another individual is shown by an experiment (Braud, 1978) in which the agent caused significantly greater GSR activity in the subject during trials in which he attempted psychically to increase the subject's GSR activity than in trials in which he tried by PK to decrease the subject's GSR activity. Psychokinetic effects on infrahuman organisms are presented in Chapter 10.

Submolar Objects

Submolar objects are of molecular size or smaller. The effect of PK on the motion of molecules is shown by temperature changes measured by a *thermistor* sealed in a thermos bottle at a distance of 25 feet from the American psychic Ingo Swann (Schmeidler, 1973). Paranormal metal-bending, in which metal objects such as keys, rings, and spoons were caused to bend at a distance from the psychic Uri Geller, may be the result of PK action on the molecules composing the object, although no temperature changes in the object were noticeable (Franklin, 1975). Increase in rate of enzyme action in bottles held by the psychic Oskar Estebany (Smith, 1968) may have been brought about by molecules responding to the influence of PK. PK may also have affected molecules in the production of images on photographic paper by the psychic Ted Serios (Eisenbud, 1969) and in the pulsating changes reported to have been induced in the mist in a cloud chamber at a distance of 600 miles by the psychic Olga Worrall (Miller & Reinhart, 1975).

PK has been tested on an electro-mechanical system consisting of an electric clock, relays, and a salt solution. The subject willed the hand of the clock to sweep faster (or slower) with the experimental system than with the control (Cox, 1965a). It is not known whether the significant results were produced by PK action on the clock hand, the relays, or the electric current, although the latter is a possibility. However, paranormal electrical conductance in a $\frac{3}{8}$ inch air space between the ends of two copper wires has been reported (Brookes-Smith, 1975). That PK may affect subatomic particles has been shown by the movement of an electron beam at a distance of 6 feet (Puthoff & Targ, 1974b) and by its apparent effect on the rate of decay of the radioactive substance uranium nitrate (Chauvin & Genthon, 1965). Also, its effect on the decay of radioactive strontium-90 has been demonstrated with the use of a binary random-event generator (Schmidt, 1970a). In this apparatus, which was invented by the American physicist Helmut Schmidt (1969), the event is determined by the arrival of an electron (from a radioactive strontium-90 source) at a Geiger-Müller tube. The radioactive substance spontaneously disintegrates, and it is not possible to determine physically when the next electron will be released. Parenthetically, a paranormal increase in the amount of background ionizing radiation was suggested by the faster clicking of a Geiger counter held by Geller, although the faster count rate may have resulted from a paranormal electric effect on the instrument (Panati, 1976). PK action on subatomic particles is further suggested by the dematerialization by Geller of a part of a single crystal of vanadium carbide enclosed in a plastic capsule (Hasted et al., 1975) and by the finding that the British psychic Suzanne Padfield was consistently successful in paranormally deflecting a beam of plane-polarized light (Herbert, 1974).

That PK can affect a physical force field as well is suggested by the finding of the physicists Harold Puthoff and Russell Targ (1974) at the Stanford Research Institute that the psychic Ingo Swann was able to alter the frequency of the waves produced by a *magnetometer* containing a slowly decaying magnetic field. He succeeded in increasing or stopping the field change for periods of from 30 to 45 seconds.

CONCLUSIONS

Psi is measured in the laboratory by the use of experimental methods and controls. Although the classical methods of testing for psi by the use of cards and dice are still in use because their simplicity facilitates the preclusion of fraud and self-deception, they have been supplemented by more complicated techniques. Although most of the experimental data are statistical, some of the paranormal phenomena produced in the laboratory are of sufficient magnitude to be measured directly rather than by statistical inference.

REVIEW QUESTIONS

1. If you fail to remember any of the following terms, ascertain its meaning with the aid of the glossary and the index: around-the-die technique, chi square, closed and open decks,

critical ratio, crosschecking, cutaneous vasoconstriction, degrees of freedom, evoked potential, free-response targets, galvanic skin response, high aim, hit, low aim, magnetometer, majority-vote analysis, miss, nose peeking, one-tailed test, optional stoppage, placement PK, plethysmograph, preferential matching, probability (p and P), proxy sitter, psi hitting, psi missing, psychometry, random order, repeated-guessing technique, restricted-response targets, run, session, standard deviation, t test, thermistor, trial, two-tailed test, variance, z score.

2. What physiological reactions of the subject have been found to be related to ESP?

3. Distinguish between the basic technique, the down-through technique, the open-matching technique, the screened touch-matching technique, and the psychic shuffle.

4. What are the empty-chair test and the sealed-message test?

5. How have haunted houses been tested statistically?

6. Why must the target order be randomized, and how can this be accomplished?

7. Describe possible sensory cues in ESP tests and state how they can be prevented.

8. How can errors in recording and in checking the results be prevented?

9. Compare individual and group testing with respect to the advantages and disadvantages of each.

10. Distinguish between the evaluation of findings the experiment was designed to test and findings unexpectedly turned up by the experiment.

11. Distinguish between psi hitting and psi missing, and explain why the presence of either in an experiment can be considered evidential of paranormality.

12. What success has been achieved in attempts to send messages by ESP?

13. Describe tests of PK on randomly moving molar objects.

14. What PK tests have been successfully performed on molar objects not in random motion; on submolar objects?

15. In a test of 50 runs with an ESP deck, the subject had 280 hits. Is the score significant?

16. In a test of five subjects each with ten runs of an ESP deck, the scores were 62, 55, 50, 56, and 57. Are the results significant?

17. In a test of two groups of five subjects each, with each subject tested for ten runs of an ESP deck, the scores for group 1 were 58, 50, 55, 50, and 52, while the scores for group 2 were 50, 49, 50, 46, and 50. Is the difference significant?

18. In an ESP test, 15 believers and 6 disbelievers scored above *MCE*, while 5 believers and 14 disbelievers scored below *MCE*. Is the difference between the ESP scores of the believers and the disbelievers significant?

19. The average ESP scores of five subjects were 5.1, 5.0, 4.8, 4.9, and 5.2, while their respective IQs were 120, 100, 95, 105, and 110. Determine the coefficient of correlation and whether or not it is significant.

20. The ESP scores of ten emotionally stable subjects were 9, 3, 1, 8, 2, 6, 6, 8, 9, and 8, while the ESP scores of ten emotionally unstable subjects were 6, 5, 4, 3, 6, 4, 4, 6, 7, and 4. Is there a significant difference between the variances of the two groups?

Chapter 4

COUNTERHYPOTHESES TO PSI

A ROPER POLL conducted in 1974 indicated that 53 percent of the American people believed in the existence of ESP, 68 percent of those with a college education expressing a belief in ESP as contrasted with 26 percent of those with only a grade school education (Elgin, 1977). Of the nearly 1,500 readers of the British magazine *New Scientist* (the majority of whom are scientists or technologists) who responded to a 1973 questionnaire, 67 percent considered ESP to be an established fact or a likely possibility (Evans, 1973). Notwithstanding, parapsychology is as yet a controversial science to many individuals, and numerous alternative explanations have been offered for the paranormality of the phenomena it encompasses. These counterhypotheses are presented in this chapter together with their intended refutations.

Sensory Cues

One of the counterhypotheses to psi is that the subject identifies the target object by means of sensory cues from the target or from the agent. In tests of ESP where the subject is permitted to see the back of the target card, it is possible that the card is not completely opaque and that the face of the card is discernible through its back. Even if the card is completely opaque, it is possible that the subject can associate certain irregularities on the back of the card with its target face and can identify the card in this manner. Also, it is possible that an association between a certain body movement or facial expression of the agent and a given target can aid in the identification of the target. Successful experiments have been performed, however, in which a screen was placed between the subject on the one side and the agent and the cards on the other, thus preventing the subject from receiving visual cues from the cards or from the agent.

It is possible that the subject could associate a particular modulation of the agent's voice with a given target or, even if the agent is seemingly silent, that the subject could receive auditory cues by the latter's unconscious whispering. Successful experiments have been conducted, however, in which the percipient and the agent were separated by a distance that precluded auditory cues. Both visual and auditory cues were precluded in successful tests in which each card was placed in a separate envelope, and its target face was not seen by the agent. Furthermore, sensory cues are not possible in tests of precognition because the target is undetermined at the time of the subject's call.

Improper Statistical Methods

The statistical methods used in the analysis of the results of psi experiments have been criticized. However, they are the same as those used in other sciences. In 1937 the American Institute of Mathematical Statistics stated that the statistical analysis used in parapsychological investigations was valid and must not be attacked on mathematical grounds (Camp, 1937). This appears to be an adequate refutation of this counterhypothesis.

No Control Group

The purpose of a control group is to indicate the effect of a variable on a test object in an experiment. This is accomplished by comparing the test object in the control group with a similar test object in an experimental group in which the variable has a different value. In the control group, the variable is either completely absent or is present to a different degree than it is in the experimental group. In other respects, the two groups are as identical as it is possible to make them with respect to variables which may affect the test factor. In psi experiments, and in fact in non-psi experiments as well, it may not be possible to have a control group in which psi is completely absent. This is because it may not be possible to isolate the control group from the effects of psi, even though the participants in the experiment have no conscious intent to introduce it. Such was the case with the experiment described in Chapter 2, which was performed by Coover at Stanford University. This does not mean, however, that psi experiments cannot be controlled. First, in many psi experiments there is a specifically designated control group. Second, the results with two experimental groups or situations in which psi is expressed differently can be compared, with each serving as a control for the other. For example, if psi is expressed positively in group A and negatively in group B, then group B is, in effect, a control for group A, and group A is a control for group. B. This is exemplified in tests of high and low aim within the same experiment, both in ESP (J.B. Rhine, 1934) and in PK (Humphrey, 1947b). Third, the results of the experiment can be compared with the results expected by probability, the latter serving as a statistical control. Fourth, the calls for the actual targets can be crosschecked for their similarity to targets in a different part of the experiment. Controls have been provided in psi experimentation with significant results in these several ways.

Nonrandom Targets

If the target sequence in an ESP test is not randomly determined, it may coincide with the psychological preferences of the subject and produce a significant deviation from mean chance expectancy that is not the result of psi. Even if the targets and their sequences are in random order, they might coincide with the psychological preference of the subject and yield a deviation from mean chance expectancy that is not due to psi. The probability of this happening can be determined statistically if the targets have been randomly determined; in contrast, the probability of coincidence between calls and targets when the latter have not been randomly selected cannot be easily determined. It is essential, therefore, that the targets be randomly selected or, at least, that their nonrandomness is not sufficient to cause the scores to differ significantly from their theoretical values.

Randomness may generally be accomplished by repeated shuffling of the deck followed by cutting it twice. This has been substantiated by crosschecking the calls of one run with the targets of another (J.B. Rhine et al., 1940). In no case were the empirical values found to differ significantly from their theoretical values.

Also, Greenwood (1938) made half a million matchings of calls and target cards without significant results when the calls were not aimed at particular target cards and when the order of the cards was determined by shuffling the decks. In many successful experiments the targets have been based on a table of random digits or have been determined by a random-number generator where the target sequences were tested for randomness.

Significant deviations from chance expectancy in the matchings between two series of random digits have been reported (Spencer Brown, 1957; Hardy et al., 1973). However, the occurrence of two similar series does not indicate that they are non-random, as similar series are bound to occur within a random digit list if it is of sufficient length. What it may indicate is that ESP was used in selecting the two series of random digits which were matched (Nash, 1954). In assessing the degree of significance of similarity found betwen two series of random digits, the probability must be corrected for the number of series that were matched before the two lists were selected.

Remembering Previously Called Targets

In ESP-*feedback* experiments in which the subject is told the target after each call, it may be possible for him to increase his probability of success by remembering which targets have been used and avoiding them in subsequent calls. This has been prevented by replacing the target card in the deck and shuffling the latter after each call, or by using an open deck in which the symbols are not restricted in their frequency of occurrence. Even when one of these procedures is followed, it is still necessary to ensure that the targets and their sequences are randomly determined.

Errors in Recording, Checking, and Counting

It is possible that the experimenter in recording the calls may be inadvertently influenced by the already recorded target symbols and may write down the symbol of the target rather than the symbol of the call. Similarly, if the calls are recorded before the targets, the experimenter may be influenced to write down the symbol of the call rather than that of the target. These errors are prevented by covering the first recorded symbols, whether they be of the targets or of the calls, when making the later entries.

Errors in checking the correct calls usually consist of overlooking hits but, whatever their nature, they are practically eliminated by the use of two independent checkers. Where the two checkers disagree, they can reexamine the record and come to a mutual agreement. Errors in counting the hits are handled in similar fashion. Several rechecks of experiments have shown that any errors present were insufficient to change the significance of the results (Greenwood, 1938; J.B. Rhine et al., 1940, p. 134). In addition to this, significant results have been achieved in ESP experiments where the targets and calls were recorded on business-machine forms and were checked and counted by the machines (Kahn, 1952).

Optional Stoppage

Because of fluctuations in the cumulative score, it would be possible to stop an experiment at a point where the total score is high. However, the correction in the probability for results in which favorable stopping might have occurred causes a very small change and would be of importance only in experiments with results of relatively marginal significance (J.B. Rhine et al., 1940, p. 122). This counterhypothesis is precluded by establishing the length of the experiment before it is begun. Similarly, any scoring advantage that could be obtained by starting with several subjects and stopping each when his score is high is precluded by determining the length of the testing of each subject before the experiment is begun.

Dropping Subjects with Poor Scores

If subjects with poor scores are dropped during the course of an experiment with several subjects, it will have no effect on the total results of the experiment as long as the scores of the poor subjects up to the time they were dropped are included in the final results.

Only Successful Data or Experiments Reported

To prevent the unrecognized loss of a part of the data, numbered record sheets are used, and in some experiments with significant results, duplicate records were taken by two experimenters. It is true that many experiments are performed with only chance results which go unreported either because the experimenter does not write them up in publishable form or because journals are reluctant to publish reports of experiments with insignificant results. However, most parapsychological journals have reported insignificant results in many experiments. A survey of members of the Parapsychological Association indicated that the ratio of each investigator's unpublished to published studies was about 2 to 1 (Tart, 1973). Furthermore, the statistical significance of some experiments is so great that, if every person who had ever lived had repeated such an experiment, not one of them by chance alone would have achieved the probability obtained in them. In addition to those experimenters who have obtained odds against chance of an astronomical order, many experimenters have reported results with odds against chance varying between 100 to 1 and 1,000 to 1. The statistical significance of the published experiments is far greater than is necessary to compensate for experiments with chance results that have gone unreported. Every inhabitant of the earth would have had to guess cards continually and unsuccessfully for many centuries in order to render the published results of ESP experiments insignificant.

Pseudopsychic Phenomena Producible by Magicians

Pseudoparanormal phenomena are producible by some stage mentalists and magicians in deceptions and illusions controlled by themselves. However, they are not successful in psi tests having elements unanticipated by them and performed under laboratory conditions. Magicians critical of psi choose to ignore the phenomena they cannot fake. A magician, who has received great publicity in recent years in his claims of being able to normally produce phenomena purported to be psychical, backed down when he was challenged to do so under test conditions

(Eisenbud, 1975). Magicians who claim they can simulate the paranormal bending of a key, for example, mean that they can, on occasion, distract the attention of the audience long enough to bend a key by mechanical means without anyone noticing. In contrast, some metal objects, which the Israeli psychic Uri Geller has stroked, bend while under continuous observation by the viewers and continue to bend when he is no longer touching them (Vaughan, 1973). Geller has been criticized because of his alleged refusal to be tested by magicians (Lustig, 1976); however, he has been tested by at least three magicians who testified that the phenomena he produced were not done by trickery (Panati, 1976).

It would be a great help to parapsychologists to have the help of magicians in studying the ostensibly paranormal abilities of claimed psychics. However, it would be as much of an error to uncritically accept the claims of the magician that he can duplicate the feats by magic as to accept without evidence the claims of the psychic that he can produce the effects by psi. It is the obligation of the scientist to make these determinations, as they cannot be validly made by either the magician or the psychic who produces the phenomena.

Experimenters Biased or Credulous in Favor of Psi Phenomena

While most parapsychologists have a natural desire that the results of their experiments will be significant, some skeptical investigators have reported extrachance results from ESP tests, and some who are favorably inclined toward ESP have failed to obtain significant results (J.B. Rhine et al., 1940, p. 147).

Experimenters Incompetent or Dishonest

Several experiments have been performed with two experimenters and, while this does not preclude incompetency or fraud on the part of the experimenter, it reduces its likelihood. While there has been an occasional dishonest parapsychologist (J.B. Rhine, 1975), as there have been dishonest scientists in other fields, the critic would have to postulate that dishonesty in psychical science includes more than a hundred respected research workers in dozens of institutions throughout the world. In several experiments, evidence that fraud was not committed by the experimenter is indicated by significant psi effects unobserved by him but found in reanalysis of the results by others (J.B. Rhine, 1975).

Data Tampered with by Nonexperimenters

To suppose that the occurrence of psi in the many reported papers has been the product of tampering by subjects or assistants is to suppose a great deal of something which is very rare. Furthermore, in certain researches the hypothetical tampering was manifestly impossible, as independent records of every score were kept by the experimenters under lock and key (J.B. Rhine et al., 1940, p. 138).

Psi Not Useful

As is the case with such phenomena as electricity, the utility of psi may lag far behind the observation of its occurrence. On the other hand, psi might be a genuine occurrence and yet forever be without practical use. Usefulness is not a criterion of reality. The question is often asked why psi is not used to win at gambling. It is likely that certain individuals do occasionally use psi successfully in games of chance. In considering the outcome of betting on races and other sporting contests, it has not been possible to distinguish between those who win by chance, superior knowledge, or better judgment and those who win through the use of psi. However, even if a gambler should precognize a winning event, the house or other gamblers might prevent its occurrence by PK.

Psi Only a Probability

The evidence for psi lies not alone in statistical inference, but also in qualitative experiments and observations. Some of the phenomena produced in the laboratory are of a sufficient degree to be measured directly rather than by statistical inference. Furthermore, the evidence for most so-called scientific facts is probabilistic in its final analysis. The Scottish philosopher David

Hume showed that the relationship between cause and effect can only be discerned by experience and, since the mind is never able to perceive a necessary or invariable relationship between cause and effect, the reality of the relationship can only be evaluated as a probability. The English astronomer Sir Arthur Eddington (1935) wrote that causal laws are no more than statistical laws, and the physicist does not predict what will certainly happen in an individual case, but what will probably happen in a group. Counterhypotheses concerning probability, including the counterhypothesis that probability theory may not be true, cannot be fairly levelled at psi any more than they can be directed to the observed phenomena of other sciences.

Unknown Cause of Similarity Between Calls and Targets

In contradiction to some critics, psi is not an empty correlation between two sets of events, the calls and the targets. To the contrary, there is a functional relationship between the level of performance in psi tests and certain independent variables, such as whether or not the subjects are hypnotized, whether or not they believe psi can occur in the test, and whether they possess certain personality traits. Changes in the experimental conditions and in the participants have resulted in changes in the character of the results. Although the nature of the mediation between the calls and the targets may be unknown, this is no less true of the physical mediation that is manifested by the four forces that are believed to account for all physical interactions of matter: gravitation, electromagnetic force, strong nuclear force, and weak nuclear force.

Psi is Negatively Defined

Psi is not negatively defined—a negative hypothesis remaining after all alternatives or counterhypotheses have been excluded. Psi is a positive hypothesis with a positive definition, i.e. it consists of effects between objects at least one of which is living or possesses mind, the effects being mediated either by psychic agency or by undiscovered physical means. It might be equally reasonable to say that physical action is negatively defined because its effects may be mediated by undiscovered psychical means.

Psi Incompatible with Current Scientific Theory

The property of psi of involving action at a distance without known intervening forces is not inconsistent with physical principles. Action at a distance is characteristic of gravitational, magnetic, and nuclear forces, all of which take place between two or more bodies without mediation by detectable energies. However, even if psi were considered to be at variance with prerelativity and prequantum physics, it is not incompatible with modern physics. The mechanical universe of classical physics in which objects push one another about has proved to be illusory. The elementary particles of matter are not solid material objects but are merely idealizations. An elementary particle is not definitely in one place but is a wave of probability occupying the universe. The concept of substance has disappeared from fundamental physics, and the passage of time is regarded as merely a feature of our consciousness with no objective physical significance. Time's reversal is provided by positrons traveling backwards in time as postulated by the American Nobel-laureate Richard Feynman (1949). In addition to the abandonment of absolute space and time, quantum physics has posited that certain events are acausal. With the tunneling effect, there is a finite probability that a particle in a sealed container will suddenly appear outside the enclosure. It is an effect without a cause.

Science resists innovation and abhors anomaly, particularly if the breakthrough is not consistent with the current vogue of scientific thinking. However, as new observations grow and organize themselves into an entirely new framework, the old paradigm is overthrown and replaced with a new one. The scientific community may be progressing towards a synthesis in which physics will be assimilated into categories that emerge from the science of psi.

Psi Phenomena Not Repeatable

A hierarchy exists in science with respect to the number of factors affecting a phenomenon. Physics is at the bottom, leading through chemistry and biology to psychology. In this hierarchy, each science has more variables than the one it overlies. Parapsychology, because its phenomena are affected to a greater extent by unconscious mental activity than are most of those of conventional psychology, has more variables than the underlying science of psychology. If the number of variables at each level of the hierarchy of sciences is estimated to increase by one order of magnitude over its lower lying level, for each variable in physics there are ten in chemistry, one hundred in biology, one thousand in psychology and ten thousand in parapsychology. Until all of the factors which affect a phenomenon are discovered, the experiment cannot be repeated with 100 percent certainty. The degree of repeatability of an experiment is in direct relation to the percentage of its variables that are controlled. Although undoubtedly only a small percentage of psi-relevant variables are presently known, it may be expected that the percentage will increase and that psi phenomena will become reliably repeatable.

Already ESP scores have been shown to be repeatable between the two halves of an experiment. This was accomplished by comparing the two halves of each subject's ESP scores and finding that the split-half reliabilities were statistically significant (Honorton, Ramsey & Cabibbo, 1975). Significant correlations were obtained by the American psychologist Robert Van de Castle (1974) between the scores of subjects in two experiments separated by an interval of approximately one year. Furthermore, certain gifted psi subjects have been able to produce a particular psi effect time and time again, and certain types of experiments have a high likelihood of being successful even when carried out by different experimenters.

The repeatability of findings in parapsychology may not compare unfavorably with the repeatability of findings in psychology. More than 73 percent of the 48 psi experiments reported at the Parapsychological Association Convention in 1975 were confirmations of earlier findings (Honorton, 1976). In contrast, less than 1 percent of research reports in psychological journals were replications of previous findings (Sterling, 1959; Bozarth & Roberts, 1972).

The replication of a single psi experiment in any laboratory as many times as desired with essentially the same results may be accomplishable in the fullness of time and with sufficient knowledge of the nature of the phenomena under investigation. However, even if it should turn out that the nature of psi is to be unrepeatable, it could still be studied scientifically, as are such unrepeatable phenomena as ball lightning, certain geological formations, and biological evolution. Regardless of its repeatability, the scientific propriety of psi is indicated by the fact that it recurs, can be measured, and, because it is statistically significant, is not the result of chance.

Each Experiment with a Different Weakness

It may be that, while each of the above counterhypotheses has been refuted in one or more experiments, no one psi experiment has been performed in which all counterhypotheses have been simultaneously precluded. Perhaps such an experiment is unattainable. Just as it has not been possible to construct an escape-proof prison, a fraud-proof experiment in any science may be impossible. Eventually, a resolute prisoner will escape the prison, and in time a determined critic will conceive of a normal explanation which could have produced the experimental results and which was not excluded by the experimental methods. Scientific acceptance of psi may come not from a single perfect experiment, but from the accumulated evidence of experiments so numerous that refusal to admit the existence of the paranormal would represent a lower degree of common sense than its acceptance.

CONCLUSIONS

While many scientists do not presently accept the reality of paranormal phenomena, this is at least partially because the usual scientist is a specialist in a narrow field and is poorly informed beyond his immediate area. A few scientists, who have given direct consideration to the evidence for psi and were not convinced of its reality, have advanced alternative explanations which are discussed in this chapter.

REVIEW QUESTIONS

1. What evidence is there that criticism of the statistical methods used in parapsychology is not warranted?

2. In addition to the use of control groups, give three other methods which serve as controls in psi experiments.

3. Why may the finding of similarities between two series of random digits support rather than disprove psi?

4. How can the counterhypothesis of optional stoppage be precluded?

5. How must the data be handled when poor subjects are dropped during an experiment?

6. Refute the counterhypothesis that significant psi results are obtained because only successful data or experiments are reported.

7. Why does not the production of pseudopsychic phenomena by magicians indicate that psi phenomena performed in the laboratory are fraudulently produced?

8. How do the findings of parapsychology disprove the counterhypothesis of experimenter bias or dishonesty?

9. How can the argument that psi is only a statistical probability be answered?

10. Why is psi not disproved by the criticism that the cause of the similarity between calls and targets is unknown.

11. Why is psi not incompatible with current scientific thought?

12. Why doesn't the relative unrepeatability of psi disprove its existence?

Chapter 5

MODALITIES OF PSI

A PSI EFFECT is a paranormal relationship between mental states in two individuals or between the mental state of an individual and the physical state of an object. The physical object in a psi effect may be inanimate or it may be an animate object such as a living brain. ESP is mental response to a state outside of the individual without sensory stimulation. PK is mental influence on a physical state without the use of motor organs. As regards the distinction between ESP and PK, it may not be possible to distinguish empirically between a telepathic effect by the agent's mind on the percipient's mind and a PK effect by the agent's mind on the percipient's brain.

When the ESP effect is a relationship between two minds, it is called telepathy. In active-agent telepathy, the agent is conceived to be the active participant and the percipient to be the passive receiver. In active-percipient telepathy, the percipient is conceived to be the active participant and the agent to be a passive source of the ESP information. When the ESP consists of a mental response to a physical state, it is termed *clairvoyance*. If it is not known whether the mental state of the percipient is responding to the mental state of the agent or to a physical state, as when the agent looks at the target, the modality is referred to as *general extrasensory perception* or *GESP*. Clairvoyance (paranormal mental response to a physical state) and PK (paranormal mental influence on a physical state) are counterparts.

When the target is not contemporaneous with the response but is in the future, the ESP event is termed *precognition* and, when the target is in the past, the act of ESP is titled *retrocognition*. Noncontemporaneous ESP may be either telepathic or clairvoyant. There is also the possibility of PK acting on noncontemporaneous targets by pre-psychokinesis or by retro-psychokinesis.

The question exists as to whether PK on objects not in random motion and producing effects such as alteration of the position or shape of stationary objects is qualitatively different from PK that affects randomly moving objects, such as electrons in a random-event generator. Even if the former and not the latter were shown to involve a physical force, such as electromagnetism, it would not indicate a basic difference between them. Psi that employed electromagnetism would not be the same as the electromagnetic waves it employed any more than sensory perception would be the same as the light waves it utilized.

Pure Telepathy

In a test of pure telepathy the targets must not only be mental but must never be recorded or spoken because, if they were, they would form physical objects which could be identified by precognitive clairvoyance (J.B. Rhine, 1945b). Purely mental targets can be obtained in random order by translating the digits in a table of random digits into mental target symbols with the use of a mental code, which is never recorded. In order for the results to be independently checked, the code for translation of the digits into mental target symbols must be made known to the checker in a purely mental way without writing it down or speaking it. The zoologist Elizabeth McMahan (1946) accomplished this with significant results by a series of oral references based on common memories of the agent and the checker. For example, if the digit is five, the agent may say to the checker, "The number is that which characterizes the size of the family you will think of first when I mention the picnic we attended." The checker may confirm the number with a reply such as, "The number is that of the day of the month when we first met." The possibility still remains that the subject may have some clairvoyant impression of the agent's nervous system, vocal cords, or other physiological concomitants of the thoughts being transmitted during the experiment. In such a case, what would appear to be telepathy would actually be the result of clairvoyance by the percipient. This is the first of three reasons that tests of pure telepathy are inconclusive.

The second reason is that the agent could affect the percipient's brain by PK to cause him to perceive the target symbol correctly (Thouless & Wiesner, 1947). In this case what would appear to be the result of telepathy would actually be caused by PK. The third reason is that in certain experimental procedures the agent may perceive the percipient's future spoken or recorded call by precognitive clairvoyance and then select the mental target that agrees with it (Nash, 1975a). According to this hypothesis, the agent precognizes the percipient's calls and thinks corresponding thoughts. To illustrate, suppose *A* says to *P*, "Try to read my mind." *A* then clairvoyantly precognizes the statements *P* will make, and thinks thoughts corresponding to those statements. In this case, what would appear to be the result of telepathy by *P* would actually be the result of precognitive clairvoyance by *A*.

Pure Clairvoyance

In a test of pure clairvoyance, the targets must be purely physical and never become known to any individual, thus precluding their identification by precognitive telepathy. This has been accomplished with the blind-matching technique in which the subject places each card in the ESP deck opposite one of the five key cards turned face downwards (Pratt, 1937). When the experimenter examines the target cards placed opposite the key cards, he does not know the order that the target cards had in the deck before they were distributed into the five piles. To illustrate, consider the bottom card in the pile opposite the square symbol. The experimenter does not know whether this was the first card in the deck, or the second, or the third, etc. Thus there is no future knowledge of the symbol on the target card in the deck that the subject could use as a target for precognitive telepathy. Tyrrell's experiment with light boxes (Chap. 2) also ruled out precognitive telepathy, as the record on the tape gave no indication of which box had been opened at any trial. Experimental evidence supports the existence of pure clairvoyance, but it does not support the existence of pure telepathy if matter is real as it is held to be in materialism and in *dualism*. However, if the universe is entirely mental, as it is conceived to be in idealism, ESP can only occur between mental objects and hence can consist only of telepathy and not of clairvoyance.

Pure Retrocognition

It may be that psychometry of an object's past history is accomplished by retrocognition. However, it has been impossible to prove pure retrocognition empirically because, in order to test ESP of a past event, a record of the event must be in existence and hence be subject to contemporaneous ESP. Evidence for retrocognition might come from a psychic's deciphering an archeological record written in an ancient language for which there is no Rosetta stone. However, even if evidence were obtained of ESP of a past event for which there is no present earthly record, it could be explained by the contemporaneous ESP of light waves whose journey into space began at the instant of the occurrence of the event and continue today. In order to make this understandable, it can be pointed out that the way a star appears to us is not due to the condition of that star as it is at the time we see it but to its state as many as several billion years ago depending upon how long it took for light from it to reach the earth.

Pure Precognition

A test of pure precognition has not been achievable because of the possibility that the results are due to PK. First, if the targets in the precognition test are the future order of the cards after they are shuffled, PK could affect the cards during the shuffling so as to cause them to be in a similar order to the calls (J.B. Rhine, 1945c). Second, if the targets are determined by a randomly selecting, mechanical apparatus such as Tyrrell's light boxes or Schmidt's random-event generator, or if the cutting of the deck or the entry point in the table of random digits is determined by a procedure involving a calculator, PK could affect the action of the instrument. Third, if the point of the cutting of the deck or the entry point in the table is determined by a completely public event such as the temperature on a future day, it is possible that the thermometer used could be affected by PK. Significant results have been obtained in precognition tests with the use of a weather cut involving a thermometer (J.B. Rhine, 1942). Significant findings were also obtained with the use of the stock-market closing-average on a future date (Nash, 1960a); however, the possibility exists that an event even as public as that could be affected by PK.

Pure Psychokinesis

In PK tests with randomly moving objects such as dice, a favorable die face could be selected as the target by precognizing which face most of the dice will have uppermost when they come to rest (Mundle, 1950). The significant results would be due to precognition rather than to PK. Even in the around-the-die method of target selection, where each face of the die is used as the target an equal number of times, a favorable precognitive selection could be made as to how many times each face would be used as the target before continuing to the next target face (Nash, 1951). The results obtained with a random-event generator could also be attributed to precognition as well as to PK (Schmidt, 1970a). Since the sequence of generated events depends on the time the test run began, precognition might have enabled the experimenter or the subject to start the run at a time when the conditions for the generation of the target would be favorable. However, if the extent of the change of the target object at the time of the test exceeded its normal range of fluctuation, it would be indicative of PK rather than of precognition. This may have been the case in tests of PK with a magnetometer and with a thermistor (Chap. 3). Also, changes in the target object that would not normally take place at all, such as the bending of metal objects or the movement of stationary objects, are not explainable by precognition and in the absence of fraud are evidence of pure PK.

Retro-Psychokinesis

In a sense, retro-psychokinesis is opposite to precognition. In precognition a later event affects the earlier state of mind of the subject, and in retro-PK the subject's mental state affects an earlier event. An experiment was performed by Schmidt (1975a) in which the subjects, ostensibly by retroactive PK, increased the frequency of signals from a random-event generator, which had been recorded on tape. Significant results were obtained suggesting that the subjects used retro-PK to affect the earlier random event before it was recorded on tape. It is not apparent whether the retro-PK consisted of a present PK act of the subject affecting the past random event or whether it consisted of a future PK act of the subject affecting the present random event, although the latter seems more likely. This is because a past event could not logically be affected by a present act, as the past event has already been determined. This objection, however, does not apply to a future act affecting a present event, as the latter is undetermined until the moment of its occurrence. As Schmidt recognized, the significant results could also be accounted for by the experimenter's use of contemporaneous PK to influence the random-event generator at the time it was producing the signals.

Pre-Psychokinesis

Pre-psychokinesis consists of a present volition paranormally affecting a future event. To illustrate, subjects could will dice to land with certain faces uppermost, the dice being mechanically released at a later time without the knowledge of the subjects. However, it is not apparent how contemporaneous PK could be precluded in a test of pre-PK.

Combination of Psi Modalities

In experiments where the experimenter looks at the target, before it is called, it is not known whether the modus of ESP is telepathy, or clairvoyance, or a combination of these two psi modalities. In such a case, the process is referred to as general extra-sensory perception (GESP). That ESP and PK may operate at the same time is indicated by hidden-target PK experiments in which the dice are thrown for a hidden target face discernible only by ESP (Thouless, 1951). The nature of psi may be such that neither ESP nor PK can occur in the absence of the other, both being aspects of the same act of psi. ESP of the target may be necessary in order for a PK effect upon it to occur, and the target object may be psychokinetically affected when it is extrasensorially perceived. The modalities of psi may be no more than distinctive conditions for the expression of a single underlying psi function.

CONCLUSIONS

Although the different modes of psi may be no more than distinctive conditions under which a single underlying psi-function operates, some of these conditions seemingly restrict psi to a specific modality. Although pure clairvoyance stands on its own as a modality of ESP, conditions precluding psi modes other than telepathy have not been met in tests of pure telepathy. Precognition can be alternatively explained as psychokinesis; however, PK of stationary objects cannot be attributed to precognition. Empirical evidence of retrocognition has not been conclusive.

REVIEW QUESTIONS

1. Distinguish between the concepts of active-agent and active-percipient telepathy.

2. What constitutes a test of general extrasensory perception?

3. Give three reasons why tests of pure telepathy are inconclusive.

4. Give experimental evidence of pure clairvoyance.

5. Why has it not been possible to prove pure retrocognition?

6. How may PK interfere with a test of pure precognition?

7. How may apparent PK with randomly moving objects actually be due to precognition?

8. Why does the counterhypothesis of precognition not apply to PK with stationary targets?

9. Why has it not been possible to prove retro-PK and pre-PK?

Chapter 6

THE TARGET

A N ACT OF PSI REQUIRES a target, a subject and, perhaps, an agent or experimenter. This and the following two chapters delineate these three sides of the psi triangle.

THE TARGET IN ESP

In tests of psi gamma the target may be mental as in telepathy, it may be physical as in clairvoyance or, as is more frequently the case, it may be mental and/or physical as in GESP. Some targets that have been used are ESP cards, reproductions of paintings in dream experiments, lighted boxes (Tyrrell, 1938), concealed material objects in psychometry tests, buried coins (Cadoret, 1955), remote geographical areas (Targ & Puthoff, 1974), and sensations of the agent such as taste, smell, pain, and touch (Guthrie, 1885). The target may be contemporaneous, existing at the present time, or it may be noncontemporaneous, existing in only the future or past.

Time Duration

With respect to ESP of targets existing only in the future, the question arises as to whether the time duration between the precognition and the precognized event has an effect. In a study of spontaneously precognized happenings, 10 percent of the events came to fruition within 30 seconds, 24 percent took place within an hour, 50 percent within 24 hours, 85 percent within a month, and 91 percent within a year (Persinger, 1974). The number of spontaneous cases reported decreases with increase of time to the event (Orme, 1974). That the decline is not solely due to forgetting is indicated by a study in which dreams were recorded and compared with events on subsequent days up to two and one-half months (Dalton, 1974). The results show that a falling-off with time does really occur. However, it may be explained by a greater interest of the subject in more immediately occurring future events and, hence, a tendency to precognitively dream about them more frequently than about events occurring in the more distant future. Anderson (1959b) obtained significant results in the precognition of targets one year before they were determined, and Nash (1960a) obtained significant results in which the time duration was one and a half years.

Distance

Several experiments show a decrease in ESP scores with distance between the subject and the target (Osis, 1965). However, this may be due to the participant's attitude being less positive at the greater distance. In one experiment, Osis found a decline with distance by comparing subjects' scores at three distances from the targets (Osis & Turner, 1968). This may have been caused by differences between the three agents, each of whom was at a different stimulus station. In a later experiment, in which the percipients' scores were compared at four distances as the agent with the targets traveled around the world, the deviations from chance of the total ESP scores did not vary significantly with distance, although distance was reported to be significantly related to some weighted ESP variables (Osis, Turner, & Carlson, 1971). Without greater experimental evidence than has been offered so far, it cannot be concluded that ESP decreases with distance. In fact, the many experiments which have displayed ESP at considerable distances suggest that the degree of spatial separation between the percipient and the target is not a contributive factor to the scoring level except as it may affect the percipient psychologically.

As to the distance over which ESP has been shown to be effective, extrachance results were obtained in a test in which the agent and the target were near the moon and the percipients were on Earth at a distance of almost a quarter of a million miles (Mitchell, 1971). There is even some suggestion of clairvoyance having taken place of the planet Mercury at a distance of 57 million miles, based on similarity between the psychic's impressions and radio messages sent back to the earth by the spacecraft Mariner 10 (Mitchell, 1975).

Screening

Significant results in ESP tests have been obtained when the percipient and agent were separated by a lead screen (Soal & Bateman, 1954). They were also obtained when the subject was placed in a sealed iron chamber; the chamber was impervious to electromagnetic waves in the range between x-rays and waves of one kilometer and was capable of attenuating both longer and shorter waves (Vasiliev, 1963). Other ESP tests have produced extra-chance findings when the percipient was in an airtight copper chamber which in turn was inside a copper cage (Puharich, 1973). Metal chambers and cages that are designed to prevent the transmission of most electromagnetic waves, called Faraday cages, have not been found to reduce the level of ESP expression.

High- and Low-Aim Targets

Subjects have succeeded in getting a low score in ESP tests as well as in getting a high score (J.B. Rhine, 1934, p. 53, 94). The percipients showed about the same deviation below chance expectation when they were trying to guess wrong as they showed above chance expectation when they tried to guess right.

The P Value

The P value or probability of success per trial is the reciprocal of the number of different choices or targets when each kind of target has an equal probability of occurrence. For example, with an ESP deck of five symbols, $P = 1/5$. The ESP quotient, which is based on the frequency of ESP hits per trial and excludes chance hits, is greatest at this value of P and falls away in both directions from it, with the exception of a relatively greater degree of ESP expression in the cases of $P = 1/10$ and $P = 1/52$ (J.B. Rhine et al., 1940). With P values greater than 1/5, the subject may experience boredom because of the few target choices. With P values less than 1/5, the subject may become discouraged at the infrequency of hits and may have difficulty in remembering the several target choices. The P values of 1/10 and 1/52 are exceptions because the ten digits and the 52 playing cards are easily remembered targets.

With a given frequency of ESP hits per trial, the CR varies inversely with the P value. With the same frequency of ESP hits per trial the results will have a higher statistical significance the lower the P value. To illustrate, if 10 ESP hits are obtained in 100 trials with a P value $= \frac{1}{2}$, the number of hits $= 10$ ESP hits $+ 90/2$ chance hits $= 55$; the deviation $= +5$; and the $CR = 1.0$. In contrast, if 10 ESP hits are obtained in 100 trials with a P value $= 1/10$, the number of hits $= 10$ ESP hits $+ 90/10$ chance hits $= 19$; the deviation $= +9$; and the $CR = 4.6$. That this relationship is real rather than solely theoretical is indicated by experimental data (J.B. Rhine et al., 1940, tables 5 & 18).

Multiple-Aspect Targets

A *multiple-aspect* target is one that has two or more characteristics that must be ascertained in order to identify the whole target. Playing cards afford multiple-aspect targets, one aspect being the number of the card and the other being the suit. In ESP experiments with multiple-aspect targets, some subjects scored better on the whole target while others scored better on one of its aspects (Foster, 1952; Mangan, 1957).

Physical Characteristics of Target

No significant differences in scores were found between large and small symbols used as ESP targets, the symbols ranging from $1/32$ to $3\frac{1}{2}$ inches; nor was the score affected by the number of times the symbol appeared on the target card, a comparison being made between one and five representations of the symbol (L.E. Rhine, 1937). Colors as targets were found to be as effective as shapes (Carpenter & Phalen, 1937), and the shape of the symbol had no effect on the scoring level even when it was grossly distorted (MacFarland & George, 1937).

Psychological Characteristics of Target

Psychological preferences for particular targets vary with the subject. Subjects scored significantly higher with symbols that were new to them than with symbols with which they had been previously tested (Pratt & Woodruff, 1939); with erotic pictures than with ESP symbols as targets (Fisk & West, 1955) ; with symbols that they had individually selected than with ESP-card symbols (Rao, 1962) ; with emotionally loaded targets such as the names of persons known by the subject than with names of unknown individuals when physiological arousal was the mode of ESP response (Dean & Nash, 1967) ; with pleasant than with unpleasant targets (Johnson & Nordbeck, 1972) ; and with targets in an unknown foreign language and identified in English than with targets in English (Rao, 1963a), suggesting that the challenge imposed by the foreign language exerted a stimulating effect. Extrachance scores were obtained with *multiply determined* targets provided by simultaneous visual and auditory stimulation of the agent (Moss & Gengerelli, 1968). However, these results were not compared with tests in which the target consisted of a single sensory modality. Scores were found to be significantly higher in GESP than in clairvoyance (Palmer, Tart & Redington, 1976), suggesting that ESP is easier when the target is multiply determined by being both a thought and a physical object.

THE TARGET IN PK

PK is the influence of an individual on the physical state of an object without physical contact or known physical intermediary. Paranormal influence on stationary objects was called *telekinesis* before the discovery of PK on randomly moving objects, but it is now generally referred to as psychokinesis.

Characteristics of the Target

That the shape of the target object in PK has no significant effect is indicated by tests with cubes, spheres, and disks (L.E. Rhine, 1951a). The number of target objects employed in a single trial appears to have no effect on the scoring level, as shown by dice tests with from one (Hilton, Baer, & Rhine, 1943) to 96 dice per roll (Averill & Rhine, 1945). Neither the size, nor the weight, nor the density of the object appears to impose a physical limitation with respect to randomly moving targets as evidenced by tests with dice of various weights and sizes (Hilton, Baer, & Rhine, 1943) and of various densities (Cox, 1971). The physical composition of the target object has not been shown to be an effective factor, extrachance results having been obtained with dice composed of paper, wood, plastic, aluminum, and steel (Forwald, 1952) and with wooden dice covered with various metal coatings (Forwald, 1959). PK has been observed with molecules, subatomic particles, and even the nonparticulate magnetic field (Chap. 3), although its effect on the latter may have been accomplished by PK action on the magnetometer.

In contrast to the absence of an effect of the weight of the object on PK with randomly moving objects, the effect of the weight of stationary objects on PK is not clear. Although paranormal movements of objects such as a heavy marble statue, which normally needed three men to move, have been reported (Geley, 1927, p. 32), measurements of the PK force with scales (Medhurst, 1972; Puthoff & Targ, 1974a) have not indicated it to exceed the normal physical limitations of the psychic.

Test Conditions

Extrachance positive scoring at a distance of thirty feet between the participants and the dice was found to be no lower than the scoring at a distance of three feet (Nash & Richards, 1947). Significant scores were also obtained at a distance of 27 yards between the participants and the dice (Fahler, 1959). Significant results were obtained even with the ostensible subject no less than a mile from the dice (McConnell, 1955a); however, the possibility of PK effects by other individuals who were nearer to the dice than was the intended subject was not precluded. The scoring level was significantly greater in light than in darkness in one experiment (Gibson & Rhine, 1943), and significantly greater in darkness than in light in another (McMahan, 1947). It appears that the effect of light on PK scoring with dice is psychological and depends upon the preferences of the percipients. Higher scores were obtained when the surface upon which the dice were allowed to roll was hard than when it was soft (Forwald, 1961), presumably because the dice bounced more times on the harder surface. Scores were significantly higher with targets produced by a random-event generator at the slower rate of 30 per second than at the more rapid rate of 300 per second (Schmidt, 1973).

CONCLUSIONS

The psychological characteristics of the target but not its physical characteristics appear to be effective in ESP. This is also true of the PK target, except that there appears to be a weight limit for stationary objects movable by PK.

REVIEW QUESTIONS

1. Does empirical evidence indicate that the efficiency of precognition decreases with the time interval to the event?

2. What is the maximum time span of precognition that has been indicated by experimental work?

3. Does ESP decrease with distance?

4. Is ESP prevented by screening?

5. How does success on low-aim targets compare with success on high-aim targets?

6. How is ESP affected by the P value?

7. Distinguish between multiple-aspect targets and multiply determined targets.

8. Is ESP affected by the physical characteristics of the target?

9. What psychological characteristics of the target affect the ESP score?

10. Is PK of randomly moving objects affected by their physical characteristics?

11. Are PK scores with randomly moving targets affected by distance?

12. Is there a limit to the weight of stationary objects that are movable by PK?

Chapter 7

THE SUBJECT

IN PARAPSYCHOLOGY, a subject is an individual who is tested for psi. He may be an agent in telepathy or in PK, or he may be a percipient or recipient in telepathy, clairvoyance, or PK. In self-testing experiments, he is also the experimenter.

Induction and Development of Psi

From a study of the literature concerning the procedures used by psychically gifted percipients to manifest ESP, Rhea White (1964) determined that they consisted of a series of several steps. The first is a state of deep physical and mental relaxation which is facilitated by sensory deprivation. After the percipient has achieved the proper degree of relaxation, he engages the attention of his conscious mind on a mental image, even if it be one of blankness, so that it will not wander. This involves passivity as well as concentration on the mental image. Next a conscious demand is made for an answer. This is followed by a period of waiting for the answer during which tension mounts as the percipient is concentrating on an image that he knows is not what he seeks, while simultaneously he is entertaining an awareness of a void wherein lies the sought-for answer. Finally, the tension is dispelled by the response entering the consciousness. In experiments in which the subjects were optimized for ESP retrieval by such procedures, ESP was found to be more efficient than in conventional ESP-guessing studies (Honorton, 1975b).

Milan Ryzl (1962) reported some success in developing ESP by intensive training of the subject during hypnosis. The individual learned to carry out increasingly complex suggestions, culminating in the development of complex and vivid visual hallucinations. Following this phase, ESP training began with suggestions for veridical hallucinations of concealed target material and immediate feedback to the subject of success or

96

failure. Finally the subject was gradually withdrawn from his dependence upon hypnosis, and controlled quantitative tests were introduced. As attempts to validate Ryzl's technique have not met with success and as he has published data on only two of the more than two hundred subjects who have passed through his hands, it is questionable how much of the ability of his two successful subjects was innate and how much was developed. The College of Psychic Science in London has also trained psychics (Vaughan, 1970); however, there is no experimental evidence to indicate the degree of their success.

The technique of transcendental meditation with the use of a *mantra* has been taught by the International Meditation Society under the direction of Maharishi Mahesh Yogi in many places throughout the world to hundreds of thousands of individuals. Practitioners of transcendental meditation and some other forms of *yoga* have generally considered the psychic powers which appear to be acquired with those practices to be manifestations of the accompanying spiritual development and not their goal. There is some recent indication that the scientific study of the paranormal abilities reportedly acquired by transcendental meditation may be encouraged by that organization as have the physiological (Wallace & Benson, 1972) and the psychological and sociological (Bloomfield, Cain, & Jaffey, 1975) effects of this practice.

Subjects, who were given immediate information following correct responses in an ESP test, obtained a higher level of scoring than did individuals who were not told of their success until completion of the session (Mercer, 1967). Experiments using immediate feedback led the American psychologist Charles Tart (1975) to conclude that persons with considerable initial ESP ability can learn to increase it by means of immediate feedback, i.e. by being immediately informed whether or not their response was correct. Other experiments with feedback performed with an ESP-testing machine yielded results consistent with a learning hypothesis (Targ, Cole, & Puthoff, 1974). The evidence for ESP learning by feedback, however, has not gone unquestioned (O'Brien, 1976; Stanford, 1977a).

Percentage with Psi Ability

The question of whether a particular subject has psi ability depends upon the modality of psi that is tested and upon the method that is used for its detection. Some gifted subjects such as Home and Geller have demonstrated outstanding ability both in PK and in ESP. The psychic Charles Stuart served successfully as the ESP agent as well as the percipient (Rhine, 1934), and in this connection, Warcollier (1938) observed that the best agents were also the best percipients. On the other hand many psychics have expressed only one modality of psi and then solely under special conditions. These subjects produced only chance scores when tested under other conditions or for a different modality of psi. The psi expression by a particular individual may be very characteristic of him and depend upon his previous experiences. For example, the Dutch psychic Croiset showed adeptness in locating missing persons, particularly drowned children. This may have resulted from his having narrowly escaped death by drowning in his childhood (Tenhaeff, 1972). Stepanek's psychic ability was shown only in his paranormal identification of whether the concealed target card had the white or the green side uppermost. Gloria Stewart was successful in tests of telepathy, but not in tests of clairvoyance (Soal & Bateman, 1954).

The test that is used to measure the psychic ability of an individual may by chance happen to be well suited for him. However, it would be impracticable, if not impossible, to test a person in enough different ways and under sufficiently varied conditions to rule out the possibility of his being able to manifest psi under some situation which had not been examined. For this reason, it is not possible from present empirical evidence to determine what percentage of individuals have psi ability. In the Census of Hallucinations conducted in England and Wales (Sidgwick, 1894), the following question was asked: "Have you ever, when believing yourself to be completely awake, had a vivid impression of seeing or being touched by a living being or inanimate object, or of hearing a voice; which impression, so far as you could discover, was not due to any external physical cause?" Out of 17,000 replies to this question, approximately 10 percent were in the affirmative. This does not give a sound index of the percentage of persons with psi ability, however, as (1) those answering the census were not a random sample of subjects, (2) it may be incorrect to attribute their experience to psi, and (3) those replying negatively to the question may have had psychic experiences other than paranormal hallucinations or which they did not remember. In a poll of a sample of 1,460 individuals in the United States, 58 percent claimed to have had some kind of ESP experience at least once or twice (Greeley, 1975).

With respect to experimental evidence of psi, Soal found two excellent subjects out or more than 160 tested (Soal & Bateman, 1954), and Ryzl (1962) published experimental results with two subjects out of 226 tested. However, the subjects tested may not have been a random sample, as they may have been prompted to undergo the tests because of their psychic ability. In experiments with a large number of subjects, it is generally not possible to determine which individuals expressed psi even if the total score of the group is above chance. This is because, in such experiments, tests of the individual are not usually sufficiently lengthy to give a meaningful indication of his psi ability. It may be true that psi is a universal trait, even though manifested in different ways by different individuals, but there is no present empirical evidence to substantiate this inference.

Culture

Psi tests of individuals in various societies have not shown that culture affects the level of scoring. This has been the case even when the state of civilization is one in which psi phenomena are generally accepted as, for example, the cultures of American Indians and Australian aborigines (Van de Castle, 1974). This may be because we have no psi tests specially adapted to other cultures and, if we did, no way to compare their results with ours.

Race and Heredity

No concerted effort has been made to compare the psychical abilities of different racial strains. However, parapsychological experiments with subjects of various races have provided no indication that individuals of any given race are more or less psychic than those of another.

The two members of identical or one-egg twin pairs had significantly greater similarity in their ESP scoring levels than did the two members of fraternal or two-egg twin pairs (Nash & Buzby, 1965). This is consistent with the hypothesis that variations in psi have a genetic basis as one-egg twins have identical inheritance, while many of the genes of two-egg twins are different between the two individuals. In this experiment it was also found that the one-egg twins had negative scores and the two-egg twins had positive scores, although the difference was not significant. A similar and significant difference between the scoring levels of one-egg and two-egg twins was found in a subsequent experiment (Charlesworth, 1975). In this experiment, the psi missing by the identical twins was attributed to their greater need to individualize, the fraternal twins remaining open to ESP with their twin because they were less subjected to a need for identity. In an experiment solely with identical twins, when alpha rhythm was evoked by closure of the eyes of one twin, a comparable rhythm appeared in the other twin although his eyes were open and he was located in a separate room (Duane & Behrendt, 1965). The extrasensory induction of alpha rhythm occurred in two out of the 15 pairs of monozygotic twins tested, but no tests were conducted on dizygotic twins with which a comparison could be made.

Flournoy (1900) reported a case in which psychic gifts and tendencies were manifested in four generations of a family and considered it to indicate that the predisposition toward psychic phenomena is hereditary in the highest degree. However, it is not known in instances where paranormal ability appears in successive generations of a family to what extent it may be due to environmental factors. While it may be true that all faculties of living organisms have a genetic basis, the inheritance of the psi faculty has not been established by empirical evidence.

Horoscope

In *astrology* it is held that the personality traits of the individual are correlated with the positions of heavenly bodies at the time of his birth. In an experiment to test whether horoscopes can indicate personality characteristics, an astrologer cast horoscopes of ten persons based on the times and places of their birth, not knowing whose birth information he had been given (Brier, 1974). When the individuals attempted to select their horoscope from the ten provided for their examination, only chance results were obtained. While this might be attributable to lack of efficiency on the part of that astrologer, a similar experiment conducted by this writer with a different astrologer also yielded only chance results. In fairness to the astrological position, however, it should be pointed out that the samples in these two experiments of ten and five subjects, respectively, were so small that a very high degree of success would have been necessary to reach a level of statistical significance. Experiments yielding nonsignificant results with a much larger number of individuals would be necessary before they could be considered to negate the astrological thesis.

Success in astrology may be attributed to the use of ESP by the practitioner. There is considerable leeway for the exercise of ESP in the casting of horoscopes, as is evidenced by the fact that astrologists are often in disagreement with one another. However, if empirical evidence should indicate that horoscopes are correlated with personality traits, a possible explanation is that the long and widely held belief in astrology by the human race may paranormally alter an individual's personality traits to correspond to his astrologically predicted nature. It is not beyond the realm of possibility that mass beliefs can exert a paranormal influence (McDougall, 1920). In fact, it has been suggested that the mass expression by a group of people with institutionalized allegiance to a religious figure may be the cause of miracles (Reichbart, 1977). However, there is no present empirical evidence to support this concept.

Sex

Whereas a medium is usually a female, a shaman is usually a male. However, both sexes have been represented by psychics and by outstanding subjects of psi experiments. In spontaneous paranormal cases, women outnumber men nearly two to one as percipients, while men are the agents in approximately 60 percent of the cases (Van de Castle, 1977). The fact that girls exceed boys about two to one in associated poltergeist phenomena has been attributed to females being more neurotic than males (Owen, 1964). The psychologist John Freeman (1970) found that girls scored higher than boys in ESP tests involving verbal ability, while boys scored higher than girls in ESP tests involving spatial relations. This follows the usual pattern of girls being more adept than boys in verbal tests and not as proficient in spatial relations. In this study, the minority of girls, who had a higher spatial IQ than verbal, scored higher on spatial ESP tests, and the minority of boys, who had a higher verbal IQ than spatial, scored higher on verbal ESP tests.

Age

An American psychiatrist, Jan Ehrenwald (1955), postulated an early mother-child relationship of symbiosis or mutual benefit, with telepathy playing the most significant part. He suggested (1976a) that telepathy has a vitally important function during the preverbal stage of communication, even though it may be superfluous or redundant at later ages. Higher ESP scores with picture cards were obtained in three-year-old children than in four-year-olds, and they were higher in the latter group than in children from five through seven years of age (Spinelli, 1977). Children constituted the majority of individuals who were found to possess psychokinetic metal-bending powers (Taylor, 1975). This may be because so much in the world about children is inexplicable to them that they do not consider metal bending to be beyond the bounds of reason and, hence, are not inhibited in its production. Many adults have also been good psi subjects, and age does not appear to be a limiting factor to psychic ability, although children may repress their psi as they grow older because of society's disapproval of its manifestation. In any case, because the aging process produces psychological changes which affect the suitability of the test, the method of testing should be adapted to the age of the subject.

Health

Some experimenters have found that ESP scores decreased at times of illness of the subject (Tyrrell, 1936; Thouless, 1951), although Soal found no reason to connect scoring failure and ill health in his experiments with Shackleton (Soal & Bateman, 1954, p. 185). While many psychics have manifested paranormal phenomena as early in life as they could remember, some dated the origin of their psychical experiences to an accident. The paranormal phenomena of the psychic Eusapia Palladino began after an accident in which she fell and cut her head on a cartwheel (Carrington, 1931, p. 87), and those of the psychic Peter Hurkos originated after a fall from a ladder following which he was unconscious for four days (Browning, 1970). Cerebral concussion may increase ESP, as patients suffering from this disorder scored significantly better in an ESP test than did a control group (Schmeidler, 1952). This was explained by their feeble, passive attitude, which made them willing to accept impressions that came to them. Epilepsy may increase the likelihood of poltergeist phenomena, which occur more often in individuals with this illness than would be expected by chance (Solfin & Roll, 1976).

Intelligence

Successful ESP experiments have been performed with mentally retarded adults. Telepathic perceptions were reported in tests of a 47-year-old man with a mentality of an 18-month-old child (de Thy, 1959), and children who were severely mentally retarded obtained high ESP scores (Shields, 1976). On the other hand, ESP scores were found to have significant positive correlations with intelligence scores (Humphrey, 1945; Nash & Nash, 1958). However, the subjects of these experiments were largely college students and generally of superior intelligence, brighter students tending to be happier in most classrooms and therefore to participate more readily in ESP tasks (Schmeidler, 1976). Similarly, a statistically significant relationship was found in elementary students' grades and their ESP scores (Anderson, 1959a). Motivation as well as intelligence may have been a causal factor in these relationships.

Creativity

Creativity, or the ability to find new relationships between things and to combine them into new wholes, is a different faculty than intelligence or reasoning power and has little correlation with it (MacKinnon, 1962). Frederic Myers (1903) believed that an uprush from the subliminal mind to consciousness characterizes the works of both the creative genius and the psychic. Subjects' ESP scores were found to vary directly with their scores on a test of creativity (Schmeidler, 1964). Similarly, artists, who by nature are generally more creative than nonartists, scored significantly higher in an ESP test than did the latter group (Moss, 1969). Creativity and psychic ability may be related because unconscious incubation of ideas fosters creativity and because psi phenomena are mediated at an unconscious level (Chap. 13).

Memory

An ESP experience is likely to be similar to a previous sensory experience which produced a memory trace, and ESP may take place by activation of a memory trace (Roll, 1966). This is in accord with the finding that remembered targets were better perceived extrasensorially than were targets which the subject had previously seen but did not recall (Kanthamani & Rao, 1974). Furthermore, individuals with good memory were found to have higher ESP scores than subjects with poor recall (Feather, 1967).

Blind versus Sighted

Blind subjects were observed to have ESP ability, but not to a significantly greater extent than did comparable sighted persons (Price, 1938). Attempts to develop skin vision in the blind by which they could read with their fingertips (Duplessis, 1975) may have resulted in improvement of their ability to distinguish objects by differences in their heat radiation (Nash, 1971) rather than in an increase of their ESP.

Visualization

Psi information is often mediated by mental imagery, and persons who were good at visualization were found to have significantly higher ESP scores than individuals who were weak imagers (Honorton, Tierney & Torres, 1974). Individuals who used visual imagery in their thinking made higher PK scores when they visualized the desired die face than when they thought of associations related to the die face, while those low in visualization did just the opposite (Stanford, 1969).

Belief and Attitude

Gertrude Schmeidler found that subjects who believed in the possibility of ESP occurring under the specific testing conditions employed in the experiment, whom she called *sheep,* scored positively, while individuals who did not believe in this possibility, whom she called *goats,* scored negatively (Schmeidler & McConnell, 1958). A study of all reported experiments on the sheep-goat effect indicated it to be statistically significant (Palmer, 1971). The sheep-goat effect, the influence of hypnosis, the effect of extraversion-introversion, and the occurrence of chronological decline are four of the most reliably replicable phenomena in experimental parapsychology.

Expectancy of success in ESP performance was found to affect the ESP scores (Taddonio, 1975). Subjects who were led to expect that they would score above chance scored significantly better than those who were led to expect that they would score at chance. Subjects tested at a time when they felt they were disposed toward and capable of psi performance scored significantly higher than when they were tested at a time fixed by the experimenter (Penwell, 1977). With respect to their attitude toward ESP, the psychologist Dallas Buzby (1967a) found that persons who felt that evidence of their own display of ESP would be very important to them had a significantly higher between-subject variance than did individuals who held the belief that such evidence would be only an interesting phenomenon. As regards the subject's attitude toward the experimenter, experiments indicated that subjects who liked the experimenter scored positively and those who did not like him scored negatively (Anderson & White, 1958; Nash, 1960b).

Mood

Pleasurable moods were found to be associated with higher ESP scores than were unhappy moods (Fisk & West, 1956). In another study, ESP scores were found to be higher with intensely pleasant or unpleasant moods than with everyday, reasonably contented ones (Nielsen, 1956). When the subject was in an interested, enthusiastic mood, the variance between ESP run-scores was significantly higher than when his mood was uninterested or unenthusiastic (Rogers, 1966), high variance representing a greater expression of ESP.

Several factors contribute to a pleasurable mood, one of these being the familiarity of the individual with the surroundings in which he is tested. This factor has been found to be associated with ESP success (Pratt, 1961). Subjects were found to have lower scores when they were intentionally distracted by an observer (Price & Rhine, 1944). On the other hand, poltergeist activity is more frequently increased than decreased by observers (Roll, 1977). The level of success was lower when the subjects were frustrated by delay in checking their scores (J.B. Rhine, 1938) or when they made their calls at a nonpreferred speed or tempo (Stuart, 1938). Informal ESP tests produced higher scores (Russell & Rhine, 1942), and gamelike testing situations met with success (Steen, 1957). Certain methods have been used to reduce the boredom resulting from routine testing, such as complimenting the subject's performance, pointing out any interesting effects that may occur in the course of the run, and permitting him to assist in counting the hits (Rhine & Pratt, 1962). Change in the experimental methods may produce a temporary inhibition of psi. For example, the scoring level of the subject Hubert Pearce temporarily dropped on nine occasions when an observer was introduced, only to return to the extrachance level when he became accustomed to the observer (J.B. Rhine, 1934). Conversely, when a subject has become inhibited with respect to an often repeated task, a change in the nature of the experiment may result in a resumption of successful scoring (Thouless, 1951).

Motivation

The individual's need to produce paranormal phenomena appears to be an important factor in causing their occurrence. Punishment of the subject by electric shock for failure (McElroy & Brown, 1950) and judiciously introduced monetary incentives (Woodruff & George, 1937) both helped to improve the ESP scoring level. Positive ESP scores may result from the subject's high motivation caused by his mood, by his attitude or beliefs, or by the psychological characteristics of the targets. Psi missing may be caused by negative motivation (Nash, 1955b), and the *differential effect,* where scores are higher in one task than in another, appears often to result from a motivational differential in the two conditions. In some cases the more difficult task resulted in higher scores, apparently by increasing the subject's motivation. This occurred in the throwing of dice in darkness (McMahan, 1947), in the employment of foreign-language targets (Rao, 1963b), and in the use of a greater target distance (J.B. Rhine & Pratt, 1954).

Sensory Deprivation

Reduction of the number of irrelevant sensory stimuli bombarding the subject may increase his ability to respond appropriately to psi stimuli. Sensory deprivation resulting in significant ESP scores has been accomplished by placing halved table tennis balls over the subject's eyes, with a diffuse light projected over the eye covers that produces an effect known as a *ganzfeld* or homogenous visual field; by exposing the individual to white noise or to a repetitious pleasant noise; and by seating the person in a comfortable position in a reclining chair (Honorton & Harper, 1974). In a later experiment, subjects under similar conditions obtained significantly higher ESP scores than did the subjects of a control group (Braud, Wood & Braud, 1975).

Relaxation

The finding that cerebral concussion patients scored significantly higher in ESP tests than patients who did not have concussion was attributed to their relaxed attitude (Schmeidler,

1952). Similarly, relaxed maternity patients had higher ESP scores than those who were tense (Gerber & Schmeidler, 1957). Subjects in a deep state of physical and mental relaxation yielded significantly higher ESP scores than did less relaxed individuals (Braud & Braud, 1974). Increased skin resistance to electricity accompanies relaxation, and ESP scores were found to be higher in subjects whose skin resistance increased during the run (Otani, 1955). In contrast, PK scores were significantly higher following suggestions for muscle tension than following suggestions for relaxation (Honorton & Barksdale, 1972). However, PK scores were significantly higher in the noneffort period immediately after cessation of effort than in the period during which an effort was being made to produce PK (Stanford & Fox, 1975). Outstanding PK psychics such as Eusapia Palladino (Carrington, 1954), Rudi Schneider (Hope et al., 1933), Ted Serios (Eisenbud, 1969), and Nina Kulagina (Ullman, 1974) have shown an increase in tension during their PK manifestations as evidenced by increased heart rate and blood pressure, loss of weight, and elevation of the respiratory rate. During some PK manifestations Palladino experienced sexual ecstasy and Schneider underwent sexual orgasm (Devereux, 1974). The French psychic Jean-Pierre Girard found that creating PK to bend a metal bar was similar to experiencing an orgasm (Dierkens, 1978). Evidence of tension during PK is also indicated by the feeling of fatigue frequently experienced at the end of psychokinetic metal-bending sessions (Taylor, 1975).

Brain Waves

The living brain generates very small electrical currents that can be recorded by connecting an electroencephalograph to the scalp with contact electrodes. Brain waves have been categorized, partially on the basis of their frequency, into beta waves at 14 to 50 per second, alpha waves at 8 to 13 per second, theta waves at 4 to 7 per second and delta waves at 1 to 3 per second. Beta waves occur during mental activity, alpha waves during eye closure and relaxation, theta waves during drowsiness, and delta waves during sleep. The proportion of time that alpha rhythms are present in an EEG record was found to be positively correlated with the ESP score (Cadoret, 1964). This may be because both ESP and alpha waves are increased by relaxation. Similarly, ESP may be related to theta waves by both of them being favored by drowsiness. The degree of increase of alpha abundance between a pretest relaxation period and an attentive ESP testing period, in both of which the eyes were closed, had a significant positive correlation with the ESP score (Stanford & Lovin, 1970). This lends substance to the theory that ESP activation is associated more with a transition of consciousness from one state to another than with a particular state of consciousness (Murphy, 1966).

Although ESP scores and alpha waves may be related because both are increased by relaxation, there is some indication that an ESP stimulus may reduce alpha wave activity. A reduction of alpha activity in the percipient, indicating an arousal response, occurred when the agent received intermittent electric shocks (Tart, 1963) or was exposed to a flashing light (Targ & Puthoff, 1974).

Meditation

Most forms of meditation attempt to reduce associative, discoursive thinking by directing the mind to a simple repetitive task such as thinking a mantra or to an object of contemplation such as a *mandala*. This produces a state which combines physical and mental relaxation with arousal and attentiveness. During transcendental meditation, the individual directs his attention to the level at which thought and action originate, until he restricts his awareness to a claimed absolute consciousness which is undifferentiated and unchanging. Meditation's core experience is an altered state of consciousness in which one's ego is diminished, while a larger sense of self-existence merged with the cosmos comes into existence. Subjects' ESP scores were found to be significantly higher following meditation sessions than they were before the session (Dukhan & Rao, 1973). Furthermore, subjects who had pursued some form of meditation in the past had higher PK scores than control subjects (Matas & Pantas, 1971).

Sensitivity to Inner State

Persons who were rated as having a penetration personality and being more responsive to internal processes had significantly larger scoring fluctuations above and below chance in an ESP guessing task than subjects who were rated as having a barrier personality (Schmeidler & LeShan, 1970). Frequency of dream recall, which may be a measure of sensitivity to the inner state, was higher in individuals with high ESP scores (Johnson, 1968). Subjects whose attention exhibited the greatest shifts from external stimuli toward internally generated stimuli scored significantly better on ESP tasks than did those individuals whose attention remained externally oriented (Honorton, Davidson & Bindler, 1971). The focus of attention was determined by having the subjects rate the degree to which their attention was focused on internal feelings and sensations.

Mysticism

The mystic experience is an altered state in which the individual's consciousness seems to become one with the absolute, eradicating the subject-object dichotomy. The psychic experience is one in which an effect occurs paranormally between the mind of an individual and an external object. Both the mystic and psychic experiences involve a union of a sort between a person's mind and an external object, and both exhibit spatial and temporal independence. Thus, it might be expected that individuals who have mystical experiences are also prone to have experiences of a psychic nature. This expectation is supported by the finding of a significant positive correlation between ESP score and religious value as measured with the Allport Study of Values (Nash, 1958). According to the authors of this study, ". . . the highest value of the religious man may be called unity. He is mystical, and seeks to comprehend the cosmos as a whole, to relate himself to its embracing totality." Similarly, in an experiment with a group of meditators (Osis & Bokert, 1971), those who did best in ESP had a "feeling of merging with the others . . . and a feeling of oneness as if the boundaries between 'what is me and what is not me' were dissolving."

Hypnosis

Paranormal phenomena in persons under hypnosis have been reported as far back as Mesmer. A number of early writers described experiments on "community of sensation" wherein hypnotized individuals became aware of tactile or olfactory stimuli presented to the hypnotist (Dingwall, 1968). Experiments were reported on the induction of hypnosis at a distance, which was dependent upon psi (Janet, 1886; Richet, 1886). In twelve contemporary experimental studies in which hypnosis and waking experimental conditions were compared, nine showed a significant advantage with hypnosis (Honorton & Krippner, 1969). An effect of hypnosis on ESP performance has been one of the most replicable of paranormal phenomena. Furthermore, the higher suggestibility of some psychics indicates that suggestibility or hypnotizability is positively related to psychic expression. Hypnosis may be conducive to paranormal expression because it dissociates the mind, allowing part of it to become strongly focused and the rest to remain quietly behind. It may facilitate ESP performance by also physically and mentally relaxing the subject.

Dreaming

Significant evidence of the telepathy of pictorial targets during dreaming has been found in nine of twelve experiments (Ullman & Krippner, with Vaughan, 1973). As there were no controls with waking subjects, it is not apparent whether the dream state is more conducive to ESP than is the waking state. A variation of the experiment was successfully conducted by inducing the dreams through hypnosis (Honorton & Stump, 1969).

Drugs

The stimulant caffein was found to significantly increase the level of PK scores (Rhine, Humphrey, & Averill, 1945). Although the stimulant amphetamine increased the variance of ESP scores (Rogers & Carpenter, 1966), it was found to decrease the scoring level (Sargent, 1977). Depressants such as alcohol were found to increase the PK scoring level when taken in moderate quantity but caused a significant decrease when taken in larger amounts

(Averill & Rhine, 1945). However, the PK psychic Ted Serios was most successful in producing psychic photographs after imbibing a considerable amount of alcoholic beverages (Eisenbud, 1969). In this case, the positive effect of alcohol on the induction of psi may have been in constituting a reward. A chlorpromazine-like tranquilizer increased the ESP scoring ability but not to a significant extent (Huby & Wilson, 1961). ESP tests of subjects under the influence of the hallucinogens LSD and psilocybin, in which the targets were photographic color prints of objects with emotional significance, provided no indication of significant scoring (Cavanna & Servadio, 1964).

Extraversion versus Introversion

The psychiatrist Carl Jung coined the terms extraversion and introversion for these two opposite types of personality. The extravert is outgoing in attention and interest, responsive to external stimuli, especially to other persons, and impulsive. The introvert directs his attention and interest inwardly with a tendency to excessive daydreaming, introspection, and careful balancing of considerations before reaching a decision.

The British psychologist H.J. Eysenck (1967) presented the belief that a large portion of personality traits can be related to two main dimensions of personality, one being extraversion-introversion and the other being neuroticism. Extraverts were reported to score significantly higher in ESP than did introverts (Humphrey, 1951), and Eysenck theorized that this relationship occurs because introverts habitually are in a state of greater cortical arousal than extraverts and because cortical arousal inhibits ESP. Also, introverts more than extraverts engage in analytical, self-conscious rationality, which tends to inhibit psi manifestation.

Eysenck considered many of the personality traits which have been found to be related to psi to be expressions of the extraversion-introversion dimension. In the case of the following pairs of opposite personality traits, he associated the first member of each pair with extraversion and the second with introversion. ESP experiments have indicated that individuals with the first or extravert trait of each pair scored significantly higher than subjects with the second or introvert trait as follows: sociable versus withdrawn (Shields, 1962), spontaneity of response versus conscious deliberation (Scherer, 1948), expansiveness or making large drawings versus compressiveness or making small drawings (Humphrey, 1946), task oriented versus ego involved (Eilbert & Schmeidler, 1950), self-confident versus timid (Nicol & Humphrey, 1953), and artists versus non-artists (Moss, 1969).

Pairs of contrasting traits not listed by Eysenck but which may be expressions of the extraversion-introversion dimension and have been found to result in a significant ESP scoring differential in favor of the extravert trait over the introvert characteristic are as follows: rapid response time versus slow rate of calling targets (Van de Castle, 1958), warm and sociable versus critical (Kathamani & Rao, 1971), attention seeking versus avoiding attention (Shields & Mulders, 1975), self-transcendent openness versus egocentricity (Nash, 1958; Osis & Bokert, 1971), penetration (view body as though surrounded by a permeable membrane) versus barrier (views body as though surrounded by a protective covering) (Schmeidler & LeShan, 1970), field dependent or global perceiving versus field independent or analytical perceiving (Buzby, 1967b), activity versus quiescence (Nash & Nash, 1967), and viewing time dynamically versus viewing time passively (Schmeidler, 1964). The association of psi with extraversion-introversion has been one of the most replicable of psi effects.

Neuroticism

In employing Rorschach tests, Schmeidler (1947) found that the differential in ESP score between sheep or believers in ESP and goats or nonbelievers in ESP was significantly greater between well-adjusted sheep and goats than between poorly adjusted sheep and goats. This indicated that well-adjusted individuals express ESP to a greater extent than do poorly adjusted persons, whether it is accomplished by psi hitting in the sheep or by psi missing in the goats. Poor adjustment is an index of neuroticism.

Nicol and Humphrey (1953) found that several personality factors which could be considered as related to neuroticism showed a significant relationship with ESP scores. Factors that were positively correlated with ESP scoring were: freedom from depression, happy-go-lucky disposition, freedom from nervous tension, emotional stability, calm trustfulness, and low irritability level. In their reaction to frustration-arousing situations, which is a measure of neuroticism, extrapunitives who blamed an outside source for their frustration in a picture-frustration test had lower ESP scores than impunitives who treated the situation impersonally (Eilbert & Schmeidler, 1950). Low ESP scores were found to be associated with high defensiveness, which is a measure of neurotic disposition (Carpenter, 1965). Anxiety is a basic component of neuroticism, and low anxious individuals had significantly higher ESP scores than high anxious subjects (Rao, 1965).

Negative correlations were found between ESP scores and all but one of the scores of neurotic and psychotic traits measured by the Minnesota Multiphasic Personality Inventory (Nash, 1966). The negative correlations were at a significant level for the neurotic traits of hypochondriasis and psychasthenia. Hypochondriasis is a term applied to individuals who are unduly worried over their health, while psychasthenia is a condition in which the person is troubled by phobias or compulsive behavior. Interests of the opposite sex, i.e. the tendency of males to have feminine interests and of females to have masculine interests, is the only trait measured by the Minnesota Multiphasic Personality Inventory that was not found to be negatively correlated with ESP scores, and it is questionable that it is a neurotic trait. A relationship may exist between homosexuality and having interests of the opposite sex, and it is the writer's observation that homosexuality occurs with greater frequency in psychics than in the general population. Consistent with this is the fact that homosexual shamans are purported to be more powerful than shamans who are heterosexual (Hardy, 1974).

The above tests of the relation between neuroticism and ESP expression were performed on individuals who were not outstanding in ESP ability. While they indicate that persons within the usual range of psychic capacity have higher ESP scores the less their neuroticism, some parapsychologists have found that psychics possess characteristics of the neurotic condition of hysteria (Assailly, 1957; Sannwald, 1962; Tenhaeff, 1962). Hysteria may be manifested in dissociations as displayed in multiple personalities, seance-room phenomena, automatic writing, use of the *Ouija*(TM) *board,* and poltergeist phenomena. Some of these manifestations may involve the expression of psi (Chaps. 11 & 12). In some instances psychic ability may induce neuroticism, the individual becoming anxious and defensive because he differs from society's norms. This may require professional advice and has given rise to the vocation of psychic counselor (Criswell & Herzog, 1977). Vice versa, the individual may dissociate in order to facilitate the expression of psi or to reduce the inhibition of psi that may be caused by conflicts (McCreery, 1969). Also, a neurotic individual may manifest psi to compensate for his not being able to function as normally as the average person. Nevertheless, some parapsychologists who have studied persons with considerable psychic ability have concluded that they are no more neurotic than individuals with less capacity (Flournoy, 1900; Richet, 1922). Schmeidler (1967) suggested that psychics fall into two groups: neurotic individuals in whom normal controls and inhibitions of ESP experience have never fully developed, and normal persons who are so well adjusted and stable that they can relax their controls without undue anxiety.

Psychoses

The paranoiac frequently alleges that he is being subjected to telepathic influences. The psychiatrist Jan Ehrenwald (1947) expressed the view that the paranoid schizophrenic lacks adequate ESP screening to background hostility and that his irrational behavior results from his attempts to ward off his uncanny experiences, which arise partly through telepathy. However, he concluded from ESP tests and clinical observations that paranoid schizophrenics seem neither more nor less susceptible to demonstrable psi phenomena than are nonschizophrenics (Ehrenwald, 1974). ESP tests conducted by several experimenters with psychotic subjects in different diagnostic categories have evidenced little more than that psychotic individuals are able to manifest ESP (Rogo, 1975) .

CONCLUSIONS

Although most individuals may have psi ability, this has not been empirically demonstrated. Furthermore, the modus of expressing whatever psi ability one has appears to vary with the individual. Sex and age affect the way psi is expressed, but they are not limiting factors to psychic ability. Paranormal expression appears to occur throughout the range of human intelligence, but it may be more pronounced in individuals who are creative or who have better memories. Certain attitudes and personality traits have been associated with psi expression, one direction of the trait resulting in a positive manifestation of psi and the opposite tendency causing psi to be negatively expressed. This is true of belief in ESP, extraversion, pleasurable mood, motivation, and emotional stability. Mental states produced by sensory deprivation, relaxation, meditation, hypnosis, and dreaming have been found to be favorable for psi expression.

REVIEW QUESTIONS

1. What are the steps used by gifted subjects to manifest ESP?
2. Can ESP be learned?
3. In what percentage of people is psi present?
4. How is psi affected by the following subject variables: age, attitude to ESP, attitude to experimenter, belief in ESP, blindness, brain waves, creativity, culture, drugs, extraversion-introversion, health, horoscope, hypnosis, inheritance, intelligence, meditation, memory, mental imagery, mood, motivation, mysticism, naivete, neuroticism, psychosis, race, relaxation, sensitivity to inner state, sensory deprivation, sex?

Chapter 8

THE AGENT AND THE EXPERIMENTER

A<small>N AGENT IS AN INDIVIDUAL</small> who is a psi sender. He may also be an experimenter or a subject. In telepathy an agent is an individual whose mental states are responded to by the percipient, while in PK he is a person who affects the physical object, which may be the brain of another individual.

Subjects in an experiment may act as agents or psi senders to one another. René Warcollier (1948) carried out drawing tests which suggested telepathic interaction between the percipients. In these tests, mental contagion seemed to occur among several subjects even when they were separated by great distances. Another suggestion of intersubject ESP is in the finding that, in a group test, resemblances in the responses occurred more frequently between percipients in adjacent positions than between those who were farther apart (Hardy et al., 1973).

That the agent may paranormally affect the telepathy scores is shown by the fact that in the same experiment the scores were significantly higher with one agent than with another even though they were several rooms away from the subjects (MacFarland, 1938). Paranormal control by the agent is indicated in an ESP experiment by Hans and Shulamith Kreitler (1972), Professors of Psychology at Tel Aviv University. Although the percipients in this experiment were unaware of using ESP or of being tested for it, the scores were higher when an agent concentrated on transmitting the target to the subject than when there was no agent. Although the agent is an important factor in the psi process, analysis of spontaneous cases indicates that the percipient is usually the individual who exercised the initiative (L.E. Rhine, 1957).

An experimenter is a person who engages in one or more of the following tasks: planning the experiment, preparing the targets, giving the test, checking the scores, or analyzing the re-

sults. Generally an experimenter does not see the targets as does
an agent; however, an experimenter may also act as the agent in a
test of telepathy or of PK. In a self-testing psi experiment, the
experimenter is also the subject. In clairvoyance experiments, an
individual who handles the targets is called an experimenter in
contrast to tests of telepathy where he is called an agent.

Paranormal influence by the experimenter is shown by the
fact that persons who prepared the targets (West & Fisk, 1953) or
who checked the scores (Feather & Brier, 1968) affected the
scoring rate even though they had no direct contact with the percipients. It is not clear how these affects are brought about. Possibly the target preparer precognizes the subject's future calls and
selects targets to coincide with them, or the score checker through
retro-PK affects the subject's calls, or the subject through precognition is influenced by the checker's vision of the targets. It may
even be that the experimenter who analyzes the data after the hits
have been checked has a paranormal influence on the subject's
calls. That the experimenter may paranormally influence the
scores is also shown by an experiment in which significantly higher
scores were obtained when the experimenter wished for the subject's success than when he wished for his failure, even though the
experimenter never saw the targets and was in a separate room
from the subject during the test (Schmeidler, 1961).

Exposure to Target

The degree of exposure of the agent to the target may affect
the scoring rate, as is indicated by the fact that drawings which
were frequently shown to the agent made better targets than
others (Carington, 1945).

Relationship with Subject

The quality of the relationship of the agent or of the experimenter with the subject may affect the scoring rate, as is indicated
by the results of several experiments. Percipients who were related to the agent by blood or marriage had significantly higher
ESP scores than those who were not (Stuart, 1946). ESP scores
were extrachance when the agent and the percipient were of op-

posite sex but not when they were of the same sex (White & Angstadt, 1963). Clairvoyance scores were significantly higher with percipients liked by the experimenter than with subjects the experimenter did not like and with experimenters liked by the subjects than with experimenters the percipients held in less favor (Anderson & White, 1958). The differential was greatest when subjects and experimenters with mutually favorable feelings were compared with subjects and experimenters who were mutually disliked. Percipients in a clairvoyance experiment who were handled by an experimenter in a positively toned manner had a significantly higher rate of scoring than subjects who were treated by the experimenter in a negatively toned way (Honorton, Ramsey & Cabibbo, 1975). Percipients who had similar experiences and memories to those of the agent had higher ESP scores than those who had not been so conditioned (Vellissaris & Vellissaris, 1977).

Belief and Expectation

Experimenters who believed in ESP and expected it to be manifested were associated with significantly higher scores in a clairvoyance experiment than were experimenters who disbelieved in ESP (Parker, 1975). Belief and expectation by the experimenter in a particular outcome of a psi experiment may paranormally affect the results to comply with the experimenter's preconceived concepts. Because of the experimenter effect, before a characteristic of psi is considered to be established, results obtained by several experimenters should be compared.

Mood

The agent's mood at the time of the experiment was found to significantly affect the ESP scoring rate, particularly with respect to his feelings of relaxation, of freedom from anxiety, and of elation and vitality, even though the agent was unknown to the subject (Osis & Carlson, 1972). The mood of the experimenter at the time she prepared the targets also significantly affected the level of ESP expression (Price, 1973).

Motivation

The motivation of the experimenter may be related to the psi-scoring level by being affected by such characteristics as his belief in ESP, his liking of the subjects, and his mood. ESP scores were significantly higher when the agent was consciously trying to transmit than when he only thought about the message (Kreitler & Kreitler, 1973).

Relaxation

Better results were obtained in ESP tests when the agent was in a state of relaxed attentiveness than when he made a strong effort (Van de Castle, 1970).

Multiple Agents

In a live television broadcast in which the ESP targets were seen by millions of potential agents, the subjects did not score significantly above chance expectancy (Nash, 1963a). On the other hand, ESP scores were significantly higher when two agents, acting together, had the same target symbol than when they had different target symbols (MacFarland, 1938). Contrary to this finding, the scores of the subject Gloria Stewart were not increased by agents working in conjunction or decreased when they worked in opposition (Soal & Bateman, 1950). The results indicated that she responded to one alone of the two agents because the scores were significantly high only on the targets he looked at. In another experiment, when two agents acted in opposition, the subjects scored significantly higher with the agent they knew better (White & Angstadt, 1963). Extrachance scores were obtained with Gloria Stewart in an experiment using two agents, one pointing to one of five blank cards and the other looking at five cards similarly arranged and each bearing a different symbol (Soal & Bateman, 1954). Each agent was concealed from the other and had only a portion of the information. A psi hit could result only if the information known to the two agents was integrated.

In a test of PK, two subjects (PK agents) working together for the same target face were more effective than when each was trying for a different target face (Humphrey, 1947a). In another

PK experiment, the variance of the run scores was greater when the two subjects tried for the same target face than when they tried for different target faces (Feather & Rhine, 1969). Séance phenomena have been observed to increase in strength when two or more mediums work in concert or when the sitters as well as the medium are psychic (Fodor, 1933, p. 237). Thus it appears that in certain situations ESP and PK are favored by an increase in the number of agents.

CONCLUSIONS

The agent or the experimenter may affect the psi performance of the subject, and the effect may be paranormal rather than merely psychological. Because of the experimenter effect, the characteristics of psi must be determined by comparisons of experiments performed by different experimenters. In so far as they have been tested, characteristics of the agent or the experimenter associated with psi expression are similar to those of the subject. These include belief in ESP, mood, motivation, and relaxation.

REVIEW QUESTIONS

1. Give evidence of intersubject ESP.
2. Distinguish between agent and experimenter.
3. What are the indications that the agent may paranormally affect the ESP score?
4. What evidence is there that the experimenter may paranormally affect the ESP score even when he has no direct contact with the subjects?
5. What characteristics of the agent or the experimenter may affect the level of psi scoring?
6. What is the effect of multiple agents on the scoring level in ESP and in PK?
7. What is the experimenter effect, and why must it be considered in determining the characteristics of psi?

Chapter 9

SPONTANEOUS PARANORMAL PHENOMENA*

IN A POLL of 1,460 individuals in the United States, 58 percent claimed some kind of ESP experience with 15 percent having had them frequently (Greeley, 1975), and in a poll of over 1,000 individuals in Iceland, two-thirds claimed to have had a psychic experience at least once in their lifetime (Haraldsson, 1977). Because of such claims, man was led to test for psi experimentally. As psi has been found to occur in the laboratory, it is reasonable to assume that some apparently paranormal spontaneous incidents are due to a psychic factor although it may be impossible to determine whether or not any given spontaneous experience is paranormal. This is because of the possibility of chance coincidence, bad observation, faulty memory, and even deliberate fraud. To prevent the effect of incorrect memory, any psychic experience should be written down right away. In the case of precognitive experiences, a written description of the predicted event should be filed with the Central Premonitions Registry (Box 482, Times Square Station, New York, N.Y. 10036) so that it can be validated if and when it occurs. Out of the thousands of participants whose predictions are on file at this registry, five individuals have provided 42 percent of the fulfilled predictions (Nelson, 1976).

Before a spontaneous case was placed in the early collections accumulated by the Society for Psychical Research, an attempt was made to validate it. This was done on the basis of the characteristics that psi was held to possess at that time. Since ESP was then believed to be telepathic, clairvoyant incidents were considered questionable. Furthermore, clairvoyant cases do not have an agent who can provide independent corroboration of the event. Because of these reasons, clairvoyance cases constitute a much

---

*Unless otherwise indicated, the spontaneous cases in this chapter are from the author's personal collection.

122

lower percentage of cases in these early collections than they do in the collection belonging to the Foundation for Research into the Nature of Mind. The cases in the latter collection, which were analyzed by Louisa Rhine, were not selected on the basis of pre- conceived notions concerning the characteristics of psi, nor was verification a prerequisite to their inclusion. While this method has the drawback of diluting the genuine cases with unreliable or spurious instances, it may be the lesser evil, as it does not elimi- nate possibly real cases of psi not recognized as such under present paradigms.

In a poll of 3,000 psychiatrists in the United States, Tornatore (1977) found that, of the 609 who responded, 171 had experienced spontaneous paranormal phenomena. On the basis of their an- swers, he concluded that the relationship between analyst and analysand is a good setting for the occurrence of psi phenomena be- cause of the mutual needs of both. He observed that within this relationship psi is most likely to occur when there is a shift of attitude or consciousness in the analysand. The Hungarian psy- choanalyst I. Hollos (1933) observed over 500 instances of telep- athy in his analytic work. He found that telepathy is a frequent occurrence between analyst and patient, especially during a diffi- cult period in the analyst's life. He concluded that when the tele- pathic process manifests itself in analysis, there is a return of what the analyst has repressed in his own mind, but the return occurs in the mind of the patient and is subject to his rules of distortion.

Although spontaneous psychical experiences are not proof of psi, their analysis and categorization suggest hypotheses about the paranormal that can be tested by laboratory experimentation. Also, living organisms do not always function under laboratory conditions as they do in the field, and it is only through the study of the expressions of psi under natural conditions as well as in the laboratory that the full range of psi capacity can be known.

Impressions

Spontaneous paranormal phenomena are divisable into five classes: impressions, dreams, hallucinations, motor automatisms, and PK phenomena. The sometimes paranormal experience of *déjà vu,* French for already seen, can be placed in the class of impressions. It is a feeling that the experience that one is having has happened before, even though there is reason to believe that this is not the case. In some instances the experiencer can predict what will happen next as, for example, what will be seen around a corner or heard in a conversation. *Déjà vu* appears to be of common occurrence, approximately 80 percent of college students polled reported having experienced it (Palmer & Dennis, 1975). The following is an example:

> In 1948 I had a most interesting experience in a sixteenth century hacienda in Bolivia. While going through the building with the owner I suddenly found myself in an area I had seen in a dream which had recurred many times over a period of twenty years. To the astonishment of the owner I accurately described the layout and appearance of an entire wing before he had opened the door leading into it. Since that time I have not had this dream.

More typically, a *déjà vu* experience is not associated with a previous dream or with any previous event.

Impressions other than *déjà vu* constitute about one fourth of reported spontaneous psi cases (Stevenson, 1970a). The impression may be a feeling that something is or is not so or will or will not happen. Or, the impression may be a compulsion that turns out to have a meaningful result, as in the following example:

> Polly lived in Winnipeg and her father lived in Philadelphia. One day she told her husband to get her a ticket and a reservation from Winnipeg to Philadelphia as her father needed her. Her husband said, "How do you know? You didn't get any letter." She said, "Daddy needs me and I must go." He obtained the tickets and she had to change over at Chicago. When she reached Chicago, her husband had her paged as he had received a telegram that her father was dangerously ill. When she arrived in Philadelphia her father was dead. He was 80 years of age, and had died of an appendectomy operation.

The impression may be a presentiment of meeting someone. A person is seen in the street and is recognized as an old friend. The next minute the mistake is perceived, yet shortly thereafter the friend comes into view in flesh and blood. The following is an example:

As I was walking through the city hall plaza in Philadelphia, I saw some distance away a woman coming toward me. "Why," I thought, "there's Helen. I haven't seen her for some time." The woman was lost in the crowd and I followed up my thought, remembering the last time I had seen her. The woman came closer, the crowd had thinned out—and it wasn't Helen. She didn't even look like her. And I laughed inside myself to think I had been so mistaken. Toward the east end of the plaza there are outlets from the subway, and as I came to one of them a woman came up and started across to the north entrance. She looked up and saw me. She waved her hand. "Hi, Florence!" she said. It was Helen.

The impression may be an emotion such as depression, and weeping may occur at the time of death of another without knowledge that the person has died or without any conscious thought of the individual.

Dreams

The spontaneous psi experience may be manifested by mental imagery in a dream. Excluding *déjà vu* experiences, reported dream cases expressing psi exceed waking paranormal experiences (L. E. Rhine, 1962b). Realistic dreams manifesting psi are reported more frequently than unrealistic dreams with fanciful detail (L.E. Rhine, 1953). The following is an example of a realistic dream from the author's files:

One morning at the crack of dawn I dreamed I saw my baby beside my bed with blood all over his face, pajamas and the side of his bed and little pools on the floor around him. I awoke screaming, "Blood! Blood! All over the place." My husband awoke and wondered what was wrong. When I told him, he said I had been watching too much TV. I then laid down and tried to go back to sleep. It was about 45 minutes later that the baby awoke crying. When I went over I was horrified to see he was covered with blood just as I had seen him, only now it was dried on his face and all over his pillow and sheet. His nose was still bleeding when he awoke. I feel if I had gotten up and looked at him when I had that dream he wouldn't have bled so much.

The following is an example of an unrealistic dream:

My mother awakened in great distress after a very vivid dream in which I was attacked by a large dog and was covered with blood. She

warned me to be very careful of my arms, much to my father's amuse-
ment, and insisted that I stay away from dogs. Later that morning my
brother was carried into the house after being attacked by a large dog
of the same breed as she had described. He bled profusely and had
to have his right arm taken care of at the hospital.

Because paranormal as well as normal dreams may involve
symbolism, their interpretation should be considered by the parapsychological investigator as well as by the psychoanalyst. Freud
offered an example of a symbolic dream that was interpretable on
the basis of psychoanalytic theory if the dream could be presumed
to involve ESP (Chap. 2). Several psychiatrists have observed that
their patients used, as dream material, events in the life of their
analyst of which they had no normal knowledge. The American
psychiatrist Jule Eisenbud (1946) described a dream of his patient
which apparently involved events in his life paranormally known
to her. "I was at Atlantic City where I met you on the board-
walk. You were dressed in a very loud sport jacket and in general
looked very 'Hollywoodish.' I was carrying some books, a paper
bag and my little notebook." Eisenbud stated that he had recently
bought a sport jacket and had been trying unsuccessfully to get his
wife to go to Atlantic City with him. It was as though his patient
had said in her dream, "If your wife does not wish to accompany
you to Atlantic City, why don't you take me with you? Then we
can really get on with our work!" The American psychiatrist Jan
Ehrenwald (1947) expressed the opinion that some of what a
therapist finds in a patient's mind the therapist has telepathically
implanted there himself. This is exemplified by the correspondence in the dream content of patients with the prevailing idea of
the school of their analyst, which he called doctrinal compliance.

Cases have occurred where the individual incorporates into his
dream a precognized event that is about to occur while he is still
asleep, possibly in an attempt to prevent the event when it takes
place from shocking him out of his sleep (Puthoff & Targ, 1974b).
The Frenchman Alfred Maury dreamed that he was brought before
the tribunal during the French Revolution, questioned by Robe-
spierre and Marat, condemned to death, and led to the place of
execution. He climbed onto the scaffold and was bound to the

plank by the executioner. The blade of the guillotine fell and he felt his head separate from his body. He awoke in great anxiety, only to find that the top of the bed had fallen down and had struck the back of his neck (Freud, 1913). It may be suggested that Maury precognized the striking of the back of his neck by the falling bed top. He then constructed dream events which would permit the blow on his neck to be logically interpreted in the dream as coming from the blade. If the blow from the falling bed top had not been sufficient to awaken him, he may have continued to sleep without remembering the dream.

Mutual or reciprocal dreams in which two dreamers share the same dream environment are less frequently reported. Hart and Hart (1932) report the following example:

> Mr. Davis dreamed one night that he was helping two ladies across the ruined planking of an old sawmill, built over black stagnant water. Something white, glimmering below, proved to be the face of his wife, just showing above the water, with her eyes looking into his, but without a motion or sound. Mr. Davis dreamed that he immediately jumped into the water and caught her round the shoulders and neck to support her. At that instant he was roused from sleep by a smothered cry from Mrs. Davis at his side. He shook her to waken her and asked what she had dreamed to frighten her. She had just been dreaming of finding herself sinking in a pond of water by the roadside, of throwing up her arms above the water, and trying to scream for help. Just as she felt her hand grasped by someone to help her, Mr. Davis spoke, and she awoke.

Hallucinations

Spontaneous psi experiences involving mental imagery may take place in hallucinations as well as in dreams. Hallucinations constitute about 10 percent of reported psychic experiences (L.E. Rhine, 1956b). The difference between hallucinations and dreams is not as pronounced as it may seem to be. When the mental imagery occurs in the *hypnagogic* period of visual and auditory sensations that may precede sleep or in the similar period that may follow sleep before fully awakening, it is a question whether to consider it as a dream or as an hallucination. An hallucination is in a sense a waking dream, embodying many of the features of the latter, with the major difference being that the individual's eyes are open instead of closed. To illustrate this fact, the following instance can be cited. An Oxford undergraduate had a very vivid dream of being chased by a figure in green (Gurney, Myers & Podmore, 1886, p. 252). He woke and saw the green figure in the middle of the room. He had no doubt that he was awake because he saw the light from the street lamp shining on his door. The hallucinated figure was not in this light, but nearer the bed, and the green tinge was very perceptible.

According to the English psychiatrist Donald West (1960), very distinct differences exist between pathological hallucinations and those of the sane. Pathological hallucinations are generally auditory, stereotyped, repetitive, vague, take place during illness, and are accompanied by loss of awareness of normal surroundings. In contrast, hallucinations of the sane are generally visual, almost unique in the life of the individual, realistic, and remembered and described with precision. However, many apparently sane mediums have hallucinations of spirits of the deceased which, far from being unique, are of frequent occurrence.

Most reported hallucinations are auditory or visual, with the auditory predominating (L.E. Rhine, 1956b). An auditory hallucination due to ESP is also called *clairaudience*. The following is an example of an auditory hallucination from the author's files:

> My daughter and two young women tried to pass a coal truck. Their car hit a snow bank at the side of the road, went up over cement steps through a bush and into a tree. The young woman who was sitting on that side was killed instantly. Later while being treated at the hospital, my daughter heard the dead woman say, "Ken, my husband—I want my husband, Ken." My daughter did not learn of her death until sometime later.

Second in frequency to auditory hallucinations are those that are visual, as in the following example:

> A girl friend and I were enjoying a movie. It was a light drama typical of the forties. All at once I saw an entirely different scene. A friend of mine named Chuck who was in the Marine Corps was standing on the bow of a ship. Bombs were bursting and the ship was in flames. A life boat was in the water. It did not seem to be full. However, it was quite a way from my friend. I burst into tears

and excused myself. Although I was badly shaken I was finally able to compose myself and enjoy the rest of the movie. Nearly six weeks later during lunch period in high school, Chuck's brother Gene stopped me in the hall to share a letter. He began to read the letter. Chuck's ship had been bombed and burst into flames. He was on the bow of the ship. The life boat was quite far away; however, it managed to get back to him. He and a few others were saved. His rescue was regarded as a miracle. The surviving crew members were hospitalized for minor burns, smoke inhalation and observation. Chuck was unharmed. Gene and I compared dates and times. The exact time and date of my "vision" in the movie theater was when Chuck's ship was hit.

A hallucination may be one of having an *out-of-body experience* (OBE) or it may be one of seeing an apparition of the person who is having the OBE (Chap. 11). If the hallucination is one of seeing a person, whether he is alive or dead, it is termed an "apparition." In a poll of 900 persons in Iceland, 31 percent reported having seen an apparition of a person who was dead, and 11 percent stated that they had perceived an apparition of a living individual (Haraldsson, 1977). The apparition may be of a person who has left to go to a certain place but is seen before he arrives there (Gurney, Myers, & Podmore, 1886). This phenomenon is often reported in Norway where a man is heard or seen by his family to arrive home—he hangs up his hat, lights his pipe, says hello—and then disappears only to arrive in the flesh a few minutes later (Knight, 1969, p. 93). Also it may be an hallucination of seeing one's double or *doppelgänger* in action. The German writer Goethe described a *doppelgänger* experience in his autobiography, *Wahrheit und Dictung:*

> I rode now on the footpath toward Drunsenheim, and there one of the strangest presentiments surprised me. I saw myself coming to meet myself, on the same way, on horseback, but in a garment such as I had never worn. It was of light grey mingled with gold. As soon as I had aroused myself from this dream, the vision entirely disappeared. Remarkable, nevertheless, it is that eight years afterward I found myself on the same road, intending to visit Frederika once more, and in the same garment which I had dreamed about and which I now wore, not out of choice but by accident. This wonderful hallucination had a quieting effect on me.

Apparitions of acquaintances have been found to occur more frequently near the time of the acquaintance's death than would be expected by chance. In the Census of Hallucinations (Sidgwick, 1894), one in 43 of such hallucinations occurred within 12 hours either preceding or following the death of the person who was seen in the hallucination. On the basis of the death rate in England and Wales at that time, only about one in 19,000 individuals died in a given 24-hour period. It would be expected therefore, on the basis of chance if no other factor were involved, that only about one in 19,000 hallucinations would be within 12 hours of the person's death instead of the one in 43 that was reported. This is indicative of paranormality.

Dying persons have been found to have hallucinations near death much above the rate of hallucinations in a normal population, and these deathbed hallucinations occur for the most part in patients who are not sedated (Osis, 1961). These hallucinations are most often of the dead, and the majority of percipients who died within ten minutes of seeing an apparition stated that the apparitions had come to take them into the next life.

The English physicist G.N.M. Tyrrell (1953) gave the characteristics of what he considered to be a "perfect apparition," which he collected from a large number of cases. If the perfect apparition were standing beside a normal human being, we should find the following points of resemblance: (1) Both figures would appear equally real and solid. (2) We should be able to walk around the apparition, viewing it from any standpoint. (3) How well we should see the figures would depend upon the light; both figures would disappear in darkness. (4) Both figures would obscure the background. (5) If the apparition happened to be wearing a rose in its buttonhole, we should probably smell the scent of it. (6) On approaching the apparition, we should hear its breathing, the rustling of its clothes, and the shuffling of its shoes on the floor. (7) The apparition would probably behave as if aware of our presence, possibly smiling and turning its head to follow our movements. It might even place its hand on our shoulder, in which case we should feel an ordinary human touch. (8) The apparition might speak to us, and possibly it might go as far as to answer a question; but we should not be able to engage it in any long conversation. (9) We should see the apparition reflected in a mirror. (10) Both figures would probably cast shadows. (11) If we shut our eyes, both figures would disappear and reappear when we reopened them. (12) In addition to its clothes, the figure might have other accessories and might be accompanied by a dog or even by another human being. (13) The apparition might seem to pick up an object in the room or open and close the door, although physically the objects would not have moved at all.

According to Tyrrell we should find the following points of difference between a perfect apparition and a normal human being. (1) If we came near the apparition, or if the apparition touched us, we might feel a sensation of cold. (2) If we tried to take hold of the apparition, our hand would go through it without encountering any resistance. (3) If we were to sprinkle powder on the floor only the real individual would leave any footprints. (4) Only the real individual would come out in a photograph or be recorded on a sound-recording apparatus. (5) After a time, which might be anything up to half an hour, the apparition would suddenly vanish, become transparent and fade away, vanish into the wall or go through the floor, or open the door and walk out. (6) The apparition might become slightly luminous. (7) It might show small details of itself when we were so far away that normally we could not possibly have seen them. To these characteristics could be added that, unlike a real person, the apparition might not be seen by everyone looking in its direction.

An analysis of accounts of apparitions made by the British psychical researchers Celia Green and Charles McCreery (1975) revealed the following characteristics: (1) The background may remain the same or it may be modified as a part of the hallucination. (2) The percipient's actions and movement while viewing the apparition may not tally with those he thought he had made. (3) The percipient may or may not realize until after the apparition ended that what he was perceiving was an apparition. (4) The apparition is usually seen quite close to the percipient. (5) It is more common for the apparition to enter the percipient's field of view as a complete figure rather than building up or solidifying

before the percipient's eyes.   (6) The large majority of apparitions appear on the ground, walking, standing, or sitting, just like
real people; however, in a few cases they appear off the ground or
floating.   (7) As well as apparitions of human beings, the visual
hallucination may be of an animal or of an inanimate object.   (8)
About one third of recognized apparitions of human beings are of
people who are alive at the time of the experience, and about two-
thirds are of people whom the percipient knew to be dead.   The
Canadian psychologist Michael Persinger (1974) reported that the
apparition is commonly smiling and that the time interval between the established death and the appearance of the apparition
in most cases is less than five days.

Many collectively perceived hallucinations have been apparitions of persons, instances of which are given in the section on
haunting in Chapter 11.   There are reports of groups numbering
from two to eight people seeing the same apparition at the same
time (Green & McCreery, 1975).   Collective perceptions of apparitions account for approximately 8 percent of the total number
of reported apparitions, and in a group situation, if one person
sees an apparition, there is a 40 percent likelihood that others will
share his perception (Tyrrell, 1953).   The following is an example
of a collectively perceived hallucination from the author's files:

> My mother and I were out riding on Delaware Drive at about
> 7 PM. It was dusk and raining very hard. As we were driving down
> the hill, we both saw an old model T Ford which looked as if it would
> crash right into the front of our car. I screamed and my mother
> swerved our car off the road. The model T was gone—there was
> nothing there. This happened right beside a cemetery.

Several theories have been presented to explain apparitions.
The theory of Frederic Myers (1903) is that the agent sends a
telepathic message to the percipient who embodies it in sensory
form, and this constitutes the apparition. To explain collectively
perceived apparitions, he postulated that the apparition occupies
space even though it can be perceived only paranormally. Edmund Gurney's explanation for collectively perceived apparitions
is one of telepathy by infection, the agent telepathically influencing
a primary percipient who transmits the apparition to another

percipient, who may transmit it to still another (Gurney, Myers, & Podmore, 1886). H. H. Price (1939), Professor of Philosophy at Oxford University, postulated that apparitions may be persistent and dynamic images in a *psychic ether* (Chap. 14), which might exist in a common unconscious. Tyrrell (1953) believed that an apparition is an aggregate of sense data in the percipient's mind caused by unconscious portions of the minds of the percipient and the agent working together. It was the belief of the sociologist Hornell Hart (1956) that apparitions are conscious entities in four-dimensional space and that they are semisubstantial with both physical and nonphysical characteristics. George Zorab (1975) postulated that some apparitions are physically structured and are produced by a phantom-forming faculty of a human being. There is also the theory that an apparition is an *astral body,* a much finer physical counterpart of the living body, and the theory that an apparition is a soul or disembodied spirit of a deceased person.

While most reported hallucinations are auditory or visual, they may be of other sense modalities such as olfactory, and somatic or body sensations (L.E. Rhine, 1956b). The following is a somatic hallucination from the author's files:

> During World War II, I was in London and worked at the Church Canteen after working hours. While there I became very attached to Teddy and his wife—he was a British soldier. He was much older than I and had no children of his own. I think I felt he had taken the place of my father who had passed away when I was seven. It was at one of these dances that I experienced a terrific burning sensation over my face, hands and arms and I mentioned it to my partner who was Teddy's buddy. The pain was almost unbearable. The following day my partner called me to say that at the exact time I had experienced the burning sensation a gas tank had exploded burning Teddy's face, hands and arms.

Motor Automatisms

Psi may be manifested spontaneously by motor automatisms, i.e. movement performed without conscious effort, such as dowsing and automatic writing, which are more frequently induced than they are spontaneous and are described in Chapter 11.

Spontaneous PK Phenomena

The spontaneous paranormal event may take the form of PK, as in the stopping of clocks and the falling of pictures without a known physical cause, and occur near the time of death of an individual previously associated with the object. Such phenomena are less than 2 percent as frequent as are spontaneous ESP experiences (L.E. Rhine, 1977). Mechanical sounds produced by PK, such as knocks, raps, and the ringing of a bell, are heard normally and are different from paranormal auditory hallucinations (L.E. Rhine, 1963). Carl Jung (1963) had two experiences, during a period in which he was writing his doctoral thesis on mediumship, that he attributed to spontaneous PK. On one occasion a round walnut dining table split apart, making a sound that reminded him of a pistol shot. Two weeks later, a similar explosive sound resulted in his finding a bread knife with its blade broken into several pieces.

An apparent spontaneous PK act that benefited the experiencer is described by a correspondent as follows:

> When I was fifteen years old I saw an ad in the paper asking for a girl to work after school and stating that applicants should apply after five o'clock. As I approached the area where the store was located I began to get nervous and I felt something was wrong. Most of the stores on the street were empty and it looked like a deserted neighborhood. I finally found the address and went in. A young man came from the back of the store and asked me to "come on back." I did and he asked me to take my coat off and I did and then I knew something was very wrong and I was more frightened than ever. He made a telephone call and said something like, "Come on over—I have a good one." The man must have been next door because he was over in no time. They started asking me personal questions and by this time I knew I was in danger and I was scared. I wanted to run but one man kept the door blocked. I wanted to scream but was too frightened. Suddenly a little bell rang and with that they both jumped and asked me if I had someone waiting for me and I said falsely, "Yes, my brother." With that they ran out the back door and I ran out the front door. I ran down the street, which was still deserted. Suddenly I felt the presence of my father. It had the most calming effect on me and I said out loud, "Oh, Dad you didn't desert me." He had died about four years before and I felt his presence so clearly. A few weeks later a ring engaged in white slavery was arrested

in that area. When I ran out the door no one was in the store and no one was on the street. The bell which had rung was just a bell at the top of the door and the door had to be pushed open for the bell to ring.

Time and Place Relationships

Persinger (1974) found more spontaneous psychic experiences occurring (1) at night than in the day, (2) in the home than in other locations, and (3) in the bedroom than elsewhere in the home. ESP experiences of contemporaneous events are more frequently reported than those of future happenings (L.E. Rhine, 1954). Contemporaneous ESP experiences occur more frequently in waking than in dreaming, while more precognitive cases are reported during the dreaming state, the ratio in each case being about two to one. Precognition seems so alien to our waking minds that we may tend to block such knowledge from coming to consciousness; but when we dream and our controls are weaker, the blocked message may arise to awareness. More precognitive dreams are unrealistic than realistic, and Persinger (1974) found 20 percent of them to be recurrent.

Retrocognition is much less frequently reported than contemporaneous ESP and precognition and is difficult to establish because a present record of the past event must exist in order to verify the retrocognition. It could be that the identification of the present record by contemporaneous ESP is the actual cause of the ostensible retrocognition. An apparent example of spontaneous retrocognition is that experienced by a principal and a vice-principal of an Oxford women's college who were on a visit to the Petit Trianon at Versailles (Salter, 1950). The location of the buildings and the dress of the individuals who were seen led them to conclude that they had seen the Trianon as it was at the time of Marie Antoinette, more than a century before. Their accounts were afterwards confirmed by documents in the French National Archives.

Agent Participation

In paranormal auditory hallucinations in which the percipient heard his name called, many of the cases had no identifiable agent, the agent was dead, or there was no actual physical calling of the percipient's name (L.E. Rhine, 1953). In many cases of telepathy, the agent may lack even unconscious intent, whereas the percipient always shows some degree of motivation (L.E. Rhine, 1956a). There are, however, many cases of telepathic impressions in which the agent seems to be an important participant in the process. The following is an example from the author's collection:

> When I was in high school, I was organist for two Episcopal churches. This meant traveling from one town to another with the priest. After the second service my mother would pick me up at noon or a little after. One morning the priest informed me that the second service would begin and end a half-hour earlier. I had no time to call my mother, nor did anyone else. All through the service I kept thinking, "Mother, come for me at 11:30." As church let out I dashed out to find my mother waiting. Her first words were, "Well, here I am." She then recalled a previous experience we had during World War II. My father was in the Navy, stationed in Gulfport, Mississippi. My mother and I were traveling down to see him. Mother had written him to meet the bus at a certain time. En route, however, we were able to get connections which would get us there five or six hours earlier. Mother told me to "think very hard of Dad." We both thought very hard, and sure enough there he was to meet the bus. He said he just "knew" we would be on that bus.

It may be questioned whether it is correct to consider such an experience as spontaneous because it was intentionally induced. However, it is spontaneous in the sense of occurring under natural conditions in everyday life rather than in the laboratory.

In spontaneous psi cases, when the agent was thinking about or calling for the percipient during a crisis, the percipient was more likely to take some specific action than when the agent was not focusing on the subject (Stevenson, 1970a). When an agent is involved in a spontaneous psi event, he is usually a relative or friend of the percipient and most frequently dying or in a near-death or emotionally traumatic situation at the time of the paranormal experience (Gurney, Myers, & Podmore, 1886).

Conviction and Intervention

In paranormal impressions, dreams and hallucinations, the ESP information reaching consciousness may be incomplete (L.E. Rhine, 1962a). Nevertheless, a majority of reported cases show conviction on the part of the percipient, i.e. he had a definite feeling of certainty about the validity of the experience (L.E. Rhine, 1951b). This may be due to spontaneous paranormal experiences without conviction being forgotten sooner than those that were convincing. Conviction occurred in about two thirds of the waking cases but only in one third of the dreaming experiences. This may be because a person is more likely to take notice of an irrational impression when awake than if it occurred in a dream where they are not unusual. In conviction cases concerning an undesirable foreseen event, nearly two thirds of the percipients did not attempt to intervene (L.E. Rhine, 1955). The following is an example of futile intervention from Rhine's study.

> My grandmother tried one morning to keep my grandfather from going to work on his farm telling him she dreamed so vividly of his falling from a load of hay and breaking his neck. He was planting that day and laughed at her, but the weather started to change, and he stopped planting to help the haying crew get the hay in. The team lunged, he fell off the top of the load and died of a broken neck.

The following is an example of successful intervention from the same study:

> About ten years ago in New York I had a dream. I heard a scream and turned around and saw my son, then two years old, falling through the window. I even heard the siren of the ambulance driving up in front of the house. When I awoke I first checked the baby and then the windows. Everything was okay. A couple of days later I put his mattress in the window for airing. The window was pulled tightly down on it. I was busy in the next room. Suddenly I remembered my dream and ran into his room. He had managed to push up the window and was up on the window sill. I grabbed him the moment he was going to fall. The mattress was already down on the street.

In the 191 cases in the study where intervention was attempted, two thirds of the attempted interventions were successful and one-third was futile. However, of the 131 cases of successful intervention, all but three had alternative explanations and, although suggestive of intervention, are not proof of its occurrence. How an event could be precognized and at the same time be intervened is a question for which a satisfactory answer has yet to be provided.

CONCLUSIONS

While spontaneously occurring, ostensibly paranormal experiences such as *veridical* intuitions, dreams, and hallucinations are not proof of the paranormal, their study indicates how psi occurs under natural circumstances rather than in the artificial conditions of the laboratory.

REVIEW QUESTIONS

1. Why may it be impossible to determine whether or not a given spontaneous experience is paranormal?

2. Give a hypothetical example of each of the five principal kinds of spontaneous paranormal experience.

3. What is *déjà vu?*

4. How do pathological hallucinations differ from those of the sane?

5. What is the evidence that there is greater likelihood of being seen as an hallucination near the time of one's death than at any other time?

6. Give the principal characteristics of an apparition.

7. Give the theories to explain apparitions.

8. How do reported contemporaneous and precognitive psychic experiences compare in frequency?

9. Do more reported contemporaneous paranormal experiences occur when awake than when dreaming?

10. Are reported precognitive experiences more frequent in waking or in dreaming?

11. To what extent does an agent participate in spontaneous psychic experiences?

12. What are the frequencies of conviction and of attempted intervention in reported spontaneous ESP cases?

Chapter 10

PSI IN LOWER ORGANISMS

IN ADDITION TO humans and inanimate objects utilized for psi manifestation, subhuman organisms may function in this capacity. In testing psi with animals, sensory cues must be precluded, just as they must be in tests with humans. The horse Clever Hans is an example of an animal picking up sensory cues to produce a seemingly paranormal manifestation. He tapped out with his hoof the correct number in answer to questions by responding to small unconscious movements made by the questioner (Pfungst, 1911). Evidence of psi in lower organisms may alternatively be the result of (1) PK by the human experimenter on the lower organism, (2) active-agent telepathy by the experimenter, (3) active-percipient ESP by the lower organism, or (4) PK by the lower organism on the test apparatus. At the present time, it is not known whether psi effects can be initiated by a lower organism, as they may be the result of PK by the experimenter instead.

Bird Navigation

The problem of navigation and homing in birds has not been adequately solved, and it may be that ESP is a factor in this activity. Since the survival of migratory bird species depends upon the reliability of their navigation and since ESP is characteristically unreliable, it seems that the use of ESP in navigation and homing would be no more than as an occasional aid. Even if ESP were used on a regular basis in bird navigation and homing, it would be difficult to establish that such was the case. It would require preclusion of the use of an internal clock, of magnetic stimuli, of the stars, and of the sun, all of which have been indicated to be made use of by birds in their navigation.

Psi Trailing

Psi trailing consists of an animal following a departed person or mate into wholly unfamiliar territory under conditions that would allow the use of no sensory trail. An example from an analysis of fifty-four apparent cases of psi trailing is that of the three-year-old Persian cat, Smoky, whose color is indicated by his name (Rhine & Feather, 1962). Smoky jumped out of his owner's car near Tulsa, Oklahoma from which city the family was en route to Memphis, Tennessee to establish a new home, a distance of around 350 miles. A year later a cat came onto the front porch of the Memphis home and jumped into the daughter's lap. It was identified by such habits as (1) jumping upon the right side of the daughter when she played the piano and placing its front paws on the keys, (2) riding in the back window of the automobile, and (3) waiting for the daughter's return by perching in the front window near the door of the house. Physical identification was made by its sex, size, hair, color, and a tuft of dark red hair under the chin.

Carrying Out Experimenter's Thought

The Russian neurophysiologist V. M. Bechterev (1949) gave silent commands to the fox terrier Piki, and the dog obeyed although the experimenter's head was shielded from the animal's view. One command was to go to the side of the room, jump upon a chair, and paw a portrait on the wall.

Identifying the Target

In a study of the horse Lady, who could spell out the answers to questions by using her nose to point out letters and numbers, the Rhines (1929), by carefully guarding against the possibility of giving sensory cues, tentatively concluded that the horse had demonstrated psychic abilities. An experiment was carried out with the dog Chris, who was taught to paw a certain number of times from one to five, representing the ESP card symbols (Wood & Cadoret, 1959). In clairvoyant testing with the cards enclosed in envelopes, significant positive scores were obtained with only the dog's owner present, and significant negative scores were obtained when a parapsychologist served as an observer. Apparently psi was expressed with this animal under both conditions.

Finding Hidden Object

An experiment was carried out with two German shepherds and their trainer in which the dog-trainer team tried to locate empty land-mine cases buried 4 inches deep in sand under 6 to 12 inches of water. Extrachance results were obtained with both dogs (J.B. Rhine, 1971a).

Choice Behavior

In an experiment with the one-called protozoan, paramecium, the organism was centered under the cross hairs of a microscope, and it moved with significant frequency into the randomly selected quadrant of the field (Richmond, 1952). Significant results were obtained with woodlice crawling out of a Petri dish into the randomly selected one of the five sectors of a circular board (Randall, 1971). Significant psi-missing occurred in an experiment testing the crawling of moth larvae onto randomly selected sectors of a Petri dish (Metta, 1972). Water fleas observed under a microscope turned in the randomly selected direction, i.e. either right or left, with significantly greater frequency than they turned in the opposite direction (Passidomo, 1977). Cats were found to correctly choose the randomly selected route to food in a two-choice maze, even though fans were blowing above the apparatus to eliminate olfactory cues (Osis & Foster, 1943). A statistically significant number of mice avoided death by making the correct precognitive selection in a two-choice maze where the correct choice was rewarded by access to a female and the incorrect choice was punished by death (Bestall, 1962). Parenthetically, in another experiment, rats were found to be significantly more active if they were killed shortly after the start of the experiment than if they were killed after an interval of at least three weeks (Craig, 1973).

Mice were found to precognitively avoid electric shock by moving away from the half of the cage that was randomly selected (Duval & Montredon, 1968). The results were statistically signicant in trials following those in which the mouse jumped to the other side of the cage even though it had not been shocked, i.e. in trials following those in which it jumped not just because it had been shocked. Extrachance results were obtained in a similar experiment with gerbils (Artley, 1974).

To a significant extent, small rodents were found to press the randomly selected one of two bars that would reward them. This was true with a water reward to mice (Schouten, 1972) and rats (Terry & Harris, 1975) and with a food reward to gerbils (Parker, 1974).

Influencing a Binary Random-Event Generator

Experiments have been performed testing PK on a binary random-event generator governed by radioactive decay. An animal is placed in a situation where one of its needs is met by an apparatus activated by the generator. Activation of the apparatus with a frequency significantly deviating from the chance expectancy value of 50 percent is indicative of PK on the radioactive decay. Significant results were obtained in an experiment with a cat in a cold room in which a heat lamp attached to the generator was psychokinetically turned on more frequently than off, thus providing the cat with pleasurable warmth (Schmidt, 1970b). In the same report, an electric grid attached to the generator was turned on more frequently than off, increasing the shocking of cockroaches that occupied its upper surface. In an experiment with aggressive tropical fish, a mirror in the aquarium was made reflective by a binary random-event generator more frequently than not, thus providing the fish with its own image to serve as a target for its aggression (Braud, 1977). In these experiments, it is not known whether the generator was affected by the animal or by the experimenter.

Growth

Increase in the growth of yeast (Haraldsson, 1973) accompanied mental effort by subjects to accelerate its reproduction. Similarly, the growth of fungus (Barry, 1968) and of tumors in mice (Elguin & Onetto, 1968) was significantly less than in the control groups when subjects attempted to mentally retard it. Experimental groups of barley plants watered by a saline solution previously held by the Hungarian psychic healer Oskar Estebany grew significantly more than control groups watered by a similar saline solution not held by the healer (Grad, 1964). In a similar experiment, the growth was significantly less in plants watered by a saline solution previously held by either of two mental patients than in plants watered by a similar solution previously held by a psychiatrically normal individual (Grad, 1967). The amount of food eaten by mice and their gain in weight were found to be related to the starvation of other mice located several floors above (Spiransky, 1975). These measurements were significantly higher than were those in a control experiment in which the mice on the upper floor were not deprived of food.

Resistance to or Recovery from Harmful Effects

An experiment was performed testing (1) the effect of psi on decreasing the rate at which goiters developed in mice on a diet which was deficient in iodine and contained thiouracil, and (2) the effect of psi on increasing the rate at which the thyroid glands returned to normal size after the mice were placed on a normal diet (Grad, 1976). Mice in cages held for two fifteen-minute periods each day by Estebany developed goiters at a significantly slower rate and recovered from them at a significantly faster rate than mice in the control group, which were given the same amount of warmth as that produced by the healer's hands. A similar experiment was performed testing the effect of psi on the rate at which wounds of mice healed, the wounds being inflicted by snipping out a small piece of skin from the back (Grad, Cadoret & Paul, 1961). Mice in cages held by Estebany had a significantly faster rate of healing than mice in the control group, which were in cages held by a different individual each day.

An experiment with pairs of mice gave evidence of a paranormal effect of a human subject in decreasing the designated mouse's recovery time from anesthesia. The mouse that the subject in an adjoining room concentrated upon to recover from anesthesia did so in significantly less time than the control mouse on

the other side of the table from it (Watkins & Watkins, 1971).
When one side of the table was used consecutively as the target
for several mice, there was a tendency in several subsequent trials
for the mice placed on that side to awaken first (Wells & Watkins,
1975). This *linger effect* occurred even with new experimenters
who were not informed as to which the target side had been.

Increased Electrical Activity of Plants

With the use of a galvanometer, the electrical activity of plants
was observed by Cleve Backster (1968) to increase significantly at
moments when the experimenter thought of injuring the plant
or when a brine shrimp was killed. Marcel Vogel (1974) obtained
similar results when he made mental threats to a plant. Both he
and Bob Brier (1969) observed increased electrical activity of
plants at moments the agent concentrated on influencing the
plant by PK. Attempts by some other experimenters to repeat
these results were unsuccessful (Horowitz, Lewis & Gasteiger,
1975). In the absence of independent evidence of the existence of
ESP in plants, it seems likely that the effect, if paranormal, was
caused by PK on the part of the experimenter.

Spontaneous Phenomena

Animals have been reported to respond in advance to impend-
ing danger to themselves or to their distant owner, to react to the
death of their absent master by howling, and to anticipate an event
such as the unexpected return home of their owner (Rhine &
Feather, 1962). Animals have acted as though they saw an apparition at the same time that a human with the animal saw the
apparition, and in many cases they acted as though they saw the
apparition first (Fodor, 1933, p. 3). That the observed response
of the animal in these cases may have been psi mediated is suggested by an out-of-body (OBE) experiment. At the time the
human subject was undergoing an OBE in which he attempted to
project to a specific location, the activity of a kitten in the target
room was significantly less than in control periods (Morris, 1974).

CONCLUSIONS

Although psi is manifested in organisms extending down to the lower end of the scale of life, it is not presently known whether psi effects can be initiated by lower organisms. However, in the light of empirical evidence of the high intelligence of great apes and cetaceans, it appears likely that psi is a faculty possessed not only by man but by at least some subhuman animals as well.

REVIEW QUESTIONS

1. Give an example of psi trailing.

2. Give examples of experiments in which animals moved in the randomly selected direction.

3. Describe small-rodent precognition tests.

4. Give examples of experiments in which animals appeared to raise the temperature by influencing a binary random-event generator.

5. Give examples of experiments in which psi affected growth and the healing of wounds.

6. What is the linger effect?

7. What reports have been made of increased electrical activity of plants due to psi?

8. Give examples of spontaneous psi in animals.

Chapter 11

QUESTIONABLE ESP PHENOMENA

IN THIS AND THE FOLLOWING CHAPTER, phenomena are presented whose reality is more questionable than some of those previously described. Many parapsychologists consider that such items should await further proof before they are given serious attention. Some of the phenomena are included not as established paranormal events but to provide a survey of those phenomena which some psychical researchers believe may have a paranormal basis. Many of the occurrences are not intrinsically paranormal, but are psychic only to the extent that they are incidentally associated with ESP or PK.

Diagnosis of Illness

Some of the early mesmerists reported that their hypnotized patients correctly diagnosed their own and others' illnesses. The American psychic Edgar Cayce, while in trance and often at a great distance, diagnosed the illnesses of thousands of persons he had never met (Sugrue, 1943). However, it has not been possible to evaluate the accuracy of his readings. Graduates of Silva Mind Control, an organization that professes to train individuals in the paranormal diagnosis of illness, were not found to be able to demonstrate this ability (Brier, Schmeidler, & Savitz, 1975).

Aura, Corona-Discharge Photography, and Acupuncture

Many psychics see what appears to them to be an aura around the human body, which varies with the individual concerned and with his mental or physical state. Psychics do not, however, agree as to the colors of the aura of any particular person (Owen, 1972a). The aura may extend from $\frac{1}{4}$ inch to 3 feet beyond the confines of the body and may be seen between the tips of the fingers of the opposing hands. A physical aura consisting of fields, radiations, and chemicals occurs around the body, which is affected by emotional and physiological states of the individual. However, the possibility that the aura seen by psychics is not a physical reality is suggested by an experiment in which the space between the subject's finger tips was visible to the psychic but the subject's fingers and hands were concealed (Ellison, 1962). The psychic was unable to tell whether the fingers were in positions on either side of a slit in a box that concealed the hands or whether the hands had been removed from the container. Other tests could be made by covering the subject with an opaque screen beyond which his aura would protrude and having the psychic tell whether the individual is near the edge of the screen or at a distance from it greater than the width of the aura (Tart, 1972b). Instead of being objective, an aura may be a way in which the unconscious mind presents paranormal information concerning another individual to the psychic's consciousness.

A photograph of an animate or inanimate object surrounded by a glowing, colored aura is produced when one electrode of a high voltage, high frequency, alternating current is applied to the object lying in juxtaposition with a photographic film that is separated by a dielectric layer from a second electrode in the same circuit. This corona-discharge photography is also known as *Kirlian* photography, after a Russian investigator of the phenomenon. The corona, consisting of ultraviolet radiation and ionized air molecules, is affected by the degree of skin hydration or sweating of the subject (Pehek, Kyler & Faust, 1976). Hence, in the case of a part of a living being such as a finger, the corona may vary with the physical and mental state of its owner. Some observers have postulated that the aura produced in this radiation-field photography is the aura seen by psychics; however, there is no evidence to associate the two. The phantom-leaf effect, which is the appearance of a corona in the cut-away portion of a leaf, has been attributed to artifacts caused by inappropriate techniques (Millar, 1974).

Because of the possibility that points on the body which produce the greatest corona discharge are the same as *acupuncture* points, it has been suggested that a relationship exists between the two (Ostrander & Schroeder, 1970). Acupuncture consists of the stimulation of a superficial point on the body, as by sticking it with a needle, which is followed by anesthesia in some other part of the body sometimes greatly removed. Specific acupuncture sites are associated with particular parts of the body that are anesthetized by the acupuncture. The physiological basis of acupuncture is uncertain. However, it may be that impulses over sensory neurons in one part of the body inhibit, in the central nervous system, the passage of impulses from sensory neurons in other parts of the body, thereby causing anesthesia of the latter (Melzack & Wall, 1965).

Telepathic Reading

Instances have been reported of children paranormally reciting passages silently read by a distant observer. A feeble-minded, nine-year-old, Latvian girl named Ilga, who was unable to read under usual conditions because of word blindness, was able to recite what was written in a book gazed at by her mother in another room. Although her mother sought to help Ilga's performance by audible aids, some of the tests succeeded without whispering on the mother's part (Bender, 1938).

Skin Vision

The French philosopher Emile Boirac (1908) reported the ability of blindfolded, hypnotized subjects to read with their finger tips. The French novelist Jules Romains (1924) reported the same phenomenon with waking individuals. Experiments performed on the blindfolded Russian subject Roza Kuleshova showed that she could distinguish colors and letters even when they were covered with glass or aluminum foil, but not in the dark (Novomeiskii, 1965). It is possible that ESP may be used in some cases; however, it should be borne in mind that blindfolding may not be sufficient to prevent the person from seeing the test object. Even when dough is applied over the eyes under the blindfold, the subject may manipulate his facial muscles to produce a chink beside the nose for "nose peeking." To prevent this, the individual can be tested (1) in the dark, (2) with the test article touched by his finger behind his back, or (3) with a head box which has a board extending beneath his chin (Nash, 1971).

Exteriorization of Sensibility

The French psychical researcher Paul Joire (1908) was the first to call attention to the phenomenon of exteriorization of sensibility. He found that the hypnotized subject was sensitive to a pointed instrument several inches from his skin. The sensitivity appeared to be exteriorized into objects such as a glass of water because when the object was pricked the subject felt a pain. If the effect was paranormal, it may have resulted from the subject's extrasensory perception that the object was penetrated by a pointed instrument.

External Divination

The practice of obtaining knowledge paranormally with the use of external objects is called external divination, in contrast to internal divination which is accomplished in trance or in dreaming. The external device may be employed to induce a revelatory hallucination as in *scrying,* in which the psychic gazes into a translucent object such as a crystal ball or a glass of water. During crystal-ball gazing, the globe appears to the gazer to become cloudy, and when the mist vanishes, a visual hallucination is seen in the ball to vanish immediately or to remain for awhile. In a premonitory crystal-ball vision reported by Sir William Barrett (1923), the psychic saw the husband of a female sitter commit suicide, and three days later when the man took his life the vision became an accomplished fact. In the form of divination called shell hearing the psychic has an auditory hallucination of hearing a voice while listening to a shell applied to his ear. In one case the percipient heard the voice of a distant friend speaking to another person and ascertained afterwards that the precise words had been said at that time (Myers, 1892, p. 492).

A form of divination called *augury* is accomplished by inferences based on the outcome of chance events. These include tea-leaf reading, card laying, casting of dice or bones, inspecting entrails, and observing the behavior of birds. In one type of augury the question is answered by means of the ancient Confucian book of divination, the *I Ching,* based on the random assortment of stalks of the yarrow plant to determine the entry point into the book. ESP may be utilized in augury to interpret the outcome of chance results in which there is considerable leeway for judgment. If the psychic paranormally knows the answer to the question, he may be influenced by this knowledge in his interpretation of the chance results. ESP may be similarly used in *palmistry* and astrology.

Divining objects may be of assistance in ESP in four ways. First, the divining object, such as the lines of the palm or the position of cast bones, may resemble the paranormally acquired information and, by reinforcing this knowledge, bring it to consciousness. Second, the use of a divining object may break the chain of associative thought and permit information acquired by ESP to enter the conscious mind. Third, it may shift much of the responsibility from the diviner to the external object, thereby producing in the practitioner a more relaxed state favorable to the use of his psi ability. Fourth, it is possible that PK is used to affect the divining object, as by influencing the position of tea leaves, thereby causing it to coincide with the psychic's paranormally acquired knowledge. That psi can work in the latter way is suggested by experiments in which dice were successfully rolled to match concealed targets knowable only by ESP (Thouless, 1951).

Dowsing

ESP may be manifested by motor automatisms, i.e. involuntary motor responses, such as moving a *dowsing* rod or a pendulum. Dowsing has been in use since ancient times to locate under ground water—as in water divining—or other underground objects such as metals. In the United States, it has been estimated that there may be as many as 40,000 water diviners (Vogt & Hyman, 1959). The diviner holds an apparatus in his hands as he walks over the area suspected to contain the water and, at a certain spot, the apparatus responds by moving. Digging is undertaken at the designated place, and often the water or other sought-for substance is located. The divining apparatus may consist of a forked stick with each arm held by one of the diviner's hands, a metal loop, a pendulum, or an angle iron with its short arm enclosed in a loose sleeve held in the hand. Sir William Barrett expressed the belief that success in divining may be due to unconscious contraction of muscles, causing the divining rod to turn downwards at the spot where the diviner locates the water through ESP (Barrett & Besterman, 1926). Richet (1922) believed that in some instances the rod may be turned by PK. The Dutch geophysicist Solco Tromp (1968) expressed the belief that the rod or the pendulum is moved by muscle reflex in response to a physical force, such as a magnetic field, produced by the underground material. Most dowsers, however, believe that the underground material exerts a direct physical influence on the divining apparatus, rather than working through their muscles. In opposition to this belief, the Jesuit Athanasius Kircher (1641) found that no movement of a rod occurred when it was balanced horizontally on a vertical support and water was placed beneath one end.

In a field test of water divining, dowsers were inferior to a geologist and a water engineer in estimating the depth of the water at spots which had been located by the dowsers (Dale et al., 1951). However, statistically significant results were obtained in testing the ability of the Maine diviner Henry Gross to determine whether the flow of water through an underground pipe was on or off (J.B. Rhine, 1950). In some cases divining is accomplished by holding a pendulum over a map of the area, which may be many miles distant, and observing at what spot or spots the pendulum responds. The Canadian physician Remi Cadoret (1955) performed an experiment with significant results in locating a penny buried in his yard by dowsing a map of the area with a pendulum. Success at dowsing from a map favors the ESP hypothesis, as there is no apparent explanation of how a physical influence could extend from the sought-for object to the pendulum by way of the map. The movement of a pendulum has also been used to give possibly paranormal answers to a variety of questions by means of a code correlated with various directions of oscillation.

The postulated physical effect on a divining apparatus by a substance not in contact with it, such as underground water or minerals, has been called *radiesthesia*. It has been used as an explanation of medical diagnosis that is made by determining the point over a patient's body at which a pendulum oscillates. Diagnostic instruments, which are superficially complex but are composed of simple parts such as a magnet and a camera, have been constructed to respond through radiesthesia to the patient's illness, sometimes from a sample of his blood (Parsons, 1961) in a process called *radionics*. Conversely, the apparatus may be used to treat the patient, who may be many miles distant. It is possible that whatever dubious success has been achieved with the use of such equipment is attributable to the action of psi.

Psychometry

Psychometry is the faculty of obtaining paranormal knowledge of persons or events connected with a physical article by holding the object, which may be concealed in a container. The article, such as a fountain pen, the clothing of a murdered victim, or an archeological artifact, is held by the psychometrist, who makes a series of statements about the owner of the object or about events associated with its history. The word "psychometry" was coined by the American physician Rhodes Buchanan (1849), who claimed that all bodies produce an emanation that gives clues to certain persons as to the nature of those bodies. The American geologist William Denton (1863) expanded Buchanan's theory by proposing that emotions and ideas impregnate objects in their vicinity, and that these emotions or ideas can be perceived by psychometry of the impregnated objects. The German physician Gustav Pagentecher (1922), who practiced in Mexico, reported the ability of one of his female patients to produce information concerning the background and history of a token object such as a stone when this was handed to her while she was in an hypnotic trance. The British electrical engineer John Hettinger (1940) worked with two psychics using articles in sealed envelopes. Statements made by the *sensitive* concerning the article were mixed up with an equal number of spurious statements. The owner of the object then determined which of the statements correctly applied to it. Of 6,631 statements made by the psychics, 39 percent were claimed by the owners to be correct, while only 29 percent of a group of control statements were considered to be accurate. The differential of over one-third in favor of the statements made by the sensitives is extremely significant statistically, although the methodology has been subject to criticism (Scott, 1949).

Psychometry of articles belonging to lost persons or victims of murder has been used in attempts to solve the mystery concerning their death or disappearance. In some cases the psychic worked with the police; however, it is difficult to assess to what extent these efforts have met with success. Perhaps, the best known psychometrists in this activity are the two Dutch sensitives, Croiset (Pollack, 1964) and Hurkos (Browning, 1970). It has not been determined whether the object is a source of paranormal information in psychometry or whether it is a psychological crutch helping the psychic to acquire the paranormal information directly from the event.

Ouija Board and Planchette

An Ouija board consists of a small platform on legs that is movable over a larger board bearing letters and other inscriptions. The fingers of one person's hand or of the hands of two individuals are lightly placed on the smaller board, which through their unconscious motor action moves over the larger board pointing to letters and spelling out answers to questions. The *planchette*, which is a step between the Ouija board and automatic writing, consists of a tripod on casters with one of its legs being a pencil that writes on an underlying sheet of paper. It is used like the Ouija board, from which it differs in that it writes the message instead of moving to the appropriate letters.

Sometimes messages received by an Ouija board or a planchette purport to come from departed spirits. A message written by a planchette used by a female participant and Hensleigh Wedgwood, brother-in-law of Charles Darwin, purportedly came from a deceased female by the name of A. Grimbold (Myers, 1893, p. 99). According to the message, she had been burned at the stake in March, 1605 for being an accomplice to the murder of her mistress, Mrs. Clarke in Leicester. The murder was carried out by two men—Bradshaw and Harrison. The latter was A. Grimbold's lover and had promised to marry her if she helped. Bradshaw was hanged; however, Harrison was released with the aid of powerful friends. Through advertising in newspapers, Wedgwood was able to locate a little-known book on the history of Leicester which corroborated the existence of Alice Grimbold and the events in the message written with the planchette.

Sometimes the Ouija board or planchette is replaced by automatic speech, as was the case with Pearl Curran (Litvag, 1972), whose works, like those of some other automatists, are of literary value. They purported to be communicated to this Twentieth century American woman by Patience Worth, who lived in England in the Seventeenth century and was killed in America by Indians. The obsolete and dialectal words not normally known by Mrs. Curran suggest that the writings were of paranormal origin.

Automatic Writing

Some individuals, if they sit with a pen or pencil in their hand and a piece of paper before them, find that they carry out automatic writing even when they are mentally engaged otherwise or are in trance. Although the automatic writings of different individuals are usually unrelated, this was not the case with a large group of messages known as the cross-correspondences. It consists of interlocking scripts produced over a period of about thirty years through automatic writing and automatic speech by several independent psychics in different parts of the world, including the American psychic Leonore Piper (Gauld, 1968). The scripts consist of phrases or sentences, many of classical allusions, each by itself without significance but which, when put together, give a clear message. They began shortly after the death of Frederic Myers and professed to originate with him and other deceased leaders of the Society for Psychical Research as a means of demonstrating their survival after death. While it is difficult to assess the part chance played in these correspondences, some of their characteristics are indicative of paranormality and, to some interpreters, are evidence of spirit communication.

Xenoglossy

Speaking a real language entirely unknown by the person in his ordinary state is called *xenoglossy*. The act of writing in an unknown foreign language is called xenography. In some cases of xenoglossy, the subject expresses phrases or longer passages of a foreign language, while in others he converses in it. The xeno-glossy may occur spontaneously, may be brought on by hypnotic regression, or may occur in a séance. Some cases of xenoglossy are suggestive of reincarnation or of spirit control. Richet (1905) re-ported the case of a French psychic who, in a state of partial dissociation, wrote long sentences in Greek, a language with which she was said to be entirely unacquainted under ordinary circum-stances. Ian Stevenson (1974), Professor of Psychiatry at the University of Virginia, reported his study of a woman who, when hypnotized by her physician husband, spoke as a man in an early Scandinavian language with which the woman had no known previous contact. However, in most of the studied cases of appar-ent xenoglossy the individual had contact with the foreign language in childhood and had forgotten about it.

Out-of-body Experiences

The events in a recent dream were sufficiently wild to cause me for a moment to wonder whether or not I was dreaming. I immediately dismissed the idea because it seemed to me that my perceptions were too realistic to experience unless I were awake. Although actually I was dreaming, I mistakenly "knew" that I was awake. More frequently, if an individual questions the reality of a dream, he realizes that he is dreaming. Such dreams are called *lucid dreams.* They may be a step towards the out-of-body experi-ence or OBE in which the individual in a dreaming or waking condition not only feels that he has left his physical body but may see it as if from a distance. Older terms for OBE are travel-ing clairvoyance and *astral projection.* The typical OBE usually contains some combination of the following elements: (1) float-ing, (2) seeing one's physical body from the outside, (3) thinking of a distant place while "outside" and suddenly finding oneself there, (4) experiencing oneself as a nonphysical body, and (5) being absolutely convinced that the experience is not a dream. The OBE was reported by 8 percent of 900 individuals polled in Iceland (Haraldsson, 1977). As well as taking place under more ordinary circumstances, OBEs have also occurred after a traumatic experience, or under anesthesia, and during periods of apparent clinical death (Moody, 1975).

The following is a spontaneous OBE reported from the author's files:

> After a warm bath as I sat thinking at the round kitchen table, I felt that I had stepped outside of this body and stood close by it. It was a very real, very vivid and haunting experience. It was a very pleasant sensation to stand there and watch. One of my roommates entered the room and sat directly across from me. She gazed at the staring eyes and slight smile of my face and began to holler, "Kathy, what's wrong? Kathy talk to me!" Looking down at my physical shell I knew I could not answer her nor did I really want to at first. Then for one short second I felt that I could not re-enter my body and I wanted to but could not respond. Within an instant I seemed to "rejoin." I felt different—heavy but relaxed. I did respond to my frightened roommate and in a few moments told her of what had happened. I was relieved of my momentary fear but left with a pleasant feeling and wonderment of exactly what had occurred.

Charles Tart (1967, 1968), Professor of Psychology at the University of California in Davis, reported tests of OBEs with two individuals in which they felt that they had left their physical bodies. One individual correctly reported what was occurring in an adjoining hallway, while the other was able to read a five-digit random target number on a ledge above her. In some instances the fully separated individual watches his physical body continuing its intelligent activity without his guidance or control. In one case a lay preacher, from the end of the church, saw and heard himself delivering a sermon (Green, 1968).

In other cases an apparition of the person having an OBE is seen by an individual at the spot where the out-of-body experiencer seems to himself to be. This has been called bilocation. An example is that of Mrs. Wilmot who, asleep in her home in Connecticut, found herself leaving her body and traveling across the sea in a storm to a steamer on which her husband was a passenger (Mrs. Sidgwick, 1891, p. 41). She entered her husband's stateroom and was much surprised to see another man in the upper berth looking at her. She kissed her husband and hurried away. The same night Mr. Wilmot dreamed that his wife came to his stateroom clad in her nightdress and, after hesitating, entered and kissed him. In the morning the other occupant, an Englishman who had passed a sleepless night owing to the storm, exclaimed, "You're a pretty fellow to have a lady come and visit you!", and related what had occurred exactly as Mr. Wilmot had dreamed it.

Tyrrell (1953) cited several nineteenth century experiments in which an individual succeeded in making his apparition visible to another person. In a recent experiment, a kitten in the room to which an out-of-body experiencer attempted to project himself, decreased its activity to a statistically significant extent during OBE periods in comparison with control periods (Morris, 1974). The most parsimonious paranormal hypothesis for OBEs is that they are the result of ESP by the out-of-body experiencer and by the individuals who perceive his presence at a distance from his body. On the *principle of parsimony*, only if this explanation should prove inadequate, would the hypothesis of projection of an astral body or etheric counterpart be justifiable.

Possession

Recurrent phenomena in an individual, which purport to come from a spirit occupying that person, constitute what is termed possession. Manifestations of possession may include poltergeist phenomena as well as ESP. The ostensible spirit invading the individual may give evidence of being evil by profane utterances and the production of violent physical phenomena. In such cases a religious ritual may be used to exorcise the invading entity. Cases of apparent insanity in which the person gave manifestations of being possessed have been treated with the aid of a medium by persuading the supposed spirit that he had died and that the body he was inhabiting was not his own (Uphoff & Uphoff, 1975, p. 96).

According to the Trappist monk Alois Wiesinger (1957), cases of genuine possession are extremely rare. He considers the case of Maria Talarico to be a borderline one. In 1936, the body of Pepe Veraldi was found underneath a bridge, and it was thought he had thrown himself into the river with the intention of taking his life. Three years later, as the seventeen-year-old Maria passed the bridge in the company of her grandmother, she collapsed and appeared to lose consciousness. When she had been taken home she said to her mother in a man's rough voice, "You are not my mother. My mother lives in the wooden hut, and her name is Catarini Veraldi. I am Pepe." Pepe's mother was summoned, and when she arrived, the girl said to her in Pepe's voice, "My friends murdered me; they threw me into the river bed, then as I lay there they beat me with a piece of iron and tried to make the whole thing look like suicide." Suddenly, after the dead man's mother asked him to leave, the girl returned to her normal state. Twelve years later a letter came from one of Pepe's friends in Argentina making Pepe's mother his sole heir and stating that he was the murderer of her son, had beaten him over the head with a piece of iron found in the river, and the injuries had proved fatal. Three of Pepe's other friends had been accessories.

Another possession case is that of Lurancy Vennum, a fourteen-year-old girl living in Watseka, Illinois (Myers, 1903). She claimed to be Mary Roff, who had died when Lurancy was about fifteen months old. Lurancy did not recognize her own parents and behaved like Mary Roff. At Mary's home, she recognized every former object, including the friends she had known, and for 14 weeks lived in that home continuing life where Mary had left off when she died thirteen years before. The visit was terminated when Lurancy returned to her old self. Many possession cases such as those of Maria and Lurancy give evidence of paranormality. Whether any of them are attributable to discarnate spirits awaits further evidence.

Mediumship

A medium is a person through whom an ostensibly deceased individual communicates. The communication occurs in some mediums in a waking state and in others in a self-induced trance or auto-hypnosis. The communication may be accomplished by speaking, automatic writing, use of the Ouija board, or table rapping. Some mediums have one or more *controls* or spirit guides who may relay messages from other deceased individuals or who may regulate the direct communication of these entities through the medium. The sitting of one or more persons with a medium for the purpose of spirit communication is called a séance. If the paranormal phenomena which are produced by the medium include PK, the sensitive is called a physical medium. The physical phenomena of mediumship, including table rapping, are described in the next chapter.

The personalities of the ostensible spirits expressed by some mediums may closely resemble their former living characteristics. The "spirit" of George Pelham, manifesting through the medium Leonore Piper, picked out 30 of his former friends from 150 persons who had sittings and made not one mistake (Hodgson, 1897). He spoke to them of their common memories and reacted towards them as the living George Pelham would have done. That the personality communicating through the medium is not necessarily that of a deceased individual, however, is indicated by communications from fictitious persons and from individuals later discovered to be still alive (Flournoy, 1900). Soal (1926) had conversations with a communicator in several séances only to find out three years later that the individual who was presumed to be deceased was still living.

Drop-in communicators are ostensible spirits who are unknown to the medium or to the sitters but who are identified after the séance as having lived and whose statements are verified (Stevenson, 1970b). Their appearance is more difficult to explain by a combination ESP and dramatization than is the appearance of a person already known to a sitter or to the medium.

In order to determine whether the personalities of the medium, the control, and the spirit communicators are measurably different, Whately Carington (1935) applied Jung's word-association tests to each of them. A list of words is read to the subject, he replies with the first word he thinks of, and his response time is measured. A reaction pattern characteristic and distinctive of the individual is formed. The response times of the medium and her control to given words were found to be negatively correlated. The countersimilarity was judged to indicate that the psychic revealed a different side of her own personality in the control than that which was present in her normal state, and that the control was a secondary personality of the medium probably formed around a nucleus of repressed material. Unlike the control, the spirit communicators did not display any such relationship with the psychic. However, the fact that a given spirit communicator did not show a similarity of response with different mediums lessens credibility for their autonomy.

Secondary and multiple personalities are known to develop in some individuals with hysteria. Sybil had 16 alternating personalities each appearing one at a time and some being unacquainted with others (Schreiber, 1973). The appearance of spirit personalities in mediumship bears some resemblance to the occurrence of multiple personalities in hysteria. Some of the spirit personalities are subconscious dramatizations of the medium based on information normally or paranormally obtained. Whether any of them are due to spirits of the deceased is a question awaiting further evidence.

Haunting

The phenomenon of haunting is characterized by recurrent, ostensibly paranormal events witnessed by different individuals at a particular locality, usually a house. Typically, hauntings are hallucinatory, i.e. only certain individuals hear or see anything, while others who are present experience nothing. However, hauntings sometimes include physical disturbances through which they form a continuum with poltergeist phenomena. In distinction to poltergeists, hauntings are not associated with a particular living individual but rather with a particular location. Also, they may go on for years, whereas poltergeists average only five months in duration and may last for only a few hours (Roll, 1977).

An example of a haunting is that reported by the British medical student R.C. Morton (1892). One evening, having gone up to her room, she heard someone at the door, opened it, and saw in the passage the figure of a tall lady dressed in black whose face was hidden by a handkerchief held in her right hand. The figure descended the stairs and Miss Morton followed; but the piece of candle she carried went out, and she returned to her room. After the first appearance she made it a practice to follow the figure downstairs into the drawing room. She spoke to the apparition but never obtained a reply; she cornered it several times in order to touch it, but it then simply disappeared. Its footsteps were audible and characteristic, and they were heard by her three sisters and by the cook. Miss Morton stretched some threads across the stairs, but the figure passed right through them without detaching them. The apparition was seen in the orchard by a neighbor as well as in the house by Miss Morton's sisters and brother, by the cook, by the charwoman, by a parlor maid, and by the gardener. Sometimes it was collectively seen, but her father could not see it, even when he was shown where it stood. The figure was seen during the day as well as at night. In all, about 20 people saw it, some of them many times, and some of them without having previously heard of the apparition or of the sounds. The figure was described in the same way by all; it wore widow's cuffs and corresponded to the description of a deceased former tenant of the house whose life had been unhappy. A dog in the house reacted twice as though he saw the apparition, running up to the mat at the foot of the stairs in the hall, wagging his tail, and moving his back in the way dogs do when expecting to be caressed. It jumped up, fawning as it would do if a person were standing there, but suddenly slunk away with its tail between its legs and retreated, trembling, under a sofa. The apparition continued to appear for seven years.

A well-publicized case of haunting is that of the rectory in the hamlet of Borley in England in which about 100 people participated (Dingwall, Goldney & Hall, 1956). The haunt was said to have been originated by a tragic event; a monk from the thirteenth century monastery on the site of which the rectory was built had fled in a carriage with a young nun, but they were caught. The monk was beheaded and the nun walled up alive in the convent. The apparition of a nun was seen by no less than 17 people singly or collectively between 1885 and 1943. The English psychic investigator Harry Price witnessed many phenomena on his several visits to the rectory, including incessant bell-ringing and showers of pebbles and keys. During the year 1937, in which he leased the rectory, he organized constant surveillance of the house with the assistance of over 40 men. The nun was seen again; many footsteps and similar sounds were heard; raps, taps, and knockings were frequent; there were many paranormal movements of objects; appearances, disappearances, and reappearances of strange articles; a luminous phenomenon; pleasant and unpleasant odors; sensations of coldness; and tactual phenomena. The next year a message received by means of a planchette announced that the rectory would be destroyed by a fire, and so it was, one day in 1939. The ruins continued to be haunted until they were completely demolished in 1944. In the cellar some bones were found which were assumed to be those of the nun, and they were given a Christian burial.

In a quantitative study of a haunted house, Schmeidler (1966) had three members of a family mark the floor plans for locations they considered to be haunted and to score a personality checklist for traits characteristic of the ghost. She then had nine sensitives perform the same task on separate lists after they individually toured the house. There were significant correspondences between the spots and traits selected by the psychics and also between the selections of the psychics and those of the family. However, because the aspects of certain spots may have normally suggested that they were haunted, a spirit explanation is not necessary.

Apparitions seen in hauntings may be retrocognitive hallucinations, or they may be the product of psychometry of the site at which they are seen, but this does not explain why hauntings are manifested at only certain places and not at others.

Reincarnation

Two classes of phenomena in which individuals claim to have been reincarnated sometimes exhibit evidences of paranormality. One of these is prenatal regression under hypnosis, and the other is the memory of a former life described by children in a waking state. Under hypnosis an individual, when regressed by suggestion to a younger age, may recall events occurring at that age, which he does not remember in the waking state. His method of writing and speaking may revert to those characteristic of the age to which he is regressed. When given the suggestion to regress to a previous incarnation, some hypnotized individuals respond as a personality with ostensible memories of a previous life. A case of prenatal regression which received wide publicity is that of a Colorado woman who, when regressed under hypnosis, expressed the personality of an individual claiming to be Bridey Murphy, who was born in 1798 in the town of Cork in Ireland (Bernstein, 1956). She gave details of her life in Ireland, which corresponded to specific facts that neither she nor the hypnotist seemed at all likely ever to have known. An investigation disclosed no evidence that a person bearing that name had actually lived at the places specified. However, verifications of obscure points in Ireland caused the American philosopher C. J. Ducasse (1960) to conclude that paranormal knowledge had been manifested. Although such cases are not proof of reincarnation, they are suggestive of ESP and particularly of retrocognition.

Ian Stevenson (1966) made a study of possible reincarnation in several countries including the United States, in which children usually between the ages of two and four remember details of a supposed former life, which are corroborated by investigation. In Asian cases the average interval between the birth of an individual and his supposed previous death is from five to ten years, and usually the person lived no more than 100 miles from his previous home. In most cases the memories begin to fade at around the age of five or six and disappear by the age of ten. One case is that of Shanti Devi (Stevenson, 1960), who lived in New Delhi and from the age of four made references to a former life in Muttra, a city she had never visited. When she was 11, she stated that she had died 12 years previously after bearing her second child and that her former husband's name was Kedar Nath Chaubey. A group of people, including her teacher, a lawyer, and a publisher, became interested, and they ascertained that her alleged former husband was still living in Muttra. They arranged a series of tests in which the girl successfully described the house in which she claimed to have lived and a number of people she had known.

Most startling of all, however, were the descriptions she gave to her "husband" of their former life together, which included details that no one but a wife could have known. He was moved to tears and commented, "It were as if that wife, now twelve years dead, stood again beside me." She told him the exact location of a box containing money which she had hidden in his parents' house. When taken to the house she pointed to the hiding place and then dug up the box. It was found to be empty, whereupon the husband stated that he had discovered the box and removed the money after his wife's death.

In many of the cases he studied, Stevenson was unable to find any indication that the child could have had normal knowledge of the facts concerning the deceased individual. Although such cases are not proof of reincarnation, the alternative explanation of detailed ESP on the part of the child of another's life may require more of the psychic faculty than has so far been established to exist.

CONCLUSIONS

Most of the phenomena presented in this chapter have not yet been studied experimentally. However, they are frequently of considerable interest and, although often lacking in adequate evidence, cannot be ignored in a true depiction of the landscape viewed by the psychical researcher.

REVIEW QUESTIONS

1. If you fail to remember any of the following terms, ascertain its meaning with the aid of the glossary and the index: acupuncture, astral projection, augury, aura, control, dowsing, drop-in communicator, exteriorization of sensibility, Kirlian photography, lucid dream, Ouija board, planchette, principle of parsimony, radiesthesia, radionics, sensitive, xenoglossy.

2. Is the aura an objective phenomenon (give reasons for your answer)?

3. How can fraudulent skin-vision be prevented?

4. How may psi be a factor in external divination, and in palmistry and astrology?

5. What evidence indicates that dowsing may be due to ESP rather than to a physical force from the underground material?

6. What evidences of OBEs are afforded by experimentation?

7. What evidence do word-association tests provide about the relationship between medium and control?

8. What relationship may exist between mediumship and hysteria?

9. Distinguish between hauntings and poltergeists.

10. How have haunted houses been studied quantitatively?

11. Give evidences of reincarnation and reasons why the phenomena may be due to ESP instead.

Chapter 12

QUESTIONABLE PK PHENOMENA

IN THIS CHAPTER, as in the previous one, the paranormality of most of the described phenomena has not been firmly established. It is hoped that their presentation will encourage research to determine whether or not they have a psychic basis.

Withstanding Physical Extremes

The extremes of physical condition that some individuals are able to withstand suggest the use of PK. Fakirs and yogis have demonstrated the ability to alter their heart beat or arterial pulse, to stop bleeding, and to withstand air deprivation and bitter cold (Carrington, 1931). Food abstinence has been practiced over long periods of time by Christian mystics as well as by others (Thurston, 1952). Bare-footed firewalking for a distance of several meters over glowing embers or red-hot stones has been practiced in many parts of the world without burning or even blistering (Gaddis, 1967). One of the principle centers of this practice is Fiji, where it is conducted about twice weekly by native melanesian Fijians who walk on red-hot stones and Hindu Indians who walk on glowing embers, hold them in their hands, and apply them to their faces. The psychic D.D. Home was observed by Crookes and others to handle red-hot coals and to put his hands and head into a fire without injury (Medhurst, 1972). Such events as these may on occasion be accomplished by trickery. Studies of biofeedback demonstrate that the heart beat, vaso-constriction, perspiration, and metabolic rate, all of which may have some effect on heat resistance, can be affected by learned control of the autonomic nervous system. However, some of these feats appear to require a psychokinetic explanation.

Dermography

In *dermography* or skin writing, a name or a date appears in the form of slightly elevated red figures on the skin and lasts for a few minutes (Brown, 1970). Figures can be produced fraudulently by writing on the skin with a blunt instrument; however, apparently genuine skin writing has been reported (Osty, 1929). Where it cannot be accounted for by control of cutaneous blood vessels through the autonomic nervous ssytem, it may be due to PK.

Stigmata

Red marks or blisterlike wounds that ooze blood and lymph corresponding to wounds suffered by Christ in his crucifixion have appeared on parts of the body of Christians and are called *stigmata*. They may last for months, years, or even a lifetime. According to the Jesuit priest Father Herbert Thurston (1952), rarely has a case occurred where a nervous disorder did not appear before the development of the stigmata. Some stigmata have been fraudulently produced by deliberate injury, and some are attributable to action of the autonomic nervous system on the affected areas; however, they are of parapsychological interest because of the possibility that some of them have a psychokinetic origin.

Psychic Healing

The percentage of illness that is medically judged to be mentally caused rather than to be organic has continually increased. Generally speaking, because psychogenic illness can be alleviated or cured by suggestion, only cures of organic illness should be seriously considered with respect to paranormality. Investigations of the results of psychic healing have revealed a few apparent cures of organic illness. The English psychiatrist Donald West (1957) made an examination of the eleven miraculous cures recorded at the Shrine of Lourdes between 1935 and 1950. In his opinion, in no instance did the history of a case both before and after the cure contain the specific information that would justify the conclusion that an organic disease had been cured. The British medical doctor Louis Rose (1955) carried out a study of 90 persons who claimed to have received benefit from psychic healers. Demonstrable organic disability was relieved or cured in one instance where a physician had a small but definite hernia that was diagnosed by a surgeon and by two other doctors. The hernia completely disappeared after four or five treatments by a healer and did not recur. Two German physicians made evaluations of objective changes in 247 patients treated by the psychic healer Kurt Trampler (Strauch, 1963). Although improvement was greater in the primarily functional diseases, it also occurred in ten patients with predominantly organic disease. The disappearance of a microscopically diagnosed malignant abdominal tumor within six months after a psychic treatment session by the American psychic healer Olga Worrall was testified to by the patient's medical doctor (Worrall, 1965). The British psychoanalyst Joan FitzHerbert (1971) referred to two medically verified cures of organic illness of persons attending healing services conducted by Kathryn Kuhlman. One was an instantaneous disappearance of an inoperable goiter and the other the instantaneous development of a sizeable piece of new bone. Several other medically verified healings of organic illness by this psychic healer are described by the American physician Richard Casdorph (1976).

The number of patients seeking the help of healers may be sufficient to result in spontaneous remissions of illness in some of them by chance alone. Spontaneous remission is a cure or improvement in the absence of discernible external factors; however, it is, itself, a medical mystery and may be paranormal regardless of whether it is accomplished by a healer or by the patient himself. That all psychic healing cannot be attributed to suggestion is indicated by the paranormal healing of wounds in mice (Grad, Cadoret, & Paul, 1961), which was described in Chapter 10.

Psychic Injury

The counterpart of psychic healing is psychic injury. That it can be accomplished in lower organisms is indicated by the paranormal inhibition of the growth of fungus (Barry, 1968). Psychic injury may be the cause of hex death or death by black magic. In a culture where the efficacy of the procedure is accepted, hex death is generally attributable to the suggestibility of the victim. However, there are numerous reports of individuals developing typical symptomatology related to hexing without any apparent knowledge that a sorcerer had conducted a hex-inducing ritual (Halifax-Grof, 1974). For example, one of the distinguishing characteristics of the process of hexing in the Jivaro tribes of Peru is that the victim is given no indication that he is being bewitched. Success under such conditions is suggestive of psi.

Psychic Surgery

Direct observations and motion pictures have been made of individuals who, although not trained in medicine, perform ostensible operations without aseptic methods and make apparent incisions with the use of crude implements or even with their fingers, the wounds closing immediately. The psychic surgeon Tony Agpaoa of the Phillipines is an example (Watson, 1974). Although some scientists who witnessed these operations were convinced that they were real, others believed that they were done by sleight-of-hand because, even though human blood appeared in some cases, bizarre objects such as grass, dead mice, and even corn cobs were sometimes removed from the patient. Defenders of the psychic surgeons claim that these objects were used, perhaps were even materialized, because the patients' culture demanded miracles as a sign of healing.

The psychic surgeon Jose Arigo, an uneducated man of Brazil, claimed to be guided in his medical activities by some deceased doctors. Before Arigo's death in 1971, he was studied by several medical doctors, including Puharich (Fuller, 1974), who became convinced of the authenticity of his work. His operations were performed with crude implements and without aseptic technique or anesthesia. He removed a tumor from Puharich's elbow by this method without pain or infection, and it healed in about half the time normally required. With our present meager knowledge of the limits of psi, it would be unwarranted to hold that psychic surgery is an impossibility. However, acceptance of its reality requires a far higher degree of evidence than has so far been supplied.

Temperature Change

Harry Price (1925) observed that the temperature of a séance room dropped as much as 20.5°F as measured by a thermometer.

These temperature drops occurred with the psychic Stella Crenshaw, while two sitters controlled her hands and feet. Schmeidler (1973) reported changes in temperature measured by a thermistor sealed in a thermos bottle, which was at a distance of 25 feet from the psychic Ingo Swann. The subject was able to raise or lower the temperature according to randomly ordered instructions. The ability of individuals to alter the temperature of distant objects supplies substance to the belief that rain-making ceremonies conducted in many parts of the world may be paranormally effective because condensation of raindrops is affected by thermal change.

Metal Bending

The psychic Uri Geller repeatedly demonstrated his ability to paranormally bend and break metal objects such as keys, rings, and spoons, sometimes without touching them (Panati, 1976). The bending sometimes continued after the object left Geller's vicinity. At the point of the bending, the solid metal became plasticized without an increase in its temperature. Examination of the fractured edges indicated that the bending resulted from an internal change in structure rather than from external pressure (Franklin, 1975). The English psychic Matthew Manning was observed to produce similar feats of paranormal bending and breaking of metal (Owen, 1975). He discovered his ability after watching Geller perform on television, as did several others (Keil, 1975), some of whom were children (Taylor, 1975). By means of a strain gauge mounted inside a key, J.G. Hasted (1976), Professor of Physics at the University of London, registered the paranormal bending of keys by several children who did not touch the objects. The French psychic Jean-Pièrre Girard was observed by Jean Dierkens (1978), Professor of Psychology at the State University in Mons, Belgium, to psychokinetically bend a steel bar without touching it, the effect being registered on a strain gauge.

Geller also repeatedly demonstrated the ability to paranormally start stopped watches. William Cox (1975), a magician as well as a parapsychologist, observed Geller start a watch which Cox had stopped by inserting a strip of tinfoil into the balance wheel. Without opening the watch, Geller caused it to run, apparently by paranormally moving the tinfoil to a harmless position. Geller also apparently affected numerous distant objects that were in various localities as reported by different observers. In one test in Germany while Geller was concentrating on the effect, 402 persons reported clocks and watches restarting, and 151 persons reported cutlery bending (Bender et al., 1975). About one fifth of these individuals considered the phenomena to be triggered through them by Geller rather than being produced by him directly. Some distant objects were reported to be affected before the tests began and also in prerecorded radio broadcasts during which time Geller was not consciously participating (Panati, 1976).

Alteration of Weight

Hare and Crookes (Chap. 2) each carried out experiments in which they measured the change in weight of a vessel of water as registered by a spring balance. In these tests, a psychic placed his hands or fingers in the water, which was in a wire gauze cage or a perforated copper vessel. The water-penetrated vessel was suspended in a larger, water-filled container without any contact between the two. Hare observed an increase in the weight of the outer vessel of as much as eighteen pounds. More recently, the psychic Uri Geller was observed to increase by $1\frac{1}{2}$ grams the weight of a 1 gram mass as measured by a precision laboratory balance under a bell jar (Puthoff & Targ, 1974a).

Movement of Objects

Sir William Crookes observed the paranormal movement of many objects by the psychic D.D. Home. More recently, the psychic Ingo Swann was observed to increase or decrease pendulum motion on command while sitting quietly 1 meter from a bell jar containing the pendulum (Puthoff & Targ, 1975). The Russian psychic Kulagina was observed to psychokinetically deflect compass needles as well as to paranormally move objects weighing up to 380 grams (Ullman, 1974). Her best working distance was $\frac{1}{2}$ meter from the object, which underwent several moves of a few centimeters each. Another Russian psychic, Alla

Vinogradova, was observed to produce similar effects (Ullman, 1974).

The movement of the object may take the form of levitation. Crookes reported the paranormal rising and suspension of objects in bright light with the psychic D.D. Home (Medhurst, 1972). Julian Ochorowicz (1909) photographed levitations of small objects by the psychic Stanislawa Tomczyk and observed rays extending from her fingers; he was able to move his hand through the rays without disrupting the levitation. The Italian psychic Eusapia Palladino caused the levitation from the floor in full light of a table on which her fingers rested (Fielding et al., 1909). Although she had previously admitted to cheating when she was not adequately controlled, the researchers in this case considered that the conditions of control made cheating impossible. Two separate experimental groups in England levitated tables weighing from 6 to 40 pounds in darkness or in dim light, with the sitters hands or fingers touching the table top (Batcheldor, 1966; Brookes-Smith & Hunt, 1970). The adequacy of the control of the sitters in these tests, however, is questionable because it relied partly upon their personal integrity.

Raps

Raps on tables, walls, floors, and various articles of furniture without apparent physical cause have been frequently reported. Jung reported a rapping experience he had when he met Freud in 1909 (Jaffé, 1963). He was interested to hear Freud's views on parapsychology and Freud rejected the entire subject. Jung wrote the following:

> While Freud was going on this way, I had a curious sensation. It was as if my diaphragm were made of iron and were becoming red-hot—a glowing vault. And at that moment there was such a loud report on the bookcase, which stood right next to us, that we both started up in alarm, fearing the thing was going to topple over us. I said to Freud: "There, that is an example of so-called catalytic exteriorization phenomenon." "Oh come," he said, "That is sheer bosh!" "It is not," I replied. "You are mistaken, Herr Professor. And to prove my point I now predict that in a moment there will be another such loud report!" Sure enough, no sooner had I said the words than the same detonation went off in the bookcase. To this day I do not know what gave me this certainty. But I knew beyond all doubt that the

report would come again. Freud only stared aghast at me. I do not know what was in his mind, or what his look meant. In any case, this incident aroused his mistrust of me, and I had the feeling that I had done something against him. I never afterwards discussed the incident with him.

However, years later Freud acknowledged the possibility of paranormal phenomena and went so far as to say that if he had a chance to start his career all over again, he would dedicate himself to psychical research (Jones, 1957).

In some cases the raps respond to the listeners by means of a code which the latter establish, such as two raps for "yes" and one rap for "no." It was through such rappings with the Fox sisters in 1849 that modern spiritualism originated (Chap. 2). Paranormal raps that respond to questions do not necessarily originate with a departed spirit. This is shown by the fact that a group of sitters in Canada communicated with a spirit of their own creation by table raps produced in response to their questions (Owen & Sparrow, 1974). The responses were consistent with the history and the character they had constructed for the imaginary spirit. The possibility must be considered that the imaginary spirit was not solely a manifestation of the cooperative unconscious minds of the individuals of the group but was a quasi-*autonomous* mental entity created by the group.

When sitters place their hands on the top of a table, raps may occur on it or be made by the table tilting and rapping with one of its feet. The English physicist Michael Faraday (1853) found that when a pile of cards was placed between the sitter's fingers and the table the displacement of each card, when the table tilted or turned, increased with the nearness of the card to the sitter's fingers. This indicated that the force was coming from the sitter rather than from the table itself. However, movement of a table without contact with the sitters has been reported (Batcheldor, 1966). Some knowledge of the characteristics of the rap is afforded by study of its sound envelope. A comparison of paranormal and control raps of the same loudness showed that the former were of shorter duration and ended more abruptly than the latter (Whitton, 1975).

Voices on Tape

Putatively paranormal voices recorded on magnetic tape were first reported by the American psychical researcher Raymond Bayless (1959). Later the Swedish film producer Frederich Jürgenson (1964) noticed some faint voice extras on tapes on which he had recorded bird songs. Since then he has made many recordings to obtain these extras, as did the German psychologist Konstantin Raudive (1971). The voice extras appear to consist of short sentences or phrases often comprising words from each of several languages. Sometimes they give names and make relevant comments, but often they are incoherent or nonsensical. Many of them are so indistinct that they are interpreted differently by different listeners (Ellis, 1975). Those which were made in proximity to a radio tuned between stations may have been produced by indistinct fragments of radio transmission, and the ones made by an open microphone may have resulted from normal sounds picked up by the apparatus even though they were not heard by the persons who were present. Further experimentation may determine whether any taped voices are psychokinetically produced.

Direct Voice

Some mediums, e.g. D.D. Home, Gladys Leonard, and Margery Crandon, produce a phenomenon in which the voice of an ostensible communicator seems to come directly from a point in space, generally a few feet from the medium, and which may involve psychokinesis. The communications that Soal (1926) received from his supposedly deceased but actually still-living friend were obtained through a direct-voice medium.

Psychic Photography

Almost since the beginning of photography, photographs have been produced in which, in addition to the sitter, pictures of one or more individuals not in the area appeared in the photograph. Usually the extras were individuals who were deceased or who could not be identified. As these photographs were not produced under controlled conditions, they could be fraudulent. However, in view of the later establishment of the paranormal production of images on photographic film, it seems likely that some of these spirit photographs were produced by psi.

One of the first attempts to conduct controlled experiments on the effect of thought on photographic plates was made by Tomo-kichi Fukurai (1931), Professor of Psychology at Tokyo Imperial University. Sensitive photographic plates wrapped in black paper were held by a psychic, and imprints of Japanese characters assigned for her concentration appeared on the plates. More recently the psychiatrist Jule Eisenbud (1969) obtained paranormal photographs on Polaroid® film with the psychic Ted Serios. The camera was pointed at Serios's face, at the wall, or at some object in the room. Usually the psychic pressed against the lens a short hollow cardboard tube which was about 1 inch long and 1 inch in diameter. Although most of the exposures showed no picture, some of the prints were totally white or totally black, and many showed buildings, parts of buildings, or other familiar objects such as an airplane. Some of the pictured objects were identified, while others were not. Occasionally, pictures were produced with cameras and film supplied by outsiders with no contact by Serios allowed. Some images were obtained with the psychic inside a Faraday cage and the camera and tube outside the room. A team of two photographers, by using a small tube with a lens at one end and a photographic transparency in the other, simulated the psychic photography (Reynolds & Eisendrath, 1967). However, of the numerous scientists and photographic experts present in the tests of Serios, none ever saw evidence to indicate that he used such an apparatus. Because in some instances pictures were made of objects inside the camera even though the lens was covered with masking tape, Giles (1977) postulated that the photographs resulted from the paranormal production of light within the camera.

Weeping or Bleeding Human Images

Numerous reports have been made of statues or pictures, most commonly of Christ or of the Madonna, that have wept or bled without apparent normal cause (Rogo, 1977). In some cases the blood was analyzed and found to be real. Some of these effects may have been the result of PK and resemble some of the phenomena occurring in poltergeist cases.

Teleportation

The paranormal transportation of a physical object from one place to another is termed *teleportation*. If the teleported object is conveyed into a room or other container with walls that have no openings through which the object might ordinarily pass, it is called an apport. Many such cases are undoubtedly due to fraud, and few, if any, have occurred under controlled conditions. Johann Zöllner (1888), Professor of Physics at the University of Leipzig, reported several instances of apports and attributed them to passage of the object through a fourth dimension of space. Another hypothesis of apportation is that it results from dematerialization of the object at one point of space and its rematerialization at another. Because this is what would appear to happen if the object moved through a fourth dimension of space, it may be difficult to distinguish empirically between the two hypotheses. That dematerialization should be considered seriously is indicated by the finding of a team of four British scientists working with Uri Geller that he was able to cause a part of a vanadium carbide crystal to vanish (Hasted et al., 1975). The crystal was encapsulated so it could not be touched and was placed so it could not be switched with another by sleight of hand.

Poltergeists

Poltergeist is German for "noisy spirit"; however, the paranormal physical events associated with this phenomenon may be due to the spirit of a living person rather than to that of a deceased individual. Its alternative term, recurrent-spontaneous-psychokinesis, gives an indication of its characteristics. Poltergeist phenomena have been reported since ancient history and in many cultures of the world (Carrington & Fodor, 1951). The range of apparently psychokinetic events in poltergeist cases includes raps and other noises; movement, levitation, teleportation, and apportation of objects; fire igniting; lights; and apparitions (Owen, 1964).

Poltergeistry differs from haunting in that poltergeist phenomena are associated with particular persons rather than with particular places, the physical disturbances are generally more frequent than they are in haunting, and the phenomena are usually of shorter duration than in hauntings. In certain poltergeist cases, an individual is bombarded with stones. The stones may follow him into a house, penetrating the latter through openings or even dropping from the ceiling, seemingly formed in the air. Household objects move with a controlled type of flight, sometimes navigating corners and seldom causing physical injury to the observers, although fragile objects may be broken. Some of the effects, such as the turning of radiator valves and electric fuses or the appearance of water on stairways, may produce spectacular results. The phenomena start unexpectedly and continue for a few hours to several months or even a few years. Gradually they fade out and cease altogether.

Some poltergeist phenomena are fraudulently produced; however, eyewitnessed observations and/or videotaped occurrences of moving objects, made by Hans Bender (1968) and by William Roll (1974) during the activities, indicate that some are genuine. The events tend to be concentrated within a particular house or area and within a special location in that area, such as a room or a shelf (Roll, 1977). Sometimes a special object or class of objects, such as stones, is singled out. Roll has found a decrease in the frequency of the paranormal movements with distance from the associated individual. The events generally center around a particular person, ordinarily one between the ages of ten and twenty and more likely a female (Owen, 1964). The psychoanalyst Nandor Fodor believed that poltergeist manifestations are produced by PK and result from a dissociation of the personality —an explosive loosening of an infantile part of the psyche in which severe conflicts have been kept repressed (Carrington & Fodor, 1951). Individuals who are centers of poltergeist activity are not conscious of their causal relationship to the paranormal phenomena, and tests have indicated that they possess hostility which cannot be expressed in normal ways (Roll, 1974). The production of poltergeist phenomena permits expression of the hostility without the individual feeling responsible for it.

Materialization

Materialization is the postulated paranormal appearance of temporary, more or less organized substances in various degrees of solidification and usually possessing human physical characteristics such as hands, faces, and full figures. Although it is one of the least accepted of psychic phenomena, the two parapsychologists who may have gained the greatest recognition in fields outside of psychical research, Crookes and Richet, were thoroughly convinced of its reality. Richet coined the term *ectoplasm* to denote a physical substance which is molded by thought to form the temporarily materialized object. It is described as emerging from orifices of the psychic and returning thereto when the form disintegrates. It is said to be sensitive to bright light, which may cause its rapid return to the psychic's body with possible damage to the latter. In bright light with the psychic D.D. Home, Crookes observed the apparent materialization of a hand, but his most remarkable success consisted of the witnessing and photographing of what appeared to be fully formed materializations with the psychic Florence Cook (Medhurst, 1972). Studies of materialization phenomena by several observers are described in Chapter 2.

Of more common occurrence than visible materializations are the touches a sitter may experience in a completely dark séance room. Whether or not they are the result of contact with objects materialized by the medium, their paranormality is indicated by the delicate precision with which they are administered in complete darkness even to portions of the sitter's face. The part materialization may play in séance room phenomena, psychic photography, psychic surgery, and poltergeist occurrences has yet to be scientifically determined.

Levitation and Teleportation of the Human Body

Levitation or rising into the air without normal means has been described as taking place in numerous saints and mystics (Thurston, 1952). The classic example is that of St. Joseph of Copertino, who in the seventeenth century was reportedly often seen to levitate during religious observances and at other times. Several psychics have been reported to levitate, including D.D.

Home, of whom there are at least 100 recorded instances of his rising from the ground. The most remarkable account was that of his floating in the air, his body horizontal, out of the window of an upper room, and in again through the window of an adjoining room (Dunraven, 1924). Teaching officials of the Transcendental Meditation organization, who underwent training by Maharishi Mahesh Yogi in which they claim to have developed the ability to levitate, present courses to impart this purported faculty to other meditators.

Most claimed instances of human teleportation or paranormal transportation of the body from one place to another have been unwitnessed. However, witnesses have attested to its occurrence in India (Osis, 1975). The psychic Ray Stanford (1974) stated that he was teleported on three occasions, and the psychic Uri Geller (1975) also claimed to have had this experience.

CONCLUSIONS

The complex nature of some of the possibly paranormal physical phenomena set forth in this chapter indicates that their proof and their explanation requires more than the present development of parapsychology affords.

REVIEW QUESTIONS

1. What evidence is there of the possibly paranormal withstanding of physical extremes?
2. Distinguish between dermography and stigmata.
3. What evidence is there of paranormal healing?
4. Give a paranormal explanation of poltergeist phenomena.
5. What is the experimental evidence for each of the following paranormal phenomena: alteration of weight, dematerialization, levitation, materialization, metal bending, psychic photography, raps, taped voices, and temperature change?

Chapter 13

CHARACTERISTICS OF PSI

ALTHOUGH THE SCIENCE of parapsychology is in its infancy, certain characteristics and principles of psi have been indicated through the study of its spontaneous manifestations, its induced occurrences, and its experimental expressions.

Life or Mind Requiring

The occurrence of psi apparently requires that at least one of the objects involved in the process is live or possesses mind. There have been no indications of paranormal relations solely between nonliving objects and, if a psi event did take place entirely between two inanimate things, it would be difficult to rule out the agency of a living organism. How far down the evolutionary scale psi occurs and whether it exists in discarnate spirits are questions that have not been resolved.

Extraphysical

Psi may be extraphysical, on the basis of classical physics, in the sense of being independent of space, time, and physical causality. Experiments have failed to establish a decrement in psi with distance or with time. That psi is not a physical force is suggested by the failure of metal chambers and cages to prevent its occurrence, even though these containers are impervious to the transmission of most electromagnetic waves. With randomly moving objects, PK scores are not lowered by an increase in the weight or in the number of the affected objects. On the other hand, the movement of stationary objects by PK has not been found to greatly exceed the normal physical capacity of the subject, thus suggesting a weight limit to static PK. Although psi is not encircled by the present boundaries of physics, changes in the concepts of the latter science may eventuate in its inclusion of paranormal phenomena. On the other hand, if mind proves to

180

be basic to matter and physical phenomena are found to be only special manifestations of psychical activity, the science of psi will subsume physics rather than becoming encompassed by the latter.

Rate of Scoring

Apparently the first subject to correctly name all 25 cards in an ESP deck was a nine-year-old girl named Lillian (Reeves & Rhine, 1942). Most outstanding subjects, however, have a much lower average rate of scoring than this. For example, of Rhine's exceptional subjects, Pearce had average scores of 9 or 10 hits per run of 25 trials instead of the expected 5, Linzmayer averaged 6.7 hits per run, and Stuart averaged 6.0 hits per run (J.B. Rhine, 1934). Of Soal's two exceptional subjects, Shackleton averaged 7.3 hits per run and Stewart averaged 6.8 (Soal & Bateman, 1954). The lowest of these five individuals, Stuart, had an average of 6 hits per run. However, not all of the hits of these subjects were ESP hits, as some of them were due to chance. Using the formula, ESP hits = positive hit deviation/probability of failure per trial (Timm, 1973), it can be ascertained that Stuart averaged only $1\frac{1}{4}$ ESP hits per run of 25 calls, i.e. one ESP hit in every 20 calls. However, a scoring rate much lower than this would be quite significant if it extended over a sufficient number of runs. The probability against naming all 25 cards correctly in an ESP deck is equal to 5^{25} to 1, or over 10^{17} to 1. Although this is an astronomical figure, some subjects who scored at a much lower rate had much higher odds against chance than this because of a greater number of trials. For example, with an average score of 6.8 hits per run versus a chance expectancy of 5, Stewart's odds against chance were in the order of 10^{70} to 1 (Soal & Bateman, 1954). The immensity of this number is indicated by comparing it with the number of protons in the universe, which has been estimated to have a magnitude of 10^{80}.

Although the above scoring rates are for contemporaneous ESP, the scoring level appears to be no lower in precognition. For example, Shackleton's rate of scoring was no less in those of his trials requiring precognition than in those involving contemporaneous ESP. On the other hand, although tests of PK have revealed many successful subjects, no PK subjects has had a prolonged scoring rate equal to those of the outstanding ESP subjects.

Singularization

Psi can be directed to the target deck, to a particular card in that deck, or to a particular die out of the several that are rolling at the same time. For example, when dice of two different colors were simultaneously thrown, high scores were obtained with dice of the color selected for high aim and low scores with dice of the color chosen for low aim (Humphrey, 1947b). *Singularization* was also evidenced with the sensitive Stepanek who, to a statistically significant degree, consistently called certain cards correctly and miscalled others although he was trying to identify all of them. The cards were concealed in numbered envelopes, and the focusing effect, as this tendency was called, took place even when the card-containing envelopes were placed inside larger opaque covers (Pratt, 1973).

Voluntary

Generally one is unable to purposely make psi events happen. More often they occur spontaneously without conscious voluntary effort on the part of those involved. The voluntary nature of psi, however, is shown by the fact that it can be intentionally directed to a particular card or die. Furthermore, it can be used to miscall the target in a low aim trial as well as to call it correctly in a trial of high aim (J.B. Rhine, 1934). In an experiment testing the ability of the subject to voluntarily dream of the target, correspondences were obtained with targets aimed at by the individual but unknown to him. Agreements did not occur with dream targets, which the experimenter without the subject's knowledge attempted to telepathically transmit to him (Krippner & Zirinsky, 1971). This suggests that psi effects in dreams are to some extent under the volition of the dreamer.

Unconscious Relations

Psi may be unconscious either with respect to the subject's intent to use it or with respect to his cognizance of success in using it. In the first case, the subject employs psi without conscious intent, i.e. it is nonintentional, although it may be used to fulfill a need or desire. In the second case, he uses psi intentionally but without consciousness of whether or not he is succeeding.

Most, but not all, spontaneous paranormal events are nonintentional. Cases with agent intent to send information or with percipient intent to receive information are classified as spontaneous if they occur in everyday situations rather than in the laboratory. An apparently nonintentional spontaneous case concerns the writing of a novel (Robertson, 1898). In the story, a huge steamship called the *Titan,* which was considered unsinkable, did sink after collision with an iceberg. Like the *Titanic,* which sank fourteen years later, she also carried too few lifeboats and went down with an appalling loss of life.

That ESP may be used unconsciously to fulfill a need or desire is indicated by the results of several studies. In one research, William Cox (1956) obtained passenger statistics for railway accidents and found that significantly fewer passengers traveled on the trains on the days of the accidents than on comparable days. Although some of the passengers may have consciously precognized the train wreck, most of them presumably avoided the train on that day without realizing their true motive. In another study, Cox (1957) found that families with four children of the same sex were more likely to have a child of the opposite sex as their fifth child. On the likely assumption that most of these families preferred that their fifth child be of the opposite sex to that of their first four children, he interpreted this to suggest that the sex of the offspring was affected in the desired direction by psi. On the basis of his studies of ESP effects in dreams, the American psychiatrist Montague Ullman postulated that the dreamer scans his psi field of space and time to see if hostile or threatening influences external to himself must be dealt with (Ullman & Krippner, with Vaughan, 1973). Whether or not these dreams are consciously remembered, they may affect the dreamer's subsequent activity. Rex Stanford (1974) proposed a model for spontaneous psi events which he refers to as psi-mediated instrumental response (PMIR). According to this model, the organism uses

psi unintentionally to scan its environment for need-relevant objects or events. Once having obtained the information, the organism tends to act in ways which are instrumental in satisfying its
need in relation to the particular object or event apprehended.

That subjects may use ESP unintentionally and without conscious awareness of being tested was first indicated experimentally
by Carroll and Catherine Nash (1963). They found that individuals who knew that they were being tested for subliminal
perception and thus had the need to identify the targets, but did
not know that at the same time they were being tested by inter-
spersed trials of ESP, gave significant results with ESP. That psi
can be unconsciously used to satisfy a need is also indicated by the
results of the following four experiments. In one of them, a
binary random-event generator was affected by PK to increase the
time in which a heat-giving electric bulb remained lighted in a
cold room inhabited by a cat (Schmidt, 1970c). In the second
experiment, students did significantly better on examination questions for which answers were hidden inside sealed envelopes that
were attached to the answer sheets, the students not knowing that
the answers were enclosed (Johnson, 1973). In a similar experiment, a significant positive correlation occurred between the total
errors on the examination and the scores on the questions for
which answers were hidden (Braud, 1975). This suggests that the
greater the subject's need to obtain the answer, the greater was his
use of ESP to do so. In the fourth of these experiments, human
subjects were found to unconsciously shorten their reaction time
to a randomly selected word in word-association tests when its decrease resulted in their subsequent exposure to a pleasant and
somewhat erotically arousing condition (Stanford & Stio, 1976).
The subjects were unaware that reduction in their reaction time
to the word would reward them.

When making his call the subject is usually not conscious of
whether his attempt at intentionally expressing psi has been successful (Woodruff & George, 1937). The unconsciousness of ESP
is also suggested by failure to set up a conditioned reflex with an
ESP target as the conditioned stimulus (Woodruff & Dale, 1952).
However, after the run but before the results were checked, sub-

jects were able to determine in which of their runs they had done the best (Eilbert & Schmeidler, 1950). Humphrey and Nicol (1955) asked each of their subjects to say "check" when he felt confident that a call was correct, and found significant statistical evidence of checking success, which they attributed to the individual's consciousness of ESP when it occurred. The Nashes (1958) corroborated the phenomenon of success in confidence calls. However, they pointed out the possibility that the correct checking of a hit in a confidence call may itself be a second act of ESP rather than the result of consciousness of the successful application of ESP. Nevertheless, Kanthamani and Kelly (1974) found in an ESP experiment with the American psychic Bill Delmore that the success in his confidence calls was so much greater than the success in his ordinary trials that it could not be attributed to secondary acts of ESP. Instead it suggested that he was conscious of when he was applying ESP.

Another indication that the subject may be conscious of applying ESP is the fact that some experiments using immediate feedback of success to the subject have resulted in a higher level of scoring (Targ, Cole, & Puthoff, 1974; Tart, 1975; Braud & Wood, 1977). If the subject did not have some consciousness of his mental or physical state when he was applying ESP, he would not be able to learn to improve its production by causing that mental or physical state to occur again. Such success in the positive reinforcement of the ESP act in some individuals suggests that subjects can learn to produce ESP. However, learning has not so far been indicated in PK where, despite immediate feedback after each trial, scoring decline rather than incline has been typical.

Hit Distribution

Analysis of the results of both ESP and PK experiments provided no evidence of trial-by-trial grouping of success and failure within the run (Pratt, 1947). In another experiment, however, periods of success with as many as 20 consecutive ESP hits alternated with periods of chance expectancy scoring (Marino & Benetti, 1976).

Displacement and Reinforcement

In some cases, instead of the actual target being identified, a hit is made on a target near to it either in space or in time. Whately Carington (1940) observed temporal displacement in an experiment in which a different drawing was utilized as the target on each of ten consecutive days. The calls on each day were compared with the targets for all ten days. Although most hits occurred on the correct target, the next most hits occurred on the targets for the day before and the day after the correct one, and third in order of hits were the targets displaced two days in the past or in the future.

Because of this, Soal was persuaded to recheck his own apparently unsuccessful data with 160 subjects (Soal & Bateman, 1954). He found −1 and +1 displacement, i.e. hits on the cards immediately before and immediately after the target card, in two of his subjects. In further tests, his subject, Basil Shackleton, produced −2 and +2 displacement when calling the targets at a rapid rate. He obtained higher displacement scores when the −1 and +1, or −2 and +2, targets were of the same symbol, the images reinforcing each other. Displacement has since been reported in several ESP experiments and is a fairly common characteristic of ESP. It is indicative of the imprecision with which the psi faculty is often focused in space and time.

Significant negative displacement for both −1 and +1 targets occurred in Gloria Stewart's work (Soal & Bateman, 1954). Tart (1978) interpreted such results as indicative of a transtemporal inhibition in which the subject suppresses ESP information of past and future events in order to enhance ESP of the present.

Linger Effect

Some evidence has been provided that PK exerted in a particular locus may linger or continue to produce an aftereffect in that area. A compass needle, deflected by PK in a particular area in a room, was redeflected, when returned to that area even though the psychic, Felicia Parise, was no longer at that spot (Watkins & Watkins, 1974). Mice recovered more rapidly from anesthesia when the same side of the table was used for several trials than when the sides were randomly varied, and this effect lasted approximately 30 minutes (Wells & Watkins, 1975). These results are suggestive of the establishment of a PK field that requires time to dissipate. The *linger effect* is consistent with the phenomenon of haunting, in which a place rather than a person or an object is the basis of the activity. On the other hand, the linger effect may be due to the agent's continued direction of PK to the spot after he has left it.

Declines

The fact that subjects tend to make their highest scores at the beginning of a psi test bears a resemblance to beginner's luck, which may be a manifestation of psi. In addition to a chronological decline through the experiment as a whole, declines may occur within units of the experiment such as the session, the page, or the run. Declines may occur in the variance as well as in the scoring level (Rogers & Carpenter, 1966). In some PK tests, declines have proceeded both vertically down the run as recorded on the page and horizontally across the page from run to run. This resulted in the upper left-hand quarter of the page having a higher score than the lower right-hand quarter, which is called *quarter distribution* or *QD* (Rhine & Humphrey, 1944). Chronological decline in ESP may be due to a decrease in spontaneity as the subject becomes increasingly entangled by associative tendencies (J.B. Rhine, 1941). On the other hand, chronological decline may result from a decrease in the subject's motivation as he proceeds through the task (Schmeidler, 1944). Tart (1966) considered chronological decline on the basis of learning theory, and attributed it to the extinction of psi resulting from failure to immediately reward each trial in which psi was expressed. According to Thouless (1972), decline in ESP results from the automatic reinstatement of the normal suppression of the primitive psi-function, a suppression that arose with the development of the more effective perceptual system provided by the sense organs and the central nervous system. Beloff (1972) presented the similar view that ESP results from leaks in the filter constituted by the brain and that decline is due to the filter undergoing repair.

Reliability and Duration

Paranormal ability was observed by Crookes to fluctuate even in the outstanding psychic D.D. Home (Medhurst, 1972), and its unpredictability has been characteristic of all sensitives. In addition to its unreliability, most psychics have lost their paranormal ability in time, e.g. Shackleton after three years and Stewart after four years (Soal & Bateman, 1954). Several experimenters also have lost their ability to obtain significant results, and some have prolonged their productivity by participating in experiments with fresh coexperimenters. While psychic phenomena can be induced and are subject to experimentation, they have not been reliably predictable in their occurrence. This has led to the question of whether a repeatable psi experiment will ever be possible. However, when enough of the variables affecting the expression of psi are identified and controlled, a reliably repeatable experiment may be forthcoming (Chap. 5).

Psi Missing

Not only may psi scores fluctuate and decline, but they may sometimes be significantly negative or below chance expectancy. This phenomenon—called psi missing (J.B. Rhine, 1952)—is not an absence of psi, which would result in scores near chance expectation, but is an expression of psi in a way that causes a result opposite to the conscious intent. In order for the subject to miss the target to an extrachance extent, he must use psi to avoid the target, as otherwise he would produce hits on it with chance-expectancy frequency. Consistent missing, i.e. regularly miscalling a symbol by a particular incorrect symbol (Cadoret & Pratt, 1950), has been shown to be a method by which psi missing may be brought about (Timm, 1969).

Psi missing has been attributed to consistent error on the part of the subject resulting from his tension (J.B. Rhine, 1952). An alternative hypothesis is that it is conative and results from the subject's unconscious desire to produce the opposite effect. Psi missing may result from negative moods or personality factors, from dislike of the experimenter or of the technique, from disbelief in ESP, and from participation in a dual-condition experiment in which psi missing may be exercised in the less favorable situation in order to cause the scores in the favored condition to be relatively higher.

Psi missing is not confined to the action of the subject and may be caused by the agent (Schmeidler, 1961). In conditions where both the agent and the subjects engage in psi missing, positive deviations may arise from the double psi missing that occurs (Nash, 1975c). In this case, a negative effect by the subject is reversed by a negative effect by the agent, thereby resulting in psi hitting in the actual score.

When psi missing takes place in certain units of the experiment at the same time that psi hitting occurs in others, the variance or spread of the scores of these units around their mean is increased. Because of this, high variance between units generally indicates the presence of psi missing in some of the units, particularly if the overall scoring level is not above chance expectation. Psi missing may also result in low variance between units when psi missing in one part of the unit cancels psi hitting in another part (Stanford, 1966).

Terminal Salience

Higher scores at both ends of the experiment or experimental division and a lower score in the middle result in a U-shaped curve. The effect is called *terminal salience*. The phenomenon has been attributed to differences in the subject's motivation in relation to the beginning, middle, and end of his task (Schmeidler, 1944). Another possible cause is that there is more opportunity for displacement in the middle trials. Because displacement reduces the number of hits on the target, it would cause the scores in the middle portion to be lower than the scores at either end (Nash, 1977a).

Differential Effect

The use of two contrasting conditions in the same experiment may result in a significant difference between the scoring rates in the two situations. Usually this differential effect consists of a positive score in one condition and a negative score in the other. Early evidence of the effect was afforded in an ESP experiment by

Stuart (1946) in which the scores were significantly positive with percipients and agents who were closely related and significantly negative with unrelated pairs. A differential response was first observed in a PK experiment by Nicol and Carington (1947) in which the subjects obtained positive scores on high value faces of the dice (4, 5, and 6) and negative deviations on low faces (1, 2, and 3). The difference, however, may have been the result of die bias.

The production of a negative deviation in the less favored condition, instead of a somewhat lower positive deviation than in the more favored condition, may be a means of accentuating the difference between the effects of psi in the two situations. This is suggested by the numerous instances in which a negative deviation was obtained in the less favored condition even though a positive deviation occurred when the same condition was tested by itself in a separate experiment. In Stuart's experiment above, the subjects who were unrelated to the agent had a negative deviation even though in the large majority of the many published experiments, in which only subjects unrelated to the agent were tested, the deviation was positive.

Because of the differential effect, the direction of the expression of psi in a particular condition or task should be determined in an experiment testing only that factor. For example, it should not be concluded that introverts typically engage in psi missing solely on the basis of their psi scores being negative when they are tested in an experiment with extraverts. It is quite possible that the introverts would express psi in a positive direction if they were tested by themselves in a separate experiment.

That the differential effect may embody more than a single experiment is suggested by the statistically significant negative correlation between the scores of the same subjects in two contemporaneous ESP experiments with two closely related experimenters (Nash & Nash, 1962). It may also include two ESP experiments performed at different times with different subjects and the same experimenter. This is suggested by the finding that, in two such experiments performed four months apart, each of the nine target paintings was selected, from a group of four paintings, less frequently by the subjects in the first experiment than it was selected by a different group of subjects in the second experiment when it was not the target (Nash, 1976b).

The production of a positive deviation in one part of an experiment, or in one of two linked experiments, and the production of a negative deviation in the other may be brought about by an increase in *negentropy* or information in the one part that is gained by an increase in entropy or a decrease in information in the other. To the extent that the experiment or experiments constitute a closed system, an increase of negentropy or information in one part would result in an increase of entropy or a decrease of information in another part.

Psi Masking

Analyses of some psi experiments suggests that psi may be used to cover up its own manifestation—a phenomenon that has been called *psi masking* (Nash, 1977b). Low variance between the run scores of an experiment may be due to psi missing in one part of the run to cancel the effects of psi hitting in another part of the run, or vice versa (Stanford, 1966). This would cause the run score to be nearer mean chance expectation and lower the variance between the run scores. Psi masking may also be the cause of low variance between subjects' scores. In this case, high scoring runs of a subject would be cancelled by low-scoring runs of that subject and vice versa. This would cause the subject's total score to be nearer mean chance expectation and lower the variance between the scores of the subjects.

Psi masking may be a cause of the differential effect in which a positive score under one situation is counterbalanced by a negative score under another condition, thereby preventing the manifestation of psi in the overall scoring. In addition, psi masking may be the cause of the paranormal disappearance of paranormally produced effects and objects, which has been associated with Uri Geller and some others.

Psi masking may result from negative moods or negative personality factors, from dislike of the experimenter or of the technique, or from disbelief in ESP. Another possible cause of the use of psi to cover up its own footprints is the fear of omnipotence, which originates when the child feels that he may use psi to injure his parents in his ambivalent feelings to them. Psi masking may also result from fear that psi may erase the boundaries of the ego and cause its dissolution upon merging with the external.

Two Step Process

The ESP target may not be perceived in its entirety, or it may be modified in its perception. In tests with multiple-aspect targets such as playing cards, either the suit or the number of the card may be extrasensorially perceived alone (Mangan, 1957). Furthermore, when drawings are used as targets, their perception may be modified (Warcollier, 1938). Various changes were observed, including the following: (1) Either the idea or the form of the target is perceived without the other. (2) Only a fragment of the target picture is perceived. (3) Important elements of the picture are juxtaposed. (4) Certain portions of the picture are inverted. (5) Elements of the target picture are reorganized into an identifiable form different from the original configuration. (6) The target picture is elaborated. (7) The target picture is transformed into a different but visually similar image. (8) The target picture is represented symbolically or by an associated idea. Spontaneous ESP also may be incomplete or modified, with a part of the extrasensorially perceived event being obscure, distorted, missing, or wrong (L.E. Rhine, 1962b). The facts that the external event may be significantly miscalled without conscious intent in psi missing, that it may not be perceived in its entirety, and that it may be modified in its perception suggest that ESP is a two step process. Tyrrell (1947) postulated that in the first step, which is unconscious and paranormal, an item of information becomes accessible without sensory mediation. According to him, the second step consists of the normal mediation of the information to the consciousness through psychological machinery, during which it may be altered, the conscious product taking a form such as an impulse, a dream, or a hallucination.

Partial ESP

It was pointed out by J.B. Rhine (1952) that, although the deviation in low aim with an ESP deck would be expected to be

1/5 as great as the deviation in high aim, the deviations are roughly equal. The rationale for expecting the deviation to be 1/5 as great in low aim as in high aim is as follows. By chance alone the target in an ESP deck would be called incorrectly in 4/5 of the trials, while it would be correctly identified 1/5 of the time. Therefore, a low aim act of ESP would increase the chance of a miss from 4/5 to 1 (an increase of 1/5), whereas a high aim act of ESP would increase the chance of a hit from 1/5 to 1 (an increase of 4/5). Because of this, the ratio of the effect of low aim to the effect of high aim is 1/5 to 4/5, or 1/4. Therefore, low aim would be expected to result in an excess of misses that would be only 1/4 as great as the excess of hits produced in high aim. In spite of this, the deviations in low aim and in high aim are roughly equal.

To explain this, Rhine (1952) formulated the hypothesis of partial ESP, which takes account of the fact that less knowledge of a target may be sufficient for its avoidance than may be necessary for its identification. This would cause the deviation in low aim to be as great as the deviation in high aim. Evidence of partial ESP is afforded by experiments with clock cards in which extrachance positive scores were obtained on an hour next to the target hour, which were less positive than on the target hour (Fisk & Mitchell, 1953). Apparently, in some trials the subject perceived the target sufficiently to discern the approximate position of the clock hand but not sufficiently to determine the exact hour to which it was pointing.

Uses Memory Trace

It is characteristic of memorization for there to be success in recalling the beginning and ending of a memorized selection with failure in remembering the middle portion. The similarity between this expression and the *U*-shaped curves characteristic of ESP scores suggests a relationship between ESP and memory (Pratt, 1949). ESP calls in tests with restricted-response targets are, in a sense, memory responses (Roll, 1966). Before the ESP responses are begun, certain memory traces are laid down in the subject by his familiarizing himself with the target symbols. Similarly in tests with free-response targets, the responses which appear to the mind of the percipient may spring exclusively from his memory, although stimulated to do so by ESP.

Tenhaeff (1953) observed that sensitives were more efficient in the use of ESP associated with memories of childhood events, which are generally stronger than later memories. Remembered targets were found to be better extrasensorially perceived than were targets that the subject had previously seen but did not recall (Kanthamani & Rao, 1974). In an experiment in which the target could be correctly identified by either of two responses, Stanford (1973) found that individuals were significantly more accurate when they used the commonly employed or best established response than when they used the less popular response. These findings suggest that readily available associations or memories make more effective vehicles for the expression of ESP.

Response Bias

The American psychologist Rex Stanford (1967) hypothesized that, in identifying an ESP target, a less used response is more likely to be correct than is a more frequently made response. This is because the fewer the calls of a symbol the more the scoring rate will be increased by a psi-mediated hit on that target symbol. To illustrate, in a closed deck where the number of targets of each symbol is the same, an ESP hit on one of the five square targets would result in a higher scoring rate on the square symbol if it were called four times than if it were called six times. This should not be interpreted to indicate that ESP is better mediated by a less frequent response. In fact, the reverse is indicated to be true, i.e. a more frequent response provides a more facile means of psi mediation (Nash, 1978a).

Brain Locality

In an experiment by Hans and Shulamith Kreitler (1973), the ability to identify a subliminal sensory stimulus was diminished by a contradictory, simultaneous ESP message. However, it was not aided by a concordant ESP message. This suggested to them that ESP information is communicated through a different neural channel than the one used for sensory stimuli. The rationale is that switching of attention from the sensory channel to the ESP channel would not increase the frequency of correct calls of the sensory target when it was the same as the ESP target. However, it would decrease the frequency of correct calls of the sensory target when the ESP target differed from it. The finding of a negative correlation between ESP score and subliminal-perception score (Rao & Puri, 1977) also suggests separate neural channels for the two means of information.

There is some evidence that the right cerebral hemisphere may be utilized in the manifestation of psi. Experiments on persons who have undergone hemispherectomy and on split-brain individuals, in which the two cerebral hemispheres are separated, reveal that the left hemisphere excels in linguistic, mathematical, logical, temporal, abstract, sequential, and analytical skills. The right hemisphere excels in tasks involving music, facial recognition, imagery, spatial performance, simultaneous processing, and holistic judgments (Ornstein, 1973). Experiments designed to indicate whether psi is exercised more by the right hemisphere than by the left have not yielded easily interpretable results. Persons who were given an analytical cluster of tasks presumably engaging the left hemisphere produced psi missing in an ESP test immediately following (Braud & Braud, 1975). In a comparable experiment, individuals whose left hemisphere had been exercised scored significantly below chance expectancy in a PK test immediately following, while subjects whose right hemisphere had been exercised scored significantly high (Andrew, 1975). Use of the right hemisphere in ESP by selecting wooden blocks with the left hand to match the concealed targets, when the left hemisphere was occupied in counting, resulted in ESP scores about chance expectancy (Broughton, 1976). The latter experiment suggests that ESP in a spatial task by the right hemisphere was facilitated when the left hemisphere was occupied in another activity. Maher and Schmeidler (1977) obtained extrachance results when the left hemisphere was used in an ESP task involving selection of word targets with the right hand, while the right hemisphere was occupied in pattern recognition. They concluded that each hemisphere is better at processing the kind of ESP that corresponds to the sensory activity it processes better, and this appears to be the proper judgment on the basis of the evidence.

Ehrenwald (1976b) noted a close relationship between telepathic drawings and drawings made by patients with lesions in the left hemisphere, both showing a marked distortion and disorganization of the picture. He attributed the resemblance to use of the right hemisphere in both cases. He further suggested that it is the reticular formation in the brain which serves as a screen, protecting the person from being flooded and overwhelmed by a steady influx of psi stimuli; ESP occurs when the reticular formation fails to carry out this function. On the other hand, Beloff (1974) suggested that, rather than being brought about by the more recently evolved portions of the brain, the psi process is mediated by limbic and midbrain mechanisms which permit cognition without consciousness.

Diametric

Several experimental findings indicate that psi acts diametrically, i.e. it combines into a single act what may seem to require more than one act of psi, and produces an effect in a unified way rather than through a series of separate steps. One of these findings is that ESP is as successful in the blind matching of two cards as it is in the naming of either card alone, even though blind matching might appear to require two acts of psi to identify the two cards (Foster, 1940). Psi also appeared to work diametrically in a PK experiment in which the subject was blind to the target face of the die (Thouless, 1951). Ostensibly the task required two acts of psi in the same trial, an act of ESP to determine the target face and an act of PK to make it land uppermost. However, the rate of scoring was too high for it to be likely that two acts of psi were employed to produce a single hit. This is because the probability of the occurrence of two independent acts of psi in the same trial is the product of their separate probabilities and consequently is much lower than the probability of the occurrence of a single act of psi.

Another experiment suggesting that psi acts diametrically was performed with split agents, each possessing a separate piece of the information necessary to identify the target (Soal & Bateman, 1954). Each agent and the five cards he looked at were concealed from the other agent as well as from the subject. While one agent looked at five cards arranged in a set order with each bearing a different symbol, the other agent pointed to the target card, which was one of five blank cards corresponding in position to the cards being observed by the first agent. It was necesssary for the subject to obtain information from both agents in order to correctly name the target. Nevertheless, the score was as high as it was in tests with single agents.

Goal Oriented

Multiple acts of psi are ostensibly involved in the successful completion of a psi task, such as causing a complex, binary random-event generator to produce more heads than tails (Schmidt, 1974a). In order to succeed in this task, the subject has to cause the electrons from the radioactive decay to arrive at the Geiger counter at the moment when the high frequency oscillator is in the right phase. When the task was made twice as complicated by combining two generators, the PK scores were not lowered. Furthermore, the PK score was no less with a complex generator, the binary output of which was based on the majority decision of a rapid sequence of 100 binary events, than with a simple generator that produced a one step binary output (Schmidt, 1974b). These facts led Schmidt to postulate that psi is goal oriented or teleological in the sense that it aims successfully at a final outcome no matter how intricate the intermediate steps may be. The distinction between the diametric and teleological characteristics of psi may be that the former combines two or more contemporaneous acts of psi into a single paranormal effect whereas the latter involves a series of successive psi acts. It is the hypothesis of Stanford (1977c) that psi tends to act in the most economical way. The diametric and teleological nature of psi supports this proposition.

Holistic

Although the psi score is associated with the subject who makes the calls or throws the dice, the subject's score is determined by the whole experiment of which it is a part (Nash, 1974). The whole experiment is contributed to by all of the participants, although one of them may have a dominant effect (Nash, 1975b). One evidence of the *holistic* nature of psi is the finding that the frequency with which a symbol was called varied directly with the frequency with which it occurred in the deck, even when correction was made for the calls that were hits (Child & Kelly, 1973). For example, comparison of symbols appearing seven times in the deck with symbols appearing only three times showed a deviation of calls, corrected for hits, of +101 in the former and −68 in the latter. These results suggest that ESP responds to the frequency with which the symbol appears on the cards in the deck as a whole, rather than responding solely to the target card for that trial.

The holistic character of psi is also shown by the differential effect in which the less favored condition has a psi score below *MCE*. A negative deviation in the less favored condition (instead of a somewhat lower positive deviation than in the more favored condition) is presumably brought about because it accentuates the difference between the expression of psi in the two situations. The differential effect gives evidence of the holistic nature of psi, i.e. that the expression of psi in a part of an experiment is determined by the role played by that part in the experiment as a whole. The holistic operation of psi may be facilitated by its ability to respond diametrically in one instant to the experiment as a whole and everyone taking part in it (White, 1976).

The paranormal bending of metal objects at nearly the same time by numerous, distantly separated individuals in association with Uri Geller (Panati, 1976) may be the result of psi's holistic nature. However, it might result instead from removal of the subject's inhibition of his own paranormal metal-bending ability by watching Geller perform the feat and attributing the responsibility to him.

Relationship with Evolution

It is a fundamental question whether psi is a faculty that is evolving to become more pronounced, or whether it is better developed in lower organisms and has regressed in evolution to become less effective in man. If psi has positive survival value, it is reasonable to assume that it is increasing with evolution. However, ESP may be a faculty of living protoplasm that has been suppressed by the evolution of the brain. That the brain is an organ not for generating consciousness but rather for transmitting, limiting, and directing it is a view that extends at least back to the German philosopher Kant, who wrote, "The body would thus be, not the cause of our thinking, but a condition restrictive thereof, and, although essential to our animal and sensuous consciousness, may be regarded as an impeder of pure spiritual life." The French philosopher, Henri Bergson (1914) further developed the theory that the brain is an organ of limitation and stated that each person is potentially aware of all his past experiences and of all concurrent events. He believed that, to prevent our being overwhelmed by useless knowledge, the brain suppresses all information except what is relevant to our present practical needs. Sigmund Freud (1933) wrote that telepathy "may be the original archaic method by which individuals understood one another, and which has been pushed into the background in the course of the phylogenetic development by the better method of communication by means of signs apprehended by the sense organs." The English psychologist Robert Thouless suggested that psi was probably the primitive way in which organisms managed to orientate themselves to their environment and that the evolution of sense organs was a subsequent evolutionary development of greater biological utility (Thouless & Wiesner, 1946). Similarly, the Swiss psychologist Theodore Flournoy (1900) postulated that motor organs evolved as more constant lines of force in place of a radiating influence possessed by cells and that acts of PK represent the momentary recovery of the use of these primitive forces of action at a distance.

In addition to being a product of evolution, psi may be a mechanism by which this process is brought about. The most widely accepted mechanism for evolution is neo-Darwinism. This theory is that (1) individuals possessing mutant genetic traits which make them more fit to survive and to reproduce in the struggle for existence are more likely to transmit these traits to the next generation through their germ cells than are less fit individuals, and

(2) because the next generation acquires more of its traits from the fitter individuals of the previous generation than from the less fit, the species evolves in the direction of superior adaptation to the environment. However, some scientists believe that chance mutation and natural selection are not sufficient to account for the apparent goal directed or purposive nature of evolution. To some Lamarckism or the inheritance of characteristics acquired from the environment offers a mechanism for purposive evolution. The British psychologist William McDougall found that a strain of white rats, which had been trained to avoid the lighted exit that gave them a moderate electric shock and to choose the unlighted way out of a water maze, required progressively fewer trials in successive generations to acquire this ability (J.B. Rhine, 1971b). McDougall concluded that this substantiated the theory of the inheritance of acquired characteristics. Rhine succeeded in replicating this finding; however, attempts by two others failed to do so. Perhaps, the positive results obtained by McDougall and by Rhine were paranormally caused by those experimenters.

The English biologist Sir Alister Hardy (1950) postulated that telepathy may be a factor in the evolution of structures which make a species more efficient in carrying out a new habit. As members of the species aided by mutual telepathy adopt a new behavior, for example tit birds removing milk bottle caps to get at the milk, gene combinations favorable to the new behavior pattern survive in preference to others. Through natural selection for these inheritable traits, tits became more efficient at removing milk bottle caps.

In addition to natural selection and mutation as mechanisms of evolution, psi may be a basic means by which evolution is accomplished, and not merely as an adjunct in the manner hypothesized by Hardy. Evolution may be paranormally brought about by the need-fulfilling, goal-oriented, and holistic nature of psi. Through paranormal action, members of a species may work as a whole (1) to produce preadaptive mutations whose eventual combinations within one or more individuals result in phenotypic characteristics that fulfill a need, (2) to cause the preferential survival of individuals to which these preadaptive mutations confer no survival value, and (3) to bring about mating between individuals possessing these mutations. This is not to imply that an individual produces a mutation which alters itself. That would be a logical impossibility, as a mutation occurs in a gamete, which precedes the formation of the individual. Instead, what is suggested is that members of the species paranormally cause mutations during gametogenesis, which lead to the production of beneficial phenotypic traits in individuals arising from those gametes. Psi as a mechanism of evolution does not negate chance mutation and natural selection as mechanisms in the evolutionary process. However, chance mutation and natural selection alone may be inadequate to explain the origin of such organs as the eye, which have no survival value in their early stages of evolution. As a mechanism of evolution, psi may provide the long-sought-for answer to the question of how such organs arise. In addition to mutation and natural selection, psi may constitute the third mechanism of evolution.

CONCLUSIONS

Psi appears to be unlimited by space, time, or physical causality; to act either precisely and specifically or without spatial and temporal precision; to lack reliability and durability; to require life or mind; to accomplish ends independently of the means; and to act holistically.

REVIEW QUESTIONS

1. If you fail to remember any of the following terms, ascertain its meaning with the aid of the glossary and the index: differential effect, negentropy, psi masking, quarter distribution, reinforcement, singularization.

2. Is psi nonphysical (give reasons for your answer) ?

3. What rates of ESP scoring have been reported?

4. Give possible causes of chronological decline in psi scoring.

5. How reliable and durable is psi?

6. What are the possible causes of psi missing?

7. Give possible causes of terminal salience.

8. Is ESP unconscious (give reasons for your answer) ?

9. What is the evidence that psi may be need fulfilling?

10. Give reasons for believing that ESP may function by activating a memory trace.

11. What reason is there for believing that ESP may be a two-step process?

12. What modifications of drawings have been observed when they are extrasensorially perceived?

13. In what part of the brain may ESP be located, and what is the evidence?

14. What evidence is there that psi acts diametrically?

15. What is meant by psi being goal oriented?

16. What is the evidence that psi may act holistically?

17. Is psi evolving to become more pronounced or to become less effective?

Chapter 14

THEORIES OF PSI

B ESIDES THE RELATIVE unrepeatability of psi, its lack of universal acceptance is due to the absence of a satisfactory theoretical explanation for it. Whether its true nature is adequately revealed by one of the following hypotheses, or whether it will be made intelligible only by some as yet unformulated theory is a matter of present speculation.

PSI THEORIES IN GENERAL

God's Action

According to the British philosopher George Berkeley, God causes every event in the world by willing it, and every happening in the universe is a thought in the mind of God. The objects which we see, touch, hear, etc. are presented to our minds directly by volitions of the divine mind. They are produced by the direct influence of God's mind upon our mind, which in modern terms would be called telepathy.

The chemist George Price, who suggested that the data of successful psi experiments may have been the product of fraudulent investigators (1955), later stated his belief that "God sometimes reveals to someone a little of what another is thinking, or of what is happening in a distance place, or of what will happen" (Ferguson, 1973, p. 318). The drawback to an explanation of ESP through the action of God is that it places the paranormal beyond the bounds of scientific inquiry. The same criticism may be made of several of the following psi hypotheses that are philosophical rather than scientific concepts and are not falsifiable by scientific methods.

Spirits and Postmortem Survival

Pope Benedict XIV (Haynes, 1970) wrote that St. Augustine attributed to an angelic messenger the dream of a young man he knew in Milan. The dream was that his dead father told him where to find the receipt for a debt already paid, and acting upon the dream, he found the receipt. St. Augustine also stated that an angel caused a lady to receive information in her dream that she wanted from the saint. James Hyslop (1918), Professor of Logic and Ethics at Columbia University, offered the hypothesis that a spirit may be the carrier of the mental state or stimulus which the percipient receives in telepathy and in clairvoyance. The Methodist clergyman C. Drayton Thomas (1928) explained precognition by the action of spirits who are endowed with greater inferential abilities than ourselves and who, after precognizing the future by means of these abilities, communicate that knowledge to us. Assuming the continued existence of the spirit after the death of the body, the question arises as to whether its inferential and psychic abilities are greater than when it inhabited the living body before its demise.

Some instances of each of the following possibly paranormal phenomena suggest the activity of spirits: Ouija board and planchette communication; automatic writing and cross-correspondences; xenoglossy and possession; apparitions, poltergeists, and haunting; and mediumship. However, each of these occurrences is also interpretable on the basis of the *super-ESP hypothesis* (Gauld, 1961). According to this hypothesis, such phenomena result from the use of a virtually unlimited range of ESP by living individuals, sometimes in combination with a personality constructed in the psychic's unconscious mind. With no known limits to ESP faculties, any document, object, or bit of human knowledge, even if it is only in someone's unconscious mind, may be accessible to the percipient. Because the existence of spirits has not been established, and because ESP and the human dramatizing ability are known facts, the super-ESP hypothesis may be more parsimonious than the *spirit hypothesis*. According to the principle of parsimony or Occam's razor, entities, e.g. spirits, should not be postulated to explain a phenomenon that can be accounted for without them.

Proponents of the spirit hypothesis, however, point out that ESP has not been shown to be capable of producing paranormal phenomena with the complexity of, for example, the cross-correspondences. According to them, it would require a sophistication of ESP far beyond that for which there is present evidence. They maintain that the spirit hypothesis requires fewer unsupported assumptions to explain certain paranormal phenomena than does the postulation that the psychic events are produced by complex paranormal interactions of minds at an unconscious level. They, therefore, hold that the super-ESP hypothesis is not as parsimonious as the spirit hypothesis.

Belief in postmortem survival is not in itself religious and may be subjected to scientific study. C.D. Broad (1958), Professor of Philosophy at Cambridge University, postulated a psychic factor of the mind that could persist after the death of the body and that carried some of the individual's personality traits and memories. This psi component might unite with the medium's brain and nervous system to form the basis of a temporary personality. It might slowly disintegrate and, on the basis of the fact that messages by automatic writing have been received as long as seven years after the death of the person from whom they purport to come (Lambert, 1971), the postulated temporary personality might be presumed to exist for that length of time. Such a slowly disintegrating complex might exist in addition to the spirit of the deceased individual. On the other hand, the chronological lessening of the clarity, strength, and frequence of communications from deceased individuals following their death may be accountable for by a decline in the psychic's memory of and interest in the communicator.

J.B. Rhine (1947) expressed the belief that the apparent freedom of the mind from spatial and temporal limitations, as indicated by the characteristics of ESP, suggests that the mind may not be entirely dependent upon the brain and that it may survive after the death and dissolution of this organ. He observed that parapsychology may be the science for religion, as biology is for medicine, and physics is for engineering.

Gardner Murphy (1945) suggested that the question of postmortem survival is wrongly phrased and that there is something incorrect about our approach to the time dimension and about

our conception of personality as a sharply defined thing that
either does or does not continue forward beyond a certain point
in time. According to Buddhist philosophy, there is no ego, no
self that is the subject of our varying experiences. The idea of
a separate individual self is an illusion, an intellectual concept
that has no reality. If the individual self does not exist before
death, it is a logical impossibility for it to survive death. There
can be no life after death if there is no life before death. If the
individual self is an illusion, the likelihood of its postmortem survival is not a valid question. On the other hand, if the separate-
ness of the self is an illusion and this illusion is destroyed by
death, cessation of life may result in the merging of the illusional
self into a greater whole. In this case, death would not be so
much a matter of failure of the individual to survive as it would
be a means of removing the illusional boundaries of his consciousness. Rather than annihilating the individual, death may destroy
the illusion of his individuality.

Extraterrestrial Intelligences and UFOs

The hypothesis that some paranormal phenomena are the
products of extraterrestrial intelligences may be an expression of
the times. Psychics have always sought an exterior source of their
ability. Externalization of responsibility for psi events appears
to facilitate their production. Jewish sensitives in the time of the
Old Testament interpreted some of their paranormal experiences
as being the voice of God. In the middle ages, psychic phenomena were commonly attributed to angels and demons, and in the
era of spiritualism, paranormal events were explained by actions
of spirits of the deceased. Today, with widespread interest in
space travel and the possibility of life on other planets, extraterrestrial intelligences may be a convenient external cause to which
the psychic can assign the responsibility for the paranormal phenomena with which he is associated. The psychics Uri Geller
(1975) and Ray Stanford (1974) expressed the belief that they
are under such influence.

On the other hand, there is some justification for this hypothesis, based on the enormous number of stars and planets in the

universe. The number of each may have a magnitude of 10^{22}. Since life evolved from inanimate matter on our planet in less than two billion years, it may be reasonable to conclude that it would also have evolved on other planets which provided suitable physical conditions. If only a very small percentage of planets have the requisite conditions for life, the number of life-inhabited planets in the universe would still be astronomical. It is not unreasonable to believe that the level of intelligence and technical development on an enormous number of these planets would so far exceed the level on our own that we would be of interest to their inhabitants as lower organisms are to us, and that such beings would be unable to relate to us in terms we could understand. The knowledge of psychic phenomena possessed by some extraterrestrial beings might so enormously exceed our own that they have developed techniques which liberate them from the spatial and temporal relations by which we are confined. Their UFOs or unidentified flying objects might traverse space instantaneously and might even be psychical rather than physical objects. On the other hand, the psychologist Scott Rogo (1977) believes that UFOs are semisubstantial and are psychically created by the minds of one or more of the percipients. Regardless of whether UFOs exist and have penetrated our atmosphere, the possibility of psychic communication from extraterrestrial intelligences remains a logical possibility.

Mind-Matter Theories

Dualistic interpretations of the nature of reality affirm the existence of both mind and matter. It is possible that mind is equal with matter or even primordial to it and that, in the latter case, matter is an evolutionary product of mind rather than mind arising from matter as the latter became more complex. The apparent dematerialization of physical objects through psi (Chap. 12) lends support to the position that mind is basic to matter. One dualistic explanation of the relationship of mind and matter is that of parallelism in which they are in preestablished harmony or presynchronization. According to this theory, it is the nature of spirit and matter to work together without interacting. However, parallelism does not explain why only certain minds and targets are presynchronized to produce paranormal phenomena, such as successful card calling, while others are not.

Another dualistic explanation is that of interactionism in which mind can affect matter and, in turn, be affected by it. Although interactionism is probably presently accepted by more parapsychologists as an explanation of psi than any other mind-matter theory, attempts to reveal how the paranormal interaction takes place have met with questionable success.

Because of the failure of dualistic ontologies to explain psi, it is appropriate to consider a *monistic* alternative. Modern science operates under the monistic theory of materialism in which mind either does not exist or is an epiphenomenon of the brain. However, empirical evidence suggests that psi is not bound by the limiting characteristics of space, time, and physical causality and that it can act beyond the brain. Some of the empirical observations of parapsychology are not consistent with materialistic monism.

A second monistic theory is that of idealism, in which matter is considered either not to exist or to be mind stuff. Although the empirical findings of parapsychology may be accounted for by this theory, it is difficult to explain by idealism the ostensible physical nature of commonly perceived objects. If, for example, a public object is considered to be merely a collection of sense data in the mind of the beholder, it is not clear how the sense data in the minds of several individuals simultaneously perceiving the object would be coordinated to produce its deceptive physical existence. However, if individuality is an illusion and mind is universal, this problem does not exist.

A third monistic theory to explain psi is that of neutral monism in which mind and matter are dual aspects of a neutral substance (Nash, 1976a). The neutral substance may be manifested either as mind, or as matter, or as both of them at the same time. Because the mental aspect of the neutral substance does not have extension in public space and time, information is transmitted between its elements instantaneously and without physical energy. In a psi event, information is transmitted through the substance between its manifestations, e.g. agent, physical object, and subject. Neutral monism has the advantages of being parsimoniously monistic and obviating the need for an explanation of how mind and matter interact.

Mind-Brain Interaction

The Englishmen R.H. Thouless and B.P. Wiesner (1947) hypothesized that in clairvoyance and in PK the mind of the subject acts to contact the object, while in telepathy the mind of the percipient contacts the brain of the agent or the mind of the agent contacts the brain of the percipient. They postulated that, in normal thinking or perceiving, the individual's mind is in the same sort of relation to what is occurring in the sensory part of his brain as the psychic's mind is in relation to an external event in ESP and that the connection is established by the same means, i.e. by psi gamma. Furthermore, the individual controls the activities of his nervous system by the same means as that by which the psychic controls the movement of an external object, i.e. by psi kappa.

The English astrophysicist Sir Arthur Eddington (1935) suggested that mind may act on the brain by influencing the structural constituents of the cortex within the range given by Heisenberg's *uncertainty principle*. According to this principle, the accuracy with which the position and the velocity of an elementary particle can both be determined is limited. Within limits established by Heisenberg, the elementary particle in the brain could be affected by the mind without the use of physical energy. Similarly, the Australian neurophysiologist Sir John Eccles (1953) postulated that a mental state such as the will can affect the brain by discharging a neuron poised at a critical level of excitability. In such a state the neuron can function as a detector with a sensibility of a different kind from that of any physical instrument. Within the limits of the uncertainty principle, it could be affected by the will without violating physical law.

Collective Mind

The idea of a cosmic consciousness or an absolute is an ancient mystical idea which has persisted into the age of science. The German philosopher Edward von Hartman (1885) suggested that in ESP the mind of the seer is in connection with the absolute and, through the absolute, with other individual minds. William James said, "there is a continuum of cosmic consciousness against which individuality builds but accidental fences, and into which our several minds plunge as into a mother sea or reservoir" (Murphy & Ballou, 1960). He believed that all individual minds are linked together by a common universal mind of which each individual mind, in a conscious state, is unaware but which is accessible to all subjects in a state of trance. Similar to cosmic consciousness is the concept of the Akashic records, a cosmic picture gallery and record of every thought, feeling, and action since the world began. It is a yoga belief that this record can be contacted when one is in certain psychic state of consciousness.

Frederic Myers (1903), in attempting to explain telepathy, presented the theory that each individual at a deep subliminal level is one with every other individual. Similarly, the German physician Rudolf Tischner (1925) hypothesized a super-individual subconscious mind that we gradually reach by descending from our surface consciousness and that could account for telepathy.

Whately Carington (1970) postulated a collective unconscious or group mind not only for the human but for each species of living animal. He conceived a group mind as a repository of those associations of ideas that are responsible for the instinctive behavior patterns peculiar to the species. In addition, he postulated that an idea or an object associated with sense data in one individual's mind might, if presented to another individual, cause those same sense data to arise in the latter's mind from their common unconscious (Carington, 1945). In the same vein, G.N.M. Tyrrell (1953) postulated the production of collective idea-patterns by the subconscious level of two or more minds, which could cause similar sense data to arise in each.

The American psychologist John Gowan (1975) theorized that ESP, including precognition, takes place by means of an impression on the collective unconscious, an undifferentiated ground of being or noumenon from which events can be caused by psi to be manifested in the space-time physical world. Intelligence is ephemerally particularized in the collective unconscious as individual egos that can paranormally escape restricted space-time with its physical laws by passing into an altered state of consciousness.

Universe a Unity

The concept that the universe is a unity and all of its parts are interdependent forms the basis of astrological beliefs. The astrologers believed that events in the macrocosm, the great world of stars and planets, are reflected in the microcosm, the small world of man, and vice versa. This belief led to the view of the alchemists that under the proper astrological influences a change of lead to gold might easily occur. Although paranormal phenomena are in no way dependent upon astrology for their explanation, the underlying concept of astrology and, for that matter, of quantum physics — that the universe is a unity with interdependent parts — is a view that could be used as an explanation of paranormal events. Energy is not required for information transfer between parts of a universe of undivided wholeness, because in such a universe there is no "here" and "there," no distance or travel, and all information is available at every point.

According to the bootstrap hypothesis of quantum field theory, subatomic particles are dynamically composed of one another (Chew, 1968). Each particle helps to generate other particles, which in turn generate it. The whole set of particles generates itself in this way or pulls itself up, so to speak, by its bootstraps. With each particle containing all the others, the universe would be a unity.

It has been hypothesized that the entire universe is a *hologram* (Mishlove, 1975, p. 233), which is a three-dimensional image formed by wave-interference patterns, the entire image being reconstructable from any portion of the hologram. If the universe were a hologram, it could be reconstructed from any one of its parts, and complete information concerning the universe would be contained in any of its elements. If all information is in some real sense present everywhere at any given moment, it could account for ESP. However, the hologram hypothesis appears to offer an analogy rather than a physical actuality.

The German philosopher Leibniz offered the theory that the universe is constituted of monads each of which has perception of the universe. He postulated that matter, even inanimate matter, has perception or, in modern terms, ESP. The perception, according to Leibniz, is due to psychophysical parallelism, i.e. presynchronization of mind and matter, rather than to interaction between mind and matter. A somewhat similar theory is that of primary perception, presented by Cleve Backster (1968), which holds that ESP is present in living organisms and in inanimate matter even down to the subatomic level. On the other hand, it may be that psi can occur only in an entity consisting of integrated living parts, such as a cell, an organism, a family, a nation, or an international society or religious body. It may be that psi can take place in any unit possessing living constituents that are interconnected by an integrating purpose. For example, the participants of a psi experiment may be integrated in their psi manifestation into an *autonomous* functional unit (Nash, 1974).

Seriality and Synchronicity

The Austrian biologist Paul Kammerer believed that coincidences are manifestations of a universal principle in nature, which he called *seriality* (Jung & Pauli, 1955) . It operates independently from physical causation and brings "like and like together." Such a principle, if it exists, could explain some paranormal phenomena.

Carl Jung believed that parapsychological phenomena are meaningful coincidences that result from an acausal order existing in the universe, which he called *synchronicity* (Jung & Pauli, 1955). As an example of synchronicity, he related an incident in which a woman described to him her dream of a scarab beetle and in which, at the moment of the description, a similar beetle appeared on his windowsill. He believed that the universe is so ordered that meaningful coincidences occur between unrelated events and that these coincidences account for what is called psi. He believed that synchronistic events, including those in psi experiments, are manifestations of an archetype or preformed pattern in the individual's racially inherited unconscious. In its emergence into consciousness or onto the physical plane, the archetype may split, and its parts be expressed as meaningful coincidence. If this is so, synchronized events have a common although nonphysical cause, i.e. the archetype, rather than being acausal as characterized by Jung.

The geneticist Lila Gatlin (1977) offered the hypothesis that psi phenomena are the result of matching similarly biased sources of information, such as living organisms, which causes extrachance resemblances between them. Their similarity could result from evolutionary processes, which increase the relative frequency of organisms with similar biases. Because of this, the matching of two randomly selected sources of information tends to produce extrachance results. According to Gatlin, such correspondences between two sources are acausal but meaningful coincidences. However, Jung and Gatlin to the contrary, when two events or objects have a common cause, whether the cause is the splitting of an archetype or whether it is evolution, the principle of parsimony is better served by attributing extrachance similarities between the events to their common cause than by postulating the existence in the universe of an acausal order of meaningful coincidence. The postulation of common cause in place of acausal meaningful coincidence does not indicate that all or, indeed, any paranormal events are engendered by this means. However, it replaces the mystical concept of synchronicity with the rational relationship of cause and effect.

The American philosopher Frederick Dommeyer (1977) hypothesized that psi in some instances may be entirely acausal, as when two events show a statistically significant coincidence without one causing the other and without their having a common cause.

Alteration of Probability

Helmut Schmidt (1975b) hypothesized that psi acts by a psi source, e.g. a subject, affecting the probability of an event that is rewarding to the psi source. If the psi source is a human subject, the reward could be simply a success indication, e.g. a confirmation of a hit.

Conformance Behavior

Rex Stanford (1977b) offered the somewhat similar hypothesis that psi tends to occur when there is a need for the subject to conform to the object, as in ESP, or for the object to conform to the subject, as in PK. When a need or a disposition exists, an order will tend to develop out of randomness that favors the occurrence of an event answering the need. Psi is the tendency for events to occur that conform to the needs of the organism.

Actualization of Potentialities

According to J.H.M. Whiteman (1977), Professor of Mathematics at the University of Cape Town, objects are potentialities for observation and can exist not only at the physical level but also at thought-image and ideal-purposive levels. A paranormal event is the actualization of physical and nonphysical potentialities conjointly in the physical sphere and in the subjects' thought-image sphere according to direction from the ideal-purposive level, all of the levels being linked by correspondences.

Psi Fields

The British mathematician G.D. Wassermann postulated the transmission of information by psi fields composed of hypothetical quanta so small that they do not interact with matter (Wolstenholme & Millar, 1956). Such psi fields can radiate their energy over long distances without the quanta being absorbed by matter. These psi fields are postulated to interact with behavior fields comparable to electromagnetic fields, which in turn interact with a brain or an inanimate object and, in this way, convey psi information. In evaluating this hypothesis, it should be kept in mind that the small quanta and the behavior fields are hypothetical.

William Roll (1957) postulated that every object, whether animate or inanimate, possesses a psi field that is analagous to an electromagnetic or gravitational field. In the case of ESP, a physical or mental event at the target is copied in the target's psi field. This copy is thence communicated over a channel of intermediary psi fields to the psi field of the percipient, where it interacts with his brain to produce an instance of ESP. In addition to transmitting information and energy to other psi fields, which could result in PK, a psi field is postulated to store information and thus to act as a memory record. Psychometry and haunted houses could result from the percipient's psi field interacting with the memory-stored psi field of the physical object or of the haunted house.

Somewhat similarly, Sir Cyril Burt (1968), Professor of Psychology at Oxford University, proposed the existence of mental fields that intersect to cause ESP. According to his hypothesis, the individual's mind is a kind of Leibnizian monad, an elementary particle that he termed a psychon. The psychon manifests itself as a center of an active psychic field, composed of subsidiary particles constantly interacting with the individual's brain. He suggested that an exchange of these mind particles can take place between the psychon of one individual and either the psychon or the brain of another, thereby providing ESP.

Psychic Ether

Frederic Myers (1903) postulated something intermediate between mind and matter, which he called the metetherial. It is in some sense material because it is extended in space and yet has some of the properties commonly attributed to minds. C.A. Mace (1937), Professor of Psychology at Birkbeck College in London, used the term *psychic ether* for this substantial medium, which propagates thought waves, records impressions of patterns of events, and later may produce a corresponding pattern. H.H. Price (1939) postulated that persistent and dynamic entities may exist in the psychic ether, which might be an ether of images in a common unconscious. The images could persist and interact regardless of the mind in which they originated. Such a persistent image might be tied down to a physical place, might act telepathically on a percipient near this place, and might cause him to see an apparition, thus explaining hauntings. Hornell Hart (1956) advanced the hypothesis that every physical body has an etheric counterpart, which the observer sees, if at all, with his own etheric vehicle.

Electromagnetic Waves

Julian Ochorowicz (1887) postulated that telepathic phenomena are the result of electromagnetic waves produced by the brain of the agent and received by the brain of the percipient. Sir William Crookes (1897) presented a similar hypothesis. Brain waves were finally identified by the German neurophysiologist Hans Berger in 1928. However, because they cannot be registered at a distance greater than a few millimeters from the head, he proposed instead that telepathy is accomplished by psychical waves (Berger, 1940). The Russian scientist I.M. Kogan (1967) suggested that ESP is mediated by extremely low frequency (ELF) electromagnetic waves. Michael Persinger (1975) suggested that ELF waves are used in PK as well as in ESP. These waves surround the earth and, although not generated by the brain, are postulated to be utilized by changes of the brain's electrical potential to produce paranormal phenomena. ELF waves are not stopped by a Faraday cage and travel completely around the earth with almost no attenuation. Hence, their use as psimediators avoids the failure of ESP to be hindered by a Faraday cage or by distance. It is theoretically possible that brain activity of the sender could be transduced into electromagnetic waves and that these electromagnetic waves could be transduced into brain activity of the percipient, thereby accounting for telepathy. However, it is not apparent how electromagnetic waves that can penetrate a Faraday cage could sufficiently interact with matter to mediate psi, or how they could account for clairvoyance or for precognition.

Resonance

The British theorist Ninian Marshall (1960) postulated that two complex structures with a sufficient degree of similarity, such as two human brains, can act on one another by some kind of direct resonance or sympathetic vibration without any continuous chain of intervening events or any transmission of energy. It appears that such an hypothesis is unfalsifiable.

Elementary Particles

Several physical or quasi-physical elementary particles have been postulated as the means by which psi operates. The German theorist A. Forel (1918) suggested that ESP is conveyed by means of electrons that travel to the brain of the percipient from the brain of the agent or from the extrasensorially perceived object. The American engineer A. L. Hammond (1952) postulated that the neutrino is the carrier of psi. The neutrino may be the most ghostlike of all the elementary particles as it has virtually no physical properties — no mass, no electric charge, no magnetic field. A neutrino travels with the speed of light and can go entirely through the solid body of the earth as if it were so much empty space.

Haakon Forwald (1969) suggested that PK might be carried out by means of neutrons, but that it is more likely to be accomplished by the mind of the agent affecting the object by means of gravitation, possibly by gravitons that have not yet been discovered. On the other hand, Andrija Puharich (1973) postulated that psi takes place by means of information carried by protons.

Tachyons, particles with an imaginary mass and traveling with a velocity greater than that of light, have been considered as possible carriers of ESP information (Chari, 1974). The British theorist Peter Maddock (1975) expressed belief that tachyons interact with biological macromolecules in neurons, enabling the brain to function as a sender or as a receiver of telepathic information. The British mathematician Adrian Dobbs (1965) proposed the existence of similar particles, called psitrons, as bearers of ESP information. As they have mathematically imaginary mass, they can traverse space with a velocity exceeding that of light without frictional loss of energy. If captured by critically poised neurons in the percipient's brain, they might then trigger off a chain reaction of neuron discharge.

The postulation of particles that are not intercepted by matter avoids the difficulties afforded the electromagnetic-wave hypothesis by the ineffectiveness of physical shields and the absence of distance attenuation. However, it is not apparent how particles that are not stopped by matter could be stopped by the percipient's brain. As carriers of psi, the postulation of quarks, the theoretical elementary particles of which protons and neutrons are composed (Nambu, 1977), may avoid the difficulty of accounting for the absence of psi's attenuation with distance, because the force between quarks may not decrease with distance. However, the constant force between quarks may result in their being permanently bound within the protons and neutrons, which would prevent their movement outside of the particles they constitute and prevent their carrying information beyond those narrow confines.

Bioplasma

A mixture of electrons and photons woven into an energy network and called *bioplasma* was proposed by the Soviet scientist Victor Inyushin (1970) as an energy counterpart of the living body. It is postulated that bioplasma determines the structure of the living body, although it is capable of existing beyond the physical boundaries of the latter. The Soviet neurophysiologist Genady Sergeyev (1970) hypothesized that under certain conditions bioplasma could be the cause of PK. It has also been postulated as the means by which ESP or, as the Soviets call it, biological communication takes place (Sedlak, 1975). The existence of bioplasma is questionable, and its *modus operandi* in psi has not been sufficiently formulated to warrant serious consideration.

Antimatter

The American theorist J.C. Russell (1973) suggested antimatter, which is a recognized physical entity, as an explanation of psi. By releasing persons from the limitations of matter, it may produce telepathy, clairvoyance, precognition, PK, dematerialization, and levitation and might produce a psychic existence in the form of apparitions. Antimatter can exist only momentarily in contiguity with matter because they annihilate each other upon coming in contact. This affords serious difficulty for the hypothesis of antimatter as a carrier of psi information.

Quantum Theory

In *quantum mechanics* a physical system, e.g. an atom, has an infinite number of states that are continuous, are spread out in space, and compose a state vector or wave function called *psi* (not to be confused with the psi of parapsychology). The physical system is not in one of these states alone but in the totality simultaneously. When measurement is carried out on the physical system, it undergoes a sudden discontinuous change — a collapse or reduction of the state vector or wave packet into one of its component states. Only when a measurement is performed — that is, when it is observed — does the physical system enter a single one of its component states. No energy is transferred in this process.

The American physicist Evan Walker (1975) identified the combined consciousness of the coupled observers with the hidden variables that are believed by some quantum physicists to be responsible for state-vector collapse. The consciousness of the subject and the consciousness of the experimenter are hypothesized to act together to select the particular state into which the wave function of the subject's brain and/or the wave function of the target, e.g. a card or die, are collapsed. Among those possible states of the subject's brain and of the target is one in which the call and the target are alike. Because the hidden variables are independent of space and time, they can effect the collapse of state vectors of systems that are spatially and temporally separate. Thus, equating the combined consciousness of the observers with the hidden variables provides an explanation for ESP at a distance, precognition, and PK. It would be but a step further in quantum theory to conclude that quantum events cannot occur without an observer and that they are the products of observing consciousness. Should physics take this step, it would find that its basis in the scientific hierarchy was constituted by the science of psychics.

PRECOGNITION THEORIES

Some of the psi theories that were previously described provide explanations of precognition as well as of other modalities of psi. The following are hypotheses specifically of precognition.

Prediction by Contemporaneous ESP

Instead of the ostensibly precognized event being precognized, it may be predicted by inferences made with the use of contemporaneous ESP (Nash, 1951). Some events, however, such as in precognition experiments with cards, have been predicted with an accuracy which exceeds what might be reasonably accounted for by the use of contemporaneous ESP.

Predicted Event Caused to Occur

The ostensibly precognized event may not be precognized but instead may be predicted and then caused to occur. It may be brought about by normal means or, as postulated by the Greek physician A. Tanagras (1949), it may be caused by means of PK. According to the quantum mechanical theory of psi, the predicted event is undetermined until the instant it is observed, at which moment the wave packet is collapsed to produce the predicted occurrence. The observers' minds, which collapse the wave packet, are postulated to act as hidden variables that are independent of space and time (Walker, 1975). They could cause the collapse of the wave packet of the predicted event.

The theorist I.J. Good (1963) postulated that the universe branches into myriads of distinct universes in each infinitesimal fraction of a second. To make an ordinary observation is to reduce the possible universes to the one in which we personally belong from that instant. The psychic perceives the possibilities extrasensorially and makes a selection of one of them.

Specious Present

The English psychical researcher H.F. Saltmarsh (1938) suggested that the present moment occupies a certain length of time called the specious present. If the specious present of a percipient's unconscious mind is longer than that of his conscious mind, an event in the future of his conscious mind could be a present event in his unconscious mind. If some of this knowledge rose up into conscious awareness, it would be interpreted as precognitive. A weakness of this hypothesis is the extreme length of time the specious present would have to occupy, some experiments indicating precognition of the events as long as one and one-half years in the future (Nash, 1960a).

ESP of Probabilities of Future Outcomes

According to Adrian Dobbs (1965), probabilities of future outcomes have an objective existence in a second dimension of time. These probabilities, by means of hypothetical positrons (particles with imaginary mass and traveling faster than the speed of light), transmit their information to the brain of the percipient, who then makes a precast, which has a probability of transpiring appropriate to the objective probability which caused it.

Advanced Wave

The theorist C. Mùses (1972) postulated that a precursor wave precedes an event such as the turning on of a light bulb. Similarly, the American physicist Gerald Feinberg (1975) suggested, on the basis of time symmetry, that an advanced wave travels backwards in time preceding the event that caused it, in addition to the retarded wave which propagates forwards in time. In the same vein, the Australians James Donald and Brian Martin (1976) postulated the existence of past-directed negentropy, which, by transmitting energy or information from the future to the present, could account for precognition.

Positrons

The American Nobel laureate Richard Feynmann (1949) proposed that positrons are electrons traveling backwards in time. If so, positrons may be carriers of psi information from the future into the present and, by impinging on the percipient's brain, make precognition possible. Dobbs (1965) postulated that precognition may be accounted for by a particle that, like a positron, moves backwards in time.

Extra Time-Dimensions

According to relativity theory, in which time is a fourth dimension, an event lying in the future of one observer may have already transpired with respect to a different observer of the same event. The British mathematician Charles Hinton (1904) thought of time as a fourth dimension with all objects and events — past, present and future — being spread out along the time dimension. He thought of our human consciousness as a film which moves along the time dimension from the cradle to the grave. According to this concept, both past and future events exist in the eternal present of a universe that is static except for the moving film of human consciousness.

Similarly, the Irish aeronautical engineer J.W. Dunne (1927) postulated that human beings are perceptually conscious at any moment of only a three-dimensional cross-section of this four-dimensional world. As moment succeeds moment, the observer becomes consecutively aware of another and another three-dimensional cross-section, so that in effect he seems to travel along the fourth dimension of the manifold. The effect of perceiving this series of cross-sections, each of which differs to a certain extent from that preceding it, produces the illusion that there is a three-dimensional world enduring in time and that parts of it are in motion. In periods when the normal consciousness is not active, a second observing consciousness of the same individual is free to flit backwards and forwards in this fourth dimension. The second consciousness is not only able to relive the past life of the normal consciousness, but it can precognize events in the future. Dunne presumed that the second observing consciousness must have time or a fifth dimension of space in which to move, and so on into an infinite series of observers and times. However, the Cambridge philosopher C.D. Broad pointed out that such an infinite series is not necessary to explain precognition along these lines, but only two time-dimensions are needed (Broad & Price, 1937).

World Lines

In a diagram of the conventional three-dimensional universe, an elementary particle is represented by a dot. However, in the four-dimensional, space-time continuum of Einstein and Minkowski, an elementary particle is depicted by a line. A part of this world line represents the past positions of the particle and another part represents its future positions in the four-dimensional universe. Nash (1963b) suggested that world lines, connecting the human brain with events that are remote in space and time, provide the basis of psi. By displacement of world lines within the limits of Heisenberg's uncertainty principle, information concerning the state of a target particle is transmitted to a particle in the percipient's brain without the use of energy. Through causality operating in reverse, information concerning the future state of an object is transmitted by displacement of world lines to the brain of the percipient. In PK, the effect originates in brain particles and passes by way of world lines to particles in the affected external object.

Folds in a Space-Time Matrix

Gertrude Schmeidler (1971) suggested the existence of an extra dimension through which the space-time matrix can be folded. Objects distant in space from each other could thereby be placed in continguity and, because there would be no distance between them, there would be no transmission across space. Thus the failure of psi to decrease with distance would be accounted for. It might also be postulated that temporally separated events could be placed in contiguity by such topological folding, thereby accounting for precognition because no transmission across time would be required.

PK THEORIES

Some of the psi theories described earlier in this chapter provide explanations of PK as well as of ESP. The following theories are specific for PK.

Nash (1955) suggested that Heisenberg's uncertainty principle may provide a means whereby PK could direct the movement of an elementary particle and, thereby, could influence a randomly moving molar body such as a rolling die at a moment of unstable equilibrium without the use of energy. Forwald (1961), on the other hand, expressed the belief that PK works during the whole process of the movement of the die by the mind of the subject affecting the object through gravitation possibly by gravitons, which have not yet been discovered. Empirical evidence suggesting that PK is independent of space and time is not conducive to the likelihood that its basis lies in the physical realm as the latter is presently conceived. Even if PK is nonphysical, it may sometimes utilize elementary particles or electromagnetic waves that have no contact with the subject and are spatially or temporally distant from him to produce an effect on the target object.

According to R.D. Mattuck (1977) of the University of Copenhagen, PK influences matter by utilizing the random fluctuations or "noise" occurring in the physical variables used to describe matter, such as position, velocity, voltage, magnetic field, and temperature. By supplying information directly to matter, the mind temporarily nonrandomizes the noise, causing the physical variables to attain values far above the ordinary noise level. This seems to be a variation of Maxwell's hypothetical demon, who could produce useful energy if he had the capacity to separate molecules according to their speed of motion.

In a quantum-mechanical explanation of PK, the mind of the psychic causes the collapse of the wave packet of the desired event (Walker, 1975). In quantum-field theory, elementary particles of energy and matter can arise from or be annhilated into the vacuum state. Some PK effects may be accounted for in this way.

CONCLUSIONS

It is a safe prediction that, whatever theoretical basis for psi becomes scientifically accepted, it will be modified and replaced through a succession of deeper insights into the nature of reality. A universe with psi is very different from a universe without a paranormal aspect. If, as some paranormal phenomena suggest, mind is on a par with or even underlies matter, the universe can no longer be considered to be a void, inhabited solely by a relatively infinitesimal amount of irregularly distributed matter. Instead the macrocosm takes the form of a multiplicity of holistically related events each of which occurs at the moment it is observed, the observations being spatially and temporally independent of the location of the observers whose minds are coupled into a single unit. Perhaps, there is but one mind, the universe consisting of it and the observations it makes. The relationship between God and such a universe is a theological rather than a parapsychological question.

REVIEW QUESTIONS

1. If you fail to remember any of the following terms, ascertain its meaning with the aid of the glossary and the index: autonomous, bioplasma, dualism, hologram, monism, psi field, quantum mechanics, seriality, synchronicity, uncertainty principle.

2. Distinguish between the spirit hypothesis and the super-ESP hypothesis.

3. What are the weaknesses of physical explanations of ESP by electromagnetic waves and by elementary particles?

4. Give a quantum-mechanical explanation of psi, and a quantum-field explanation of PK.

5. Explain precognition by each of the following hypotheses: extra time-dimensions, folds in space-time matrix, world lines.

APPENDICES

APPENDIX I

TABLE I

RANDOM DIGITS

11164	36318	75061	37674	26320	75100	10431	20418	19228	91792
21215	91791	76831	58678	87054	31687	93205	43685	19732	08468
10438	44482	66558	37649	08882	90870	12462	41810	01806	02977
36792	26236	33266	66583	60881	97395	20461	36742	02852	50564
73944	04773	12032	51414	82384	38370	00249	80709	72605	67497
49563	12872	14063	93104	78483	72717	68714	18048	25005	04151
64208	48237	41701	73117	33242	42314	83049	21933	92813	04763
51486	72875	38605	29341	80749	80151	33835	52602	79147	08868
99756	26360	64516	17971	48478	09610	04638	17141	09227	10606
71325	55217	13015	72907	00431	45117	33827	92873	02953	85474
65285	97198	12138	53010	94601	15838	16805	61004	43516	17020
17264	57327	38224	29301	31381	38109	34976	65692	98566	29550
95639	99754	31199	92558	68368	04985	51092	37780	40261	14479
61555	76404	82610	11808	12841	45147	97438	60022	12645	62000
78137	98768	04689	87130	79225	08153	84967	64539	79493	74917
62490	99215	84987	28759	19177	14733	24550	28067	68894	38490
24216	63444	21283	07044	92729	37284	13211	37485	10415	36457
16975	95428	33226	55903	31605	43817	22250	03918	46999	98501
59138	39542	71168	57609	91510	77904	74244	50940	31553	62562
29478	59652	50414	31966	87912	87154	12944	49862	96566	48824
96155	95009	27429	72918	08457	78134	48407	26061	58754	05326
29621	66583	62966	12468	20245	14015	04014	35713	03980	03024
12639	75291	71020	17265	41598	64074	64629	63293	53307	48766
14544	37134	54714	02401	63228	26831	19386	15457	17999	18306
83403	88827	09834	11333	68431	31706	26652	04711	34593	22561
67642	05204	30697	44806	96989	68403	85621	45556	35434	09532
64041	99011	14610	40273	09482	62864	01573	82274	81446	32477
17048	94523	97444	59904	16936	39384	97551	09620	63932	03091
93039	89416	52795	10631	09728	68202	20963	02477	55494	39563
82244	34392	96607	17220	51984	10753	76272	50985	97593	34320
96990	55244	70693	25255	40029	23289	48819	07159	60172	81697
09119	74803	97303	88701	51380	73143	98251	78635	27556	20712
57666	41204	47589	78364	38266	94393	70713	53388	79865	92069
46492	61594	26729	58272	81754	14648	77210	12923	53712	87771
08433	19172	08320	20839	13715	10597	17234	39355	74816	03363
10011	75004	86054	41190	10061	19660	03500	68412	57812	57929
92420	65431	16530	05547	10683	88102	30176	84750	10155	69220
35542	55865	07304	47010	43233	57022	52161	82976	47981	46588
86595	26247	18552	29491	33712	32285	64844	69395	41387	87195
72115	34985	58036	99137	47482	06204	24138	24272	16196	04393
07428	58863	96023	88936	51343	70958	96768	74317	27176	29600
35379	27922	28906	55013	26937	48174	04197	36074	65315	12537
10982	22807	10920	26299	23593	64629	57801	10437	43965	15344
90127	33341	77806	12446	15444	49244	47277	11346	15884	28131
63002	12990	23510	68774	48983	20481	59815	67248	17076	78910
40779	86382	48454	65269	91239	45989	45389	54847	77919	41105
43216	12608	18167	84631	94058	82458	15139	76856	86019	47928
96167	64375	74108	93643	09204	98855	59051	56492	11933	64958
70975	62693	35684	72607	23026	37004	32989	24843	01128	74658
85812	61875	23570	75754	29090	40264	80399	47254	40135	69911

Table I. From *A Million Random Digits with 100,000 Normal Deviates.*
Courtesy of the Rand Corporation.

TABLE I – *Continued*

37100	62492	63642	47638	13925	80113	88067	42575	44078	62703
53406	13855	38519	29500	62479	01036	87964	44498	07793	21599
55172	81556	18856	59043	64315	38270	25677	01965	21310	28115
40353	84807	47767	46890	16053	32415	60259	99788	55924	22077
18899	09612	77541	57675	70153	41179	97535	82889	27214	03482
68141	25340	92551	11326	60939	79355	41544	88926	09111	86431
51599	91159	81310	63251	91799	41215	87412	35317	74271	11603
92214	33386	73459	79359	65867	39269	57527	69551	17495	91456
15098	50557	33166	87904	52425	21211	41876	42525	36625	63964
96461	00604	11120	22254	16763	19206	67790	88362	01880	37911
28177	44111	15705	73835	69399	33602	13660	84342	97667	80847
66953	44737	81127	07493	07861	12666	85077	95972	96556	80108
19712	27263	84575	49820	19837	69985	34931	67935	71903	82560
68756	64757	19987	92222	11691	42502	00952	47981	97579	93408
75022	65332	98606	29451	57349	39219	08585	31502	96936	96356
11323	70069	90269	89266	46413	61615	66447	49751	15836	97343
55208	63470	18158	25283	19335	53893	87746	74531	16826	52605
11474	08786	05594	67045	13231	51186	71500	50498	59487	48677
81422	86842	60997	79669	43804	78690	58358	87639	24427	66799
21771	75963	23151	90274	08275	50677	99384	94022	84888	80139
42278	12160	32576	14278	34221	20724	27908	02657	19023	07190
17697	60114	63247	32096	32503	04923	17570	73243	76181	99343
05686	30243	34124	02936	71749	03031	72259	26351	77511	00850
52992	46650	89910	57395	39502	49738	87854	71066	84596	33115
94518	93984	81478	67750	89354	01080	25988	84359	31088	13655
00184	72186	78906	75480	71140	15199	69002	08374	22126	23555
87462	63165	79816	61630	50140	95319	79205	79202	67414	60805
88692	58716	12273	48176	86038	78474	76730	82931	51595	20747
20094	42962	41382	16768	13261	13510	04822	96354	72001	68642
60935	81504	50520	82153	27892	18029	79663	44146	72876	67843
51392	85936	43898	50596	81121	98122	69196	54271	12059	62539
54239	41918	79526	46274	24853	67165	12011	04923	20273	89405
57892	73394	07160	90262	48731	46648	70977	58262	78359	50436
02330	74736	53274	44468	53616	35794	54838	39114	68302	26855
76115	29247	55342	51299	79908	36613	68361	18864	13419	34950
63312	81886	29085	20101	38037	34742	78364	39356	40006	49800
27632	21570	34274	56426	00330	07117	86673	46455	66866	76374
06335	62111	44014	52567	79480	45886	92585	87828	17376	35254
64142	87676	21358	88773	10604	62834	63971	03989	21421	76086
28436	25468	75235	75370	63543	76266	27745	31714	04219	00699
09522	83855	85973	15888	29554	17995	37443	11461	42909	32634
93714	15414	93712	02742	34395	21929	38928	31205	01838	60000
15681	53599	58185	73840	88758	10618	98725	23146	13521	47905
77712	23914	08907	43768	10304	61405	53986	61116	76164	54948
78453	54844	61509	01245	91199	07482	02534	08189	62978	55516
24860	68284	19367	29073	93464	06714	45268	60678	58506	23700
37284	06844	78887	57276	42695	03682	83240	09744	63025	60997
35488	52473	37634	32569	39590	27379	23520	29714	03743	08444
51595	59909	35223	44991	29830	56614	59661	83397	38421	17503
90660	35171	30021	91120	78793	16827	89320	08260	09181	53622

TABLE I – *Continued*

54723	56527	53076	38235	42780	22716	36400	48028	78196	92985
84828	81248	25548	34075	43459	44628	21866	90350	82264	20478
65799	01914	81363	05173	23674	41774	25154	73003	87031	94368
87917	38549	48213	71708	92035	92527	55484	32274	87918	22455
26907	88173	71189	28377	13785	87469	35647	19695	33401	51998
68052	65422	88460	06352	42379	55499	60469	76931	83430	24560
42587	68149	88147	99700	56124	53229	38726	63652	36644	50876
97176	55416	67642	05051	89931	19482	80720	48977	70004	03664
53295	87133	38264	94708	00703	35991	76404	82249	22942	49659
23011	94108	29196	65187	69974	01970	31667	54307	40032.	30031
75768	49549	24543	63285	32803	18301	80851	89301	02398	99891
86668	70341	66460	75648	78678	27770	30245	44775	56120	44235
56727	72036	50347	33521	05068	47248	67832	30960	95465	32217
27936	78010	09617	04408	18954	61862	64547	52453	83213	47833
31994	69072	37354	93025	38934	90219	91148	62757	51703	84040
02985	95303	15182	50166	11752	56256	89546	31170	87221	63267
89965	10206	95830	95406	33845	87588	70237	84360	19629	72568
45587	29611	98579	42481	05359	36578	56047	68114	58583	16313
01071	08530	74305	77509	16270	20889	99753	88035	55643	18291
90209	68521	14293	39194	68803	32052	39413	26883	83119	69623
04982	68470	27875	15480	13206	44784	83601	03172	07817	01520
19740	24637	97377	32112	74283	69384	49768	64141	02024	85380
50197	79869	86497	68709	42073	28498	82750	43571	77075	07123
46954	67536	28968	81936	95999	04319	09932	66223	45491	69503
82549	62676	31123	49899	70512	95288	15517	85352	21987	08669
61798	81600	80018	84742	06103	60786	01408	75967	29948	21454
57666	29055	46518	01487	30136	14349	56159	47408	78311	25896
29805	64994	66872	62230	41385	58066	96600	99301	85976	84194
06711	34939	19599	76247	87879	97114	74314	39599	43544	36255
13934	46885	58315	88366	06138	37923	11192	90757	10831	01580
28549	98327	99943	25377	17628	65468	07875	16728	22602	33892
40871	61803	25767	55484	90997	86941	64027	01020	39518	34693
47704	38355	71708	80117	11361	88875	22315	38048	42891	87885
62611	19698	09304	29265	07636	08508	23773	56546	08015	28891
03047	83981	11916	09267	67316	87952	27045	62536	32180	60936
26460	50501	31731	18938	11025	18515	31747	96828	58258	97107
01764	25959	69293	89875	72710	49659	66632	25314	95260	22146
11762	54806	02651	52912	32770	64507	59090	01275	47624	16124
31736	31695	11523	64213	91190	10145	34231	36405	65860	48771
97155	48706	52239	21831	49043	18650	72246	43729	63368	53822
31181	49672	17237	04024	65324	32460	01566	67342	94986	36106
32115	82683	67182	89030	41370	50266	19505	57724	93358	49445
07068	75947	71743	69285	30395	81818	36125	52055	20289	16911
26622	74184	75166	96748	34729	61289	36908	73686	84641	45130
02805	52676	22519	47848	68210	23954	63085	87729	14176	45410
32301	58701	04193	30142	99779	21697	05059	26684	65312	75925
26339	56909	39331	42101	01031	01947	02257	47236	19913	90371
95274	09508	81012	42413	11278	19354	68661	04192	36878	84366
24275	39632	09777	98800	48027	96908	08177	15364	02317	89548
36116	42128	65401	94199	51058	10759	47244	99830	64255	40550

TABLE I – *Continued*

40603	16152	83235	37361	98783	24838	39793	80954	76865	32713
40941	53585	69958	60916	70108	90561	84505	53980	64735	85140
73505	83472	55953	17957	11446	22618	34771	25777	27064	13526
39412	15013	11442	89320	11307	49396	39805	12249	57656	88686
57994	76748	54627	48511	78646	33287	35524	54522	08795	56273
61834	59199	15469	82285	84164	91333	90954	87186	31598	25942
91402	77227	79516	21007	58602	81418	87838	18443	76162	51146
58299	83880	20125	10794	37780	61705	18276	99041	78135	99661
40684	99948	33880	76413	63839	71371	32392	51812	48248	96419
75978	64298	08074	62055	73864	01926	78374	15741	74452	49954
34556	39861	88267	76068	62445	64361	78685	24246	27027	48239
65990	57048	25067	77571	77974	37634	81564	98608	37224	49848
16381	15069	25416	87875	90374	86203	29677	82543	37554	89179
52458	88880	78352	67913	09245	47773	51272	06976	99571	33365
33007	85607	92008	44897	24964	50559	79549	85658	96865	24186
38712	31512	08588	61490	72294	42862	87334	05866	66269	43158
58722	03678	19186	69602	34625	75958	56869	17907	81867	11535
26188	69497	51351	47799	20477	71786	52560	66827	79419	70886
12893	54048	07225	86149	99090	70958	50775	31768	52903	27645
33186	81346	85095	37283	85536	72661	32180	40229	19209	74939
79893	29448	88392	54211	61708	83452	61227	81690	42265	20310
48449	15102	44126	19438	23382	14985	37538	30120	82443	11152
94205	04259	68983	50561	06902	10269	22216	70210	60736	58772
38648	09278	81313	77400	41126	52614	93613	27263	99381	49500
04292	46028	75666	26954	34979	68381	45154	09314	81009	05114
17026	49737	85875	12139	59391	81830	30185	83095	78752	40899
40870	76848	02531	97737	10151	18169	31709	74842	85522	74092
30159	95450	83778	46115	99178	97718	98440	15076	21199	20492
12148	92231	31361	60650	54695	30035	22765	91386	70399	79270
73838	77067	24863	97576	01139	54219	02959	45696	98103	78867
73547	43759	95632	39555	74391	07579	69491	02647	17050	49869
07277	93217	79421	21769	83572	48019	17327	99638	87035	89300
65128	48334	07493	28098	52087	55519	83718	60904	48721	17522
38716	61380	60212	05099	21210	22052	01780	36813	19528	07727
31921	76458	73720	08657	74922	61335	41690	41967	50691	30508
57238	27464	61487	52329	26150	79991	64398	91273	26824	94827
24219	41090	08531	61578	08236	41140	76335	91189	63312	44000
31309	49387	02330	02476	96074	33256	48554	95401	02642	29119
20750	97024	72619	66628	66509	31206	55293	24249	02266	39010
28537	84395	26654	37851	80590	53346	34385	86893	87713	26842
97929	41220	86431	94485	28778	44997	38802	56594	61366	04206
40568	33222	40486	91122	43294	94541	40988	02929	83190	74247
41483	92935	17061	78252	40498	43164	68646	33023	64333	64083
93040	66476	24990	41099	65135	37641	97613	87282	63693	55299
76869	39300	84978	07504	36835	72748	47644	48542	25076	68626
02982	57991	50765	91930	21375	35604	29963	13738	03155	59914
94479	76500	39170	06629	10031	48724	49822	44021	44335	26474
52291	75822	95966	90947	65031	75913	52654	63377	70664	60082
03684	03600	52831	55381	97013	19993	41295	29118	18710	64851
58939	28366	86765	67465	45421	74228	01095	50987	83833	37276

TABLE II
PROBABILITY VALUES OF *CR* OR *z* SCORE IN A TWO-TAILED TEST
p value

ev. / or σ	.00	.01	.02	.03	.04	.05	.06	.07	.08	.09
.0	1.0000	.9920	.9840	.9761	.9681	.9601	.9522	.9442	.9362	.9283
.1	.9203	.9124	.9045	.8966	.8887	.8808	.8729	.8650	.8572	.8493
.2	.8415	.8337	.8259	.8181	.8103	.8026	.7949	.7872	.7795	.7718
.3	.7642	.7566	.7490	.7414	.7339	.7263	.7188	.7114	.7039	.6965
.4	.6892	.6818	.6745	.6672	.6599	.6527	.6455	.6384	.6312	.6241
.5	.6171	.6101	.6031	.5961	.5892	.5823	.5755	.5687	.5619	.5552
.6	.5485	.5419	.5353	.5287	.5222	.5157	.5093	.5029	.4965	.4902
.7	.4839	.4777	.4715	.4654	.4593	.4533	.4473	.4413	.4354	.4295
.8	.4237	.4179	.4122	.4065	.4009	.3953	.3898	.3843	.3789	.3735
.9	.3681	.3628	.3576	.3524	.3472	.3421	.3371	.3320	.3271	.3222
.0	.3173	.3125	.3077	.3030	.2983	.2937	.2891	.2846	.2801	.2757
.1	.2713	.2670	.2627	.2585	.2543	.2501	.2460	.2420	.2380	.2340
.2	.2301	.2263	.2225	.2187	.2150	.2113	.2077	.2041	.2005	.1971
.3	.1936	.1902	.1868	.1835	.1802	.1770	.1738	.1707	.1676	.1645
.4	.1615	.1585	.1556	.1527	.1499	.1471	.1443	.1416	.1389	.1362
.5	.1336	.1310	.1285	.1260	.1236	.1211	.1188	.1164	.1141	.1118
.6	.1096	.1074	.1052	.1031	.1010	.0989	.0969	.0949	.0930	.0910
.7	.0891	.0873	.0854	.0836	.0819	.0801	.0784	.0767	.0751	.0735
.8	.0719	.0703	.0688	.0672	.0658	.0643	.0629	.0615	.0601	.0588
.9	.0574	.0561	.0549	.0536	.0524	.0512	.0500	.0488	.0477	.0466
.0	.0455	.0444	.0434	.0424	.0414	.0404	.0394	.0385	.0375	.0366
.1	.0357	.0349	.0340	.0332	.0324	.0316	.0308	.0300	.0293	.0285
.2	.0278	.0271	.0264	.0257	.0251	.0244	.0238	.0232	.0226	.0220
.3	.0214	.0209	.0203	.0198	.0193	.0188	.0183	.0178	.0173	.0168
.4	.0164	.0160	.0155	.0151	.0147	.0143	.0139	.0135	.0131	.0128
.5	.0124	.0121	.0177	.0114	.0111	.0108	.0105	.0102	.00988	.00960
.6	.00932	.00905	.00879	.00854	.00829	.00805	.00781	.00759	.00736	.00715
.7	.00693	.00673	.00653	.00633	.00614	.00596	.00578	.00561	.00544	.00527
.8	.00511	.00495	.00480	.00465	.00451	.00437	.00424	.00410	.00398	.00385
.9	.00373	.00361	.00350	.00339	.00328	.00318	.00308	.00298	.00288	.00279

ev. / or σ	.0	.1	.2	.3	.4	.5	.6	.7	.8	.9
3	.00270	.00194	.00137	$.0^3967$	$.0^3674$	$.0^3465$	$.0^3318$	$.0^3216$	$.0^3145$	$.0^4962$
4	$.0^4633$	$.0^4413$	$.0^4267$	$.0^4171$	$.0^4108$	$.0^5680$	$.0^5422$	$.0^5260$	$.0^5159$	$.0^6958$
5	$.0^6573$	$.0^6340$	$.0^6199$	$.0^6116$	$.0^7666$	$.0^7380$	$.0^7214$	$.0^7120$	$.0^8663$	$.0^8364$
6	$.0^8197$	$.0^8106$	$.0^9565$	$.0^9298$	$.0^9155$	$.0^{10}803$	$.0^{10}411$	$.0^{10}208$	$.0^{10}105$	$.0^{11}520$

Table II. From F.E. Croxton, *Tables of Areas in Two Tails and in One Tail of the Normal Curve*, 1949. Courtesy of Prentice-Hall, Inc.

TABLE III
VALUES OF *t*
FOR GIVEN *df* AND FOR SPECIFIED *p* VALUES
p value

df	.20	.10	.05	.025	.02	.01	.005	.001
1	3.078	6.314	12.706	25.452	31.821	63.657	127.32	636.619
2	1.886	2.920	4.303	6.205	6.965	9.925	14.089	31.598
3	1.638	2.353	3.182	4.176	4.541	5.841	7.453	12.941
4	1.533	2.132	2.776	3.495	3.747	4.604	5.598	8.610
5	1.476	2.015	2.571	3.163	3.365	4.032	4.773	6.859
6	1.440	1.943	2.447	2.969	3.143	3.707	4.317	5.959
7	1.415	1.895	2.365	2.841	2.998	3.499	4.029	5.405
8	1.397	1.860	2.306	2.752	2.896	3.355	3.832	5.041
9	1.383	1.833	2.262	2.685	2.821	3.250	3.690	4.781
10	1.372	1.812	2.228	2.634	2.764	3.169	3.581	4.587
11	1.363	1.796	2.201	2.593	2.718	3.106	3.497	4.437
12	1.356	1.782	2.179	2.560	2.681	3.055	3.428	4.318
13	1.350	1.771	2.160	2.533	2.650	3.012	3.372	4.221
14	1.345	1.761	2.145	2.510	2.624	2.977	3.326	4.140
15	1.341	1.753	2.131	2.490	2.602	2.947	3.286	4.073
16	1.337	1.746	2.120	2.473	2.583	2.921	3.252	4.015
17	1.333	1.740	2.110	2.458	2.567	2.898	3.222	3.965
18	1.330	1.734	2.101	2.445	2.552	2.878	3.197	3.922
19	1.328	1.729	2.093	2.433	2.539	2.861	3.174	3.883
20	1.325	1.725	2.086	2.423	2.528	2.845	3.153	3.850
21	1.323	1.721	2.080	2.414	2.518	2.831	3.135	3.819
22	1.321	1.717	2.074	2.406	2.508	2.819	3.119	3.792
23	1.319	1.714	2.069	2.398	2.500	2.807	3.104	3.767
24	1.318	1.711	2.064	2.391	2.492	2.797	3.090	3.745
25	1.316	1.708	2.060	2.385	2.485	2.787	3.078	3.725
26	1.315	1.706	2.056	2.379	2.479	2.779	3.067	3.707
27	1.314	1.703	2.052	2.373	2.473	2.771	3.056	3.690
28	1.313	1.701	2.048	2.368	2.467	2.763	3.047	3.674
29	1.311	1.699	2.045	2.364	2.462	2.756	3.038	3.659
30	1.310	1.697	2.042	2.360	2.457	2.750	3.030	3.646
40	1.303	1.684	2.021	2.329	2.423	2.704	2.971	3.551
60	1.296	1.671	2.000	2.299	2.390	2.660	2.915	3.460
120	1.289	1.658	1.980	2.270	2.358	2.617	2.860	3.373
∞	1.282	1.645	1.960	2.241	2.326	2.576	2.807	3.291

Table III. From R.A. Fisher, *Statistical Tables for Biological, Agricultural, and Medical Research.* Courtesy of Oliver and Boyd, Ltd., Edinburgh.

TABLE IV
VALUES OF CHI SQUARE
FOR GIVEN *df* AND FOR SPECIFIED *p* VALUES
p value

df	.30	.25	.20	.10	.05	.025	.02	.01	.005	.001
1	1.074	1.323	1.642	2.706	3.841	5.024	5.412	6.635	7.879	10.827
2	2.408	2.773	3.219	4.605	5.991	7.378	7.824	9.210	10.597	13.815
3	3.665	4.108	4.642	6.251	7.815	9.348	9.837	11.345	12.838	16.268
4	4.878	5.385	5.989	7.779	9.488	11.143	11.668	13.277	14.860	18.465
5	6.064	6.626	7.289	9.236	11.070	12.832	13.388	15.086	16.750	20.517
6	7.231	7.841	8.558	10.645	12.592	14.449	15.003	16.812	18.548	22.457
7	8.383	9.037	9.803	12.017	14.067	16.013	16.622	18.475	20.278	24.322
8	9.524	10.219	11.030	13.362	15.507	17.535	18.168	20.090	21.955	26.125
9	10.656	11.389	12.242	14.684	16.919	19.023	19.679	21.666	23.589	27.877
10	11.781	12.549	13.442	15.987	18.307	20.483	21.161	23.209	25.188	29.588
11	12.899	13.701	14.631	17.275	19.675	21.920	22.618	24.725	26.757	31.264
12	14.011	14.845	15.812	18.549	21.026	23.337	24.054	26.217	28.300	32.909
13	15.119	15.984	16.985	19.812	22.362	24.736	25.472	27.688	29.819	34.528
14	16.222	17.117	18.151	21.064	23.685	26.119	26.873	29.141	31.319	36.123
15	17.322	18.245	19.311	22.307	24.996	27.488	28.259	30.578	32.801	37.697
16	18.418	19.369	20.465	23.542	26.296	28.845	29.633	32.000	34.267	39.252
17	19.511	20.489	21.615	24.769	27.587	30.191	30.995	33.409	35.718	40.790
18	20.601	21.605	22.760	25.989	28.869	31.526	32.346	34.805	37.156	42.312
19	21.689	22.718	23.900	27.204	30.144	32.852	33.687	36.191	38.582	43.820
20	22.775	23.828	25.038	28.412	31.410	34.170	35.020	37.566	39.997	45.315
21	23.858	24.935	26.171	29.615	32.671	35.479	36.343	38.932	41.401	46.797
22	24.939	26.039	27.301	30.813	33.924	36.781	37.659	40.289	42.796	48.268
23	26.018	27.141	28.429	32.007	35.172	38.076	38.968	41.638	44.181	49.728
24	27.096	28.241	29.553	33.196	36.415	39.364	40.270	42.980	45.558	51.179
25	28.172	29.339	30.675	34.382	37.652	40.646	41.566	44.314	46.928	52.620
26	29.246	30.434	31.795	35.563	38.885	41.923	42.856	45.642	48.290	54.052
27	30.319	31.528	32.912	36.741	40.113	43.194	44.140	46.963	49.645	55.476
28	31.391	32.620	34.027	37.916	41.337	44.461	45.419	48.278	50.993	56.893
29	32.461	33.711	35.139	39.087	42.557	45.722	46.693	49.588	52.336	58.302
30	33.530	34.800	36.250	40.256	43.773	46.979	47.962	50.892	53.672	59.703

Table IV. From R. A. Fisher, *Statistical Tables for Biological, Agricultural, and Medical Research.* Courtesy of Oliver and Boyd, Ltd., Edinburgh.

TABLE V
VALUES OF *F*
FOR GIVEN *df* (n_1 and n_2) AND FOR SPECIFIED *p* VALUES

n_2	.20	.05	.01	.001	n_2	.20	.05	.01	.001
		$n_1 = 1$					**$n_1 = 6$**		
1	9.47	161.45	4,052.2	405,284	1	14.26	233.99	5,859.0	585,937
2	3.56	18.51	98.50	998.5	2	4.32	19.33	99.33	999.3
3	2.68	10.13	34.12	167.5	3	2.97	8.94	27.91	132.8
4	2.35	7.71	21.20	74.14	4	2.47	6.16	15.21	50.53
5	2.18	6.61	16.26	47.04	5	2.22	4.95	10.67	28.84
6	2.07	5.99	13.74	35.51	6	2.06	4.28	8.47	20.03
8	1.95	5.32	11.26	25.42	8	1.88	3.58	6.37	12.86
12	1.84	4.75	9.33	18.64	12	1.72	3.00	4.82	8.38
24	1.74	4.26	7.82	14.03	24	1.57	2.51	3.67	5.55
∞	1.64	3.84	6.63	10.83	∞	1.43	2.10	2.80	3.74
		$n_1 = 2$					**$n_1 = 8$**		
1	12.00	199.50	4,999.5	500,000	1	14.59	238.88	5,981.6	598,144
2	4.00	19.00	99.00	999.0	2	4.36	19.37	99.37	999.4
3	2.89	9.55	30.82	148.5	3	2.98	8.85	27.49	130.6
4	2.47	6.94	18.00	61.25	4	2.47	6.04	14.80	49.00
5	2.26	5.79	13.27	36.61	5	2.20	4.82	10.29	27.64
6	2.13	5.14	10.92	27.00	6	2.04	4.15	8.10	19.03
8	1.98	4.46	8.65	18.49	8	1.86	3.44	6.03	12.04
12	1.85	3.89	6.93	12.97	12	1.69	2.85	4.50	7.71
24	1.72	3.40	5.61	9.34	24	1.53	2.36	3.36	4.90
∞	1.61	3.00	4.61	6.91	∞	1.38	1.94	2.51	3.27
		$n_1 = 3$					**$n_1 = 12$**		
1	13.06	215.71	5,403.3	540,379	1	14.90	243.91	6,106.3	610,667
2	4.16	19.16	99.17	999.2	2	4.40	19.41	99.42	999.4
3	2.94	9.28	29.46	141.1	3	2.98	8.74	27.05	128.3
4	2.48	6.59	16.69	56.18	4	2.46	5.91	14.37	47.41
5	2.25	5.41	12.06	33.20	5	2.18	4.68	9.89	26.42
6	2.11	4.76	9.78	23.70	6	2.02	4.00	7.72	17.99
8	1.95	4.07	7.59	15.83	8	1.83	3.28	5.67	11.19
12	1.80	3.49	5.95	10.80	12	1.65	2.69	4.16	7.00
24	1.67	3.01	4.72	7.55	24	1.48	2.18	3.03	4.39
∞	1.55	2.60	3.78	5.42	∞	1.32	1.75	2.18	2.74
		$n_1 = 4$					**$n_1 = 24$**		
1	13.73	224.58	5,624.6	562,500	1	15.24	249.05	6,234.6	623,497
2	4.24	19.25	99.25	999.2	2	4.44	19.45	99.46	999.5
3	2.96	9.12	28.71	137.1	3	2.98	8.64	26.60	125.9
4	2.48	6.39	15.98	53.44	4	2.44	5.77	13.93	45.77
5	2.24	5.19	11.39	31.09	5	2.16	4.53	9.47	25.14
6	2.09	4.53	9.15	21.90	6	1.99	3.84	7.31	16.89
8	1.92	3.84	7.01	14.39	8	1.79	3.12	5.28	10.30
12	1.77	3.26	5.41	9.63	12	1.60	2.51	3.78	6.25
24	1.63	2.78	4.22	6.59	24	1.42	1.98	2.66	3.74
∞	1.50	2.37	3.32	4.62	∞	1.23	1.52	1.79	2.13
		$n_1 = 5$					**$n_1 = \infty$**		
1	14.01	230.16	5,763.7	576,405	1	15.58	254.32	6,366.0	636,619
2	4.28	19.30	99.30	999.3	2	4.48	19.50	99.50	999.5
3	2.97	9.01	28.24	134.6	3	2.98	8.53	26.12	123.5
4	2.48	6.26	15.52	51.71	4	2.43	5.63	13.46	44.05
5	2.23	5.05	10.97	29.75	5	2.13	4.36	9.02	23.78
6	2.08	4.39	8.75	20.81	6	1.95	3.67	6.88	15.75
8	1.90	3.69	6.63	13.49	8	1.74	2.93	4.86	9.34
12	1.74	3.11	5.06	8.89	12	1.54	2.30	3.36	5.42
24	1.59	2.62	3.90	5.98	24	1.33	1.73	2.21	2.97
∞	1.46	2.21	3.02	4.10	∞	1.00	1.00	1.00	1.00

Table V. From F.E. Croxton, *Values of F*, 1949. Courtesy of Prentice-Hall, Inc.

APPENDIX II

acupuncture: The insertion of a metal needle into the skin or tissue for the relief of pain or disease

agent: The psi sender in telepathy or in PK

animism: The belief that all objects possess a natural life or vitality or are endowed with indwelling souls

apparition: A visual appearance which suggests the presence of a deceased person or of a living person who is beyond the sensory range of the percipient

apport: A physical object teleported into a closed room or container, suggesting the passage of matter through matter.

archetype: Primordial form of feeling or thought

around-the die technique: Method in which each face of the die is used as the target an equal number of times

A.S.P.R.: American Society for Psychical Research

astral projection: The purported temporary separation of the nonphysical from the physical body; also known as out-of-body experience

astrology: A study that professes to interpret the influence of heavenly bodies on human affairs

augury: Divination by inference based on the outcome of chance events

aura: The multicolored halo said to surround a person, and allegedly discernible by individuals sensitive to such phenomena

automatic writing: The writing of messages without conscious effort by a person awake or in trance

automatism: An act performed without the doer's conscious effort, such as automatic writing

autonomous: Self-governing, independent, subject to its own laws

biofeedback: Confirmatory information returned to an individual concerning his success in regulating one of his physiological functions

bioplasma: Mixture of electrons and photons constituting an energy counterpart of the living body and serving as a means of ESP and PK

blind matching: An ESP card test in which the subject, holding the cards face down, sorts them into five piles attempting to match concealed key cards

call: The subject's guess or cognitive response in trying to identify the target in an ESP test

chi square (χ^2): A sum of quantities, each of which is a deviation squared divided by the expected value; also a sum of the squares of CRs

clairaudience: Auditory hallucination due to ESP

clairvoyance: Mental response to a physical state without the use of sense organs

closed deck: A pack of cards with each symbol represented the same number of times

coefficient of correlation (r): An index of the mutual relationship between two series of measurements

community of sensation: Sensory experience of a hypnotized subject corresponding to sensory stimulation of the hypnotist

control: A personality or spirit believed to actuate the utterances or performances of the medium

control group or series: A set of observations made under identical conditions to those of an experimental group or series, except that, in the control, the process being investigated cannot operate

CR (critical ratio) or score: A measure to determine whether or not the observed deviation is significantly greater than the expected random fluctuation about the average; CR is obtained by dividing the observed deviation by the standard deviation

CR_d (critical ratio of the difference): The observed difference between the average scores of two samples of data divided by the standard deviation of the difference

crosscheck: Comparison of the subject's calls with targets used in some other part of the experiment for which they were not intended.

cross-correspondences: A series of independent communications through two or more mediums, which form a complete and intelligible communication when pieced together

cutaneous vasoconstriction: Contraction of blood vessels in the skin

decline effect: Decrease in the scoring level throughout the experiment or section thereof

degrees of freedom (df): The number of values in a series that are free to vary

déjà vu: (French for "already seen.") A feeling that the experience which one is having has happened before, even though there is reason to believe that it has not previously occurred

dermography: Writing on the skin not produced by external physical means

deviation: The amount an observed number of hits is above or below the mean chance expectation of a run or other unit of trials

df: (See *degrees of freedom*)

diametric: A characteristic of psi to combine into a single act what may seem to require more than one act of psi

differential effect: Significant difference between scoring rates when subjects are participating in an experiment in which two procedural conditions such as two types of targets or two modes of response are compared

direct voice: Direct verbal communication by ostensibly discarnate entities with the living, but without the voice of a medium being used as an intermediary

direct writing: Production of a written message by PK

displacement: ESP responses to targets other than those for which the calls were intended. *Backward displacement* to the target that is one, two, three, etc. places preceding the intended target is designated as $-1, -2, -3$, etc. *Forward displacement* to the target that is one, two, three, etc. places after the intended target is indicated as $+1, +2, +3$, etc.

dissociation: The separation of an idea or desire from the mainstream of consciousness

divination: Use of ESP to discover hidden knowledge or to foretell future events *doppelgänger:* From the German, "double walker"; an apparition or double of a living person

dowsing: Locating underground water or other underground substance, usually by means of a rod or branch which in expert hands is said to exert a pull when over the underground object

dream: A succession of images or ideas present in the mind during sleep

drop-in communicator: Ostensible spirit previously unknown to the medium or to the sitters, but later identified as having lived and whose statements are verified

dualism: Philosophical system which asserts that being consists of both spirit and matter

ectoplasm: A purported fluid-like substance emanating from the body of a psychic and capable of appearing as a materialization

ESP: (See *extrasensory perception*)

ESP cards: Cards, each bearing one of the following five symbols: star, circle, square, cross (plus), and waves (three parallel wavy lines) ; a standard pack has 25 cards

evoked potential: Change in the electrical field of neurons produced by their stimulation

exorcise: To deliver a person from ostensible possession by an evil spirit

experimenter: An individual who designs, conducts, or analyzes the results of an experiment

extrachance: Not due to fortuity alone

extrasensory perception (ESP): Mental response to a state outside the mind of the percipient without the use of sense organs

F ratio: The quotient of two independent variances

fakir: An Oriental ascetic

Faraday cage: Metal chamber or cage designed to prevent the transmission of electromagnetic waves

feedback: Confirmation of the result of an action returned to its instigator

focusing effect: Significantly greater deviations with certain cards in the deck

free-response targets: Targets which are unrestricted in number

FRNM: Foundation for Research on the Nature of Mind

galvanic skin reflex or response (GSR): Decrease in the electrical resistance of the skin in response to a psycho-physiological stimulus

ganzfeld: Homogeneous visual field that may be accomplished by placing halved table tennis balls over the eyes with a diffuse light projected on the ball covers

Geiger counter: Instrument that measures the rate of radioactive decay by the number of blips on the counter

GESP (general extrasensory perception): ESP which could be either telepathy or clairvoyance or both

goat: Term for a nonbeliever in ESP

GSR: (See *galvanic skin reflex*)

hallucination: Any apparently sensory perception that has no objective reality in the field of vision, hearing, etc.

high aim: Psi directed to produce hits

high dice test: A PK technique in which the aim of the subject is to influence a pair of dice to fall with the two upper faces totaling eight or more

hit: Trial in which the response and the target correspond

holism: The belief that the determining factor is the whole and not its constituent parts

hologram: A three-dimensional image formed by wave-interference patterns; the entire image can be reconstructed from any portion of the hologram

hyperesthesia: Unusual acuteness of the senses

hypnagogic: Characteristic of the process of going to sleep

hypnotism: The induction of a mental state by the suggestions and operations of the hypnotist with whom the hypnotized subject remains in rapport, responsive to his suggestions

hysteria: A psychoneurosis characterized by losses of memory or sensation, or by functional paralyses, frequently simulating organic diseases, but probably due to mental causes, as autosuggestion, dissociation, or repressed emotion

impression: An effect produced on the intellect or feelings

induced psi phenomenon: A paranormal occurrence caused intentionally

key cards: The cards against which the subject attempts to match the target cards

Kirlian photography: Corona-discharge photography of an object in the field of a high voltage, high frequency current

levitation: The raising of objects from the floor or the ground through the agency of a psychic using no apparent physical means; sometimes the raising of the psychic himself

linger effect: PK continuing to produce an effect in a particular area after it is no longer consciously evoked

low aim: Psi directed to produce misses

low dice test: A PK technique in which the aim of the subject is to influence a pair of dice to fall with the two upper faces totaling six or less

lucid dream: Dream in which the individual is aware that he is dreaming

magnetometer: An instrument for measuring the intensity and direction of magnetic forces

majority-vote analysis: In the repeated-guessing technique, the determination of the number of targets that were called by the correct symbol more frequently than they were called by any of the incorrect symbols

mandala: An image or symbol used for concentration during meditation

mantra: In meditation, a silent utterance, the constant repetition of which is utilized to concentrate the mind

materialization: The purported appearance of temporary figures of living organisms or parts of them, shaped by an unknown agency possibly out of ectoplasm

MCE (mean chance expectation): The most likely score if only chance is involved

medium: A person susceptible to the agency of purported disembodied spirits to such an extent as to be able to impart knowledge from them or to perform actions impossible without their aid

mesmerism: Hypnotism

miss: Trial in which the response and the target do not correspond

modality of psi: One of the ways in which psi is expressed, e.g. telepathy, clairvoyance, precognition, retrocognition, and psychokinesis

molar: Of a size larger than molecular

monad: An individual unit, psychical or spiritual in nature, but constituting the underlying reality of the physical as well

monism: Belief in one principle of being or ultimate substance

multiple-aspect target: Target with two or more characteristics that must be ascertained in order to identify the target as a whole

multiply determined target: Target involving more than one sense modality

mysticism: Belief in an altered state in which the person's consciousness becomes one with the absolute

negentropy: A measure of the available energy or information in a thermodynamic system

neuroticism: Condition of psychological disorder arising from an unsuccessful attempt to deal with inner conflicts and stressful life situations

nose peeking: Seeing by a blindfolded person through a space between his nose and the blindfold

OBE: (See *out-of-body experience*)

one-tailed test: An estimate of probability when the direction of the deviation, i.e. either above or below mean chance expectation, has been specified in advance

open deck: A pack of cards in which each symbol is not necessarily represented an equal number of times

optional stoppage: Stopping an experiment at a point where the results happen to be favorable by chance alone

oracle: The revelation or utterance supposed to issue from a divinity through a medium, usually a priest or priestess

Ouija board: A device consisting of a board marked with the alphabet and other signs, and a smaller board which glides over it; used for the purpose of obtaining paranormal information

out-of-body experience: A feeling of having left one's physical body

p (probability): The fraction of times in a great number of repetitions that the observed result is expected to be equaled or exceeded

P (probability): The fraction of times that an event is expected to occur by chance alone, e.g. in chance matchings with five targets, $P = 1/5$, or one success in five trials

palmistry: The practice of telling fortunes and interpreting character by the lines and configurations of the palm of the hand

paranoiac: Person with a chronic mental disorder characterized by systematized delusions of persecution or of his own greatness

paranormal (parapsychical, parapsychological): Attributable to psi

paraphysical: Psychokinetic

parapsychology: The branch of science that deals with psi, i.e. extrasensorimotor communication with objects external to the individual's mind

percipient: The psi receiver

phantasm (phantom): Because phantom is generally restricted to visual hallucinations, phantasm is used to signify any hallucinatory sensory impression, whatever sense may happen to be affected

PK: (See *psychokinesis*)

placement PK: A PK technique in which the aim of the subject is to try to influence falling objects to come to rest in a designated area of the throwing surface

planchette: A small board supported by two casters and a vertical pencil, used for purposes of automatic writing

plethysmograph: Instrument for determining variations in the size of an organ or of its light-transmitting characteristics, and hence variations in the amount of blood it contains

poltergeist: From the German, "noisy ghost"; presumably a dissociated living person who unconsciously through PK hurls dishes, breaks objects, causes loud raps, etc.

possession: The complete control, by an ostensible, extraneous spirit-entity, of the body of a living person

precognition: Prediction of future events, the occurrence of which cannot be inferred from present knowledge

preferential matching: A method of scoring responses to free material. A judge ranks the target objects, such as pictures, with respect to their similarity to each response; or he ranks the responses with respect to their similarity to each target object

principle of parsimony: Occam's razor; economy of assumption in reasoning

probability: (See *p* and *P*)

prophet: One who foretells the future; especially, an inspired predictor

proxy sitter: A person who represents the subject at a séance but knows nothing about him

psi: A term to identify an individual's extrasensorimotor communication with objects external to his mind. Psi includes *psi gamma* or ESP, and *psi kappa* or PK. It is used as a noun and as an adjective. It is also the term in quantum mechanics for a state vector or wave function.

psi field: Portion of space possessed by an object through which it acts or is acted upon paranormally

psi hitting: Exercise of psi to correctly call the target

psi masking: The use of psi to cover up evidence of its own manifestation

psi mediation: Causation by psi

psi missing: Exercise of psi ability in a manner which has an effect opposite to the conscious intent

psi trailing: An animal's following an individual into wholly unfamiliar territory under conditions that would not allow the use of a sensory trail

psiology: Parapsychology, psychical research

psychic: An individual possessing particular psi ability; also psychical

psychic ether: Hypothetical substantial medium which propagates thought waves, records impressions of events, and produces corresponding patterns

psychic healer: Individual who effects cures of illness through thought or laying on of hands

psychic photography: The appearance on photographic film of images of objects not normally in view of the camera or of the film

psychic shuffle: Physical shuffling of a deck of cards to put it in an order paranormally corresponding to that of a target deck

psychical: Psychic or paranormal

psychical research: Parapsychology

psychics: Science of mind; also plural of psychic

psychoanalysis: A body of psychological doctrines and therapeutic techniques using free association, dreams, and blunders to reveal unconscious mechanisms and conflicts

psychokinesis (PK): Mental influence on a physical state without the use of motor organs

psychometry: The divination of facts about an object or its owner through contact with or proximity to the object

psychosis: Mental illness in which the patient fails to discriminate between stimuli arising within himself and those received from the external world

QD (quarter distribution): The distribution of hits on the record page (or in a subdivision thereof, such as the set or the half-set) as found in the four equal quarters formed by dividing the selected unit horizontally and vertically

quantum mechanics: A branch of physics concerning the emission or absorption of energy by atoms or molecules, the process taking place by steps, with each step being the emission or absorption of an amount of energy called the quantum

r: (See *coefficient of correlation*)

radiesthesia: Purported physical effect of a distant substance upon a divining apparatus

radionics: Diagnosis or treatment of a patient through radiesthesia with the use of a diagnostic instrument

random order: An order of events which displays no trends or regularities that would allow any inference regarding one event from one or more of the others in the series

reincarnation: The belief that human souls or spirits are reborn in new physical bodies, often many times

reinforcement: Higher displacement score when the backward- and forward-displacement targets have the same symbol

repeated-guessing technique: Summation of repeated attempts to identify the same sequence of targets

restricted-response targets: Targets which are limited in number and are known to the subject, e.g. the five symbols of the ESP deck

retrocognition: ESP of a past event

retro-PK: A future event paranormally affecting a present one

Rorschach test: A psychological test consisting of inkblots of various shapes and colors shown to the subject with the request to interpret them

run: A group of trials, usually the successive calling of a deck of 25 ESP cards or symbols; in PK tests, 24 single die throws regardless of the number of dice thrown at the same time

s: Unbiased estimate of the standard deviation

schizophrenia: A form of mental disorder characterized by disturbances of feeling, thought, and relationship to the outside world

score: The number of hits made in any given unit of trials, usually a run

screened-touch matching: An ESP card-testing technique in which the subject points to one of five key positions, thereby indicating what he thinks the top card is in an inverted pack held by the experimenter behind a screen; the card is then laid by the experimenter opposite that position

scrying: Crystal-ball gazing

séance: A meeting of one or more persons with a medium for the purpose of receiving spirit communications through the sensitive

secondary personality: An additional but subordinate personality resulting from dissociation

sensitive: A psychic percipient

seriality: Postulated universal principle that operates independently from physical causation and brings like things together

series: Several runs or experimental sessions that are grouped in accordance with the stated purpose and design of the experiment

session: A unit of a psi experiment comprising all of the trials of one test occasion

set: A subdivision of the record page serving as a scoring unit for a consecutive group of trials

shaman: A mediumistic priest or medicine man

sheep: Term for a believer in ESP

sigma (σ): See standard deviation

sigma (Σ): The sum of

significance: A numerical result is significant when it equals or surpasses some criterion of degree of chance improbability; the degree of chance improbability commonly used is that of .05

(odds of 20 to 1 against chance)

singularization: Directing psi to the correct one of several possible targets

soothsayer: One who foretells events

spirit: In spiritualism and similar beliefs, a disembodied entity

spirit hypothesis: The theory that individual consciousness survives death and may be communicated with by living persons

spiritualism: Belief that spirits of the dead survive and can hold intercourse with the living by means of physical signals such as rappings or by mediumistic communication

spontaneous psi phenomenon: A paranormal event occurring in the course of daily living

S.P.R.: Society for Psychical Research

stacking effect: Similarity between calls and targets due to psychological preferences when the same sequence of targets is repeatedly used

standard deviation (σ) : Usually the theoretical root mean square of the deviations; it is obtained from the formula $\sqrt{npq}$ in which n is the number of single trials, p the probability of success per trial, and q the probability of failure

stigmata: Marks produced on the bodies of certain individuals corresponding to the wounds received by Christ or other religious figure

subject: The individual who is tested for psi, either as an agent or as a percipient

subliminal: Beneath the ordinary threshold of awareness

super-ESP hypothesis: The theory that ESP by living individuals may be used to produce such complex phenomena as ostensible spirit communication

synchronicity: Occurrence of acausal but meaningful coincidences

t test: A measure to determine whether or not the observed deviation is significantly greater than the expected random fluctuation around the average; unlike the z score, it is based upon the number of subjects tested

target: In ESP tests, the physical or mental event to which the subject is attempting to respond; in PK tests, the physical process or object which the subject tries to influence, such as the terminal position of a rolling die

telekinesis: Older term for paranormal movement of a stationary object

telepathy: Mental response to the mental state of another individual, which is not caused by means of a sense organ

teleportation: The paranormal transportation of a physical object, including the human body, from one place to another

terminal salience: Higher scores at both ends of the experiment or experimental division than in the middle portion

thermistor: An instrument used for measuring temperature by its electrical resistance

trance: Condition of apparent unconsciousness during which the conscious mind rests while the deeper recesses of mental activity are given free rein

traveling clairvoyance: Type of clairvoyance in which a "mental visit" is made to a distant scene, with the returning percipient describing what occurred there; similar to OBE

trial: In ESP tests, a single attempt to identify a target object; in PK tests, a single unit of effect, to be measured in the evaluation of results

two-tailed test: An estimate of probability when the direction of the deviation has not been specified in advance

uncertainty principle: The principle that the velocity and the position of a particle are together determinable only within certain limits

variance: A measure of the dispersal of a group of scores about their mean

veridical: Truthful

witchcraft: The art or practice of a person who professes or is supposed to practice magic, sometimes for evil purposes

xenoglossy: An individual's speaking a real language entirely unknown to him in his ordinary state

yoga: The practice of directing the attention exclusively upon an object such as the supreme spirit, with a view to identification of the consciousness with that object

z score: (See *critical ratio*)

BIBLIOGRAPHY*

Anderson, M.: The relationship between level of ESP scoring and student class grade. *JP*, 23, 1-18, 1959a.

Anderson, M.: A precognition experiment comparing time intervals of a few days and one year. *JP*, 23, 81-89, 1959b.

Anderson, M. & White, R.: A survey of work on ESP and teacher-pupil attitudes. *JP*, 22, 246-268, 1958.

Andrew, K.: Psychokinetic influences on an electromechanical random number generator during evocation of "left-hemispheric" vs. "right-hemispheric" functioning. *RIP 1974*, 58-61, 1975.

Artley, B.: Confirmation of the small-rodent precognition work. *JP*, 38, 238-239, 1974.

Assailly, A.: Some characteristics of mediumship. *Proceedings of Four Conferences of Parapsychological Studies*. New York: Parapsychology Foundation, Inc., 69-71, 1957.

Averill, R.L. & Rhine, J.B.: The effect of alcohol upon performance in PK tests. *JP*, 9, 32-41, 1945.

Backster, C.: Evidence of a primary perception in plant life. *International Journal of Parapsychology*, 10, 329-348, 1968.

Barrett, W.F.: A remarkable premonitory crystal vision. *JSPR*, 21, 157-164, 1923.

Barrett, W.F. & Besterman, T.: *The Divining-rod: An Experimental and Psychological Investigation*. New Hyde Park, N.Y.: University Books, 1968. Orig. publ. by Methuen in 1926.

Barry, J.: General and comparative study of the psychokinetic effect on a fungus culture. *JP*, 32, 237-243, 1968.

Batcheldor, K.J.: Report on a case of table levitation and associated phenomena. *JSPR*, 43, 339-356, 1966.

Bayless, R.: Correspondence. *JASPR*, 53, 34-38, 1959.

Bechterev, V.M.: "Direct influence" of a person upon the behavior of animals. *JP*, 13, 166-176, 1949.

Bell, M.: Francis Bacon: pioneer in parapsychology. *International Journal of Parapsychology*, 6, 199-208, 1964.

---

*The following abbreviations are used: *JP* Journal of Parapsychology, *JSPR* and *PSPR* for *Journal, and Proceedings of the Society for Psychical Research*, *JASPR* and *PASPR* for *Journal and Proceedings of the American Society for Psychical Research*, *RIP* for *Research in Parapsychology*.

Beloff, J.: The place of theory in parapsychology. In *Psychology and Extrasensory Perception,* by Van Over, R. New York: New American Library, 1972.

Beloff, J.: The subliminal and the extrasensory. *Proceedings of an International Conference on Parapsychology and the Sciences.* New York: Parapsychology Foundation, Inc., 102-115, 1974.

Beloff, J. & Regan, T.: The Edinburgh electronic ESP tester (E.E.E.T.). *JSPR,* 45, 7-13, 1969.

Bender, H.: The case of Ilga K.: report of a phenomenon of unusual perception. *JP,* 2, 5-22, 1938.

Bender, H.: An investigation of "poltergeist" occurrences. *Proceedings of the Parapsychological Association.* 5, 31-33, 1968.

Bender, H., Hempel, R., Kury, H., & Wendtland, S.: Der "Geller-effekt"— eine interview und fragebogenuntersuchung, Part I. *Zeitschrift für Parapsychologie und Grenzgebiete der Psychologie,* 17, 219-240, 1975.

Berger, H.: *Psyche.* Jena, Germany: Gustav Fischer, 1940.

Bergson, H.: Presidential address. *PSPR,* 48, 157-175, 1914.

Bernstein, M.: *The Search for Bridey Murphy.* Garden City, N.Y.: Doubleday, 1956.

Bestall, C.M.: An experiment in precognition in the laboratory mouse. *JP,* 26, 269, 1962.

Bleksley, A.E.H.: An experiment on long-distance ESP during sleep. *JP,* 27, 1-15, 1963.

Boirac, E.: *La Psychologie Inconnue.* Paris: Alcan, 1908.

Bozarth, J.D. & Roberts, R.R.: Signifying significant significance. *American Psychologist,* 27, 774-775, 1972.

Braud, W.G.: Allofeedback: immediate feedback for a psychokinetic influence upon another person's physiology. *RIP 1977,* 1978.

Braud, W.G.: Conscious vs. unconscious clairvoyance in the context of an academic examination. *JP,* 39, 277-288, 1975.

Braud, W.G.: Psychokinesis in aggressive and nonaggressive fish with mirror presentation feedback for hits: some preliminary experiments. *JP,* 40, 296-307, 1977.

Braud, L.W. & Braud, W.G.: Further studies of relaxation as a psi-conducive state. *JASPR,* 68, 229-245, 1974.

Braud, W.G. & Braud, L.W.: The psi conducive syndrome: free response GESP performance following evocation of "left-hemispheric" vs. "right-hemispheric" functioning. *RIP 1974,* 17-20, 1975.

Braud, W.G. & Wood, R.: The influence of immediate feedback on free-response CESP performance during ganzfeld stimulation. *JASPR,* 71, 409-428, 1977.

Braud, W.G., Wood, R., & Braud, L.W.: Free-response GESP performance during an experimental hypnagogic state induced by visual and acoustical ganzfeld techniques: a replication and extension. *JASPR*, 69, 105-114, 1975.

Brier, B.M.: PK on a bio-electrical system. *JP*, 33, 187-205, 1969.

Brier, B.: Parapsychological principles from anthropological studies. *Parapsychology Review*, 5, no. 1, 3-8, 1974.

Brier, R., Schmeidler, G., & Savitz, B.: Three experiments in clairvoyant diagnosis with Silva Mind Control graduates. *JASPR*, 69, 263-272, 1975.

Broad, C.D.: *Personal Identity and Survival*. Thirteenth Frederic W. H. Myers Memorial Lecture. London: Society for Psychical Research, 1958.

Broad, C.D., & Price, H.H.: The philosophical implications of precognition. *Aristotelian Society Supplementary*, 16, 1937.

Brookes-Smith, C.: Paranormal electrical conductance. *JSPR*, 48, 73-86, 1975.

Brookes-Smith, C., & Hunt, D.W.: Some experiments in psychokinesis. *JSPR*, 45, 265-280, 1970.

Broughton, R.S.: Possible brain hemisphere laterality effects on ESP performance. *JSPR*, 48, 384-399, 1976.

Brown, S.: *The Heyday of Spiritualism*. New York: Hawthorn, 1970.

Browning, N.L.: *The Psychic World of Peter Hurkos*. New York: Doubleday, 1970.

Buchanan, J.R. *Journal of Man*, 1849.

Burt, C.: *Psychology and Psychical Research*. The 17th Frederic W. H. Myers Memorial Lecture. London: Society for Psychical Research, 1968.

Buzby, D.E.: Subject attitude and score variance in ESP tests. *JP*, 31, 43-50, 1967a.

Buzby, D.E.: Precognition and a test of sensory perception. *JP*, 31, 135-142, 1967b.

Cadoret, R.J.: The reliable application of ESP. *JP*, 19, 203-227, 1955.

Cadoret, R.J.: An exploratory experiment: continuous EEG recording during clairvoyant card tests. *JP*, 28, 226, 1964.

Cadoret, R.J. & Pratt, J.G.: The consistent missing effect in ESP. *JP*, 14, 244-256, 1950.

Cahagnet, L.A.: *The Celestial Telegraph: or, Secrets of the Life to Come Revealed Through Magnetism*. New York: Arno Press, 1976. Orig. publ. London, 1850.

Camp, B.H.: Statement in Notes section. *JP*, 1, 305, 1937.

Carington, W.: The quantitative study of trance personalities. *PSPR*, 43, 319-361, 1935.

Carington, W.: Experiments on the paranormal cognition of drawings. *JP*, 4, 1-129, 1940.

Carington, W.: *Telepathy: An Outline of Its Facts, Theory and Implications*. London: Methuen, 1945.

Carington, W.: *Matter, Mind and Meaning.* Freeport, N.Y.: Books for Libraries, 1970.

Carpenter, C.R. & Phalen, H.R.: An experiment in card guessing. *JP*, 1, 31-43, 1937.

Carpenter, J.C.: An exploratory test of ESP in relation to anxiety proneness. *Parapsychology from Duke to FRNM.* Durham, N.C.: The Parapsychology Press, 1965.

Carpenter, J.C.: Scoring effects within the run. *JP*, 30, 73-83, 1966.

Carpenter, J.C.: Unpublished research. See *JP*, 41, 43-44, 1977.

Carrington, H.: *The Story of Psychic Science.* New York: Ives Washburn, 1931.

Carrington, H.: *The American Séances with Eusapia Palladino.* New York: Garrett/Helix, 1954.

Carrington, H. & Fodor, N.: *Haunted People: Story of the Poltergeist Down the Centuries.* New York: New American Library, 1951.

Casdorph, H.R.: *The Miracles.* Plainfield, N.J.: Logos International, 1976.

Castaneda, C.: *The Teachings of Don Juan: A Yaqui Way of Knowledge.* New York: Simon & Schuster, 1973.

Cavanna, R., & Servadio, E.: *ESP Experiments with LSD 25 and Psilocybin. Parapsychological Monographs,* No. 5, New York: Parapsychology Foundation, Inc., 1964.

Chari, C.T.K.: The challenge of psi: new horizons of scientific research. *JP*, 38, 1-15, 1974.

Charlesworth, E.A.: Psi and the imaginary dream. *RIP 1974,* 85-89, 1975.

Chauvin, R. & Genthon, J.P.: Eine untersuchung über die moglichkeit psychokinetscher expieremente mit uranium und Geiger zähler. *Zeitschrift für Parapsychologie und Grenzgebiete der Psychologie*, 8, 140-147, 1965.

Chew, G.F.: Bootstrap: a scientific idea? *Science,* 161, 762-765, 1968.

Child, I.L. & Kelly, E.F.: ESP with unbalanced decks: a study of the process in an exceptional subject. *JP*, 37, 278-297, 1973.

Coover, J.E.: *Experiments in Psychical Research at Leland Stanford Junior University.* New York: Arno Press, 1975. Orig. publ. Psychical Research Monograph No. 1. Leland Stanford Junior University Publications, 1917.

Cox, W.E.: The effect of PK on the placement of falling objects. *JP*, 15, 40-48, 1951.

Cox, W.E.: A comparison of spheres and cubes in placement PK tests. *JP*, 234-239, 1954.

Cox, W.E.: Precognition: an analysis, II. *JASPR*, 50, 99-109, 1956.

Cox, W.E.: The influence of "applied psi" upon the sex of offspring. *JSPR*, 39, 65-77, 1957.

Cox, W.E.: The PK placement of falling water. *JP*, 26, 266, 1962.

Cox, W.E.: The effect of PK on electromechanical systems. *JP*, 29, 165-175, 1965a.

Cox, W.E.: A cumulative assessment of PK on multiple targets. *JP*, 29, 299-300, 1965b.

Cox, W.E.: A comparison of different densities of dice in a PK task. *JP*, 35, 108-119, 1971.

Cox, W.E.: A scrutiny of Uri Geller. *RIP 1974*, 63-66, 1975.

Craig, J.G.: The effect of contingency on precognition in the rat. *RIP 1972*, 154-156, 1973.

Crawford, W.J.: *The Reality of Psychic Phenomena*. New York: Dutton, 1918.

Criswell, E. & Herzog, L.: Psychic counseling. *Psychic*, 7, no. 6, 43-46, 1977.

Crookes, W.: Presidential address. *PSPR*, 12, 338, 1897.

Dale, L.A., Greene, R.M., Miles, W., Murphy, G., Trefethen, J.M., & Ullman, M.: Dowsing; a field experiment in water divining. *JASPR*, 45, 3-16, 1951.

Dalton, G.R.: Correspondence. *JSPR*, 47, 526-527, 1974.

Dean, D.: The plethysmograph as an indicator of ESP. *JSPR*, 41, 351-352, 1962.

Dean, E.D. & Nash, C.B.: Coincident plethysmograph results under controlled conditions. *JSPR*, 44, 1-13, 1967.

Denton, W. & Denton, E.M.F. *The Soul of Things*. Wellesley, 1863.

Devereux, G.: Trance and orgasm in Euripides: Bakchai. *Proceedings of an International Conference on Parapsychology and Anthropology*. New York: Parapsychology Foundation, Inc., 36-58, 1974.

Dierkens, J.C.: Psychophysiological approach to PK states. *Proceedings of an International Conference on Psi and States of Awareness*. New York: Parapsychology Foundation, Inc., 1978.

Dingwall, E.J.: *Abnormal Hypnotic Phenomena: a Survey of Nineteenth-Century Cases*. New York: Barnes & Noble, 1968.

Dingwall, E.J., Goldney, K.M., & Hall, T.H.: The haunting of Borley Rectory: a critical survey of the evidence. *PSPR*, 51, 1-181, 1956.

Dobbs, H.A.C.: Time and extrasensory perception. *PSPR*, 54, 249-361, 1965.

Dodds, E.R.: Supernormal phenomena in classical antiquity. *PSPR*, 55, 189-237, 1971.

Dodds, E.R.: Gilbert Murray's last experiments. *PSPR*, 55, 371-402, 1972.

Dommeyer, F.C.: An acausal theory of extrasensory perception and psychokinesis. *Proceedings of an International Conference on the Philosophy of Parapsychology*. New York: Parapsychology Foundation, Inc., 85-105, 1977.

Donald, J.A. & Martin, B.: Time-symmetric thermodynamics and causality violation. *European Journal of Parapsychology*, 1, 3, 17-36, 1976.

Duane, T.D. & Behrendt, T.: Extrasensory electroencephalographic induction between identical twins. *Science*, 150, 367, 1965.

Ducasse, C.J.: How the case of The Search for Bridey Murphy stands today. *JASPR*, 54, 3-21, 1960.

Dukhan, H. & Rao, K.R.: Meditation and ESP scoring. *RIP 1972*, 148-151, 1973.

Dunne, J.W.: *An Experiment with Time*. New York: Hillary, 1958. Orig. publ. by Macmillan in 1927.

Dunraven, E.: Experiences in spiritualism with D. D. Home. *PSPR*, 35, 1-288, 1924.

Duplessis, Y.: The Paranormal Perception of Color. *Parapsychological Monographs*, No. 16, New York: Parapsychology Foundation, Inc., 1975.

Duval, P. & Montredon, E.: ESP experiments with mice. *JP*, 32, 153-166, 1968.

Eccles, J.: *The Neurophysiological Basis of Mind*. London: Oxford University Press, 1953.

Eddington, A.: *New Pathways in Science*. New York: Macmillan, 1935.

Ehrenwald, J.: *Telepathy and Medical Psychology*. London: George Allen, 1947.

Ehrenwald, J.: *New Dimensions of Deep Analysis: A Study of Telepathy in Interpersonal Relationships*. New York: Grune & Stratton, 1955.

Ehrenwald, J.: The telepathy hypothesis and schizophrenia. *Journal of the American Academy of Psychoanalysis*, 2, (2), 159-169, 1974.

Ehrenwald, J.: Parapsychology and the seven dragons: a neuropsychiatric model of psi phenomena. *Parapsychology: Its Relation to Physics, Biology, Psychology, and Psychiatry*, edited by G.R. Schmeidler. Metuchen, N.J.: Scarecrow Press, 1976a.

Ehrenwald, J.: Psi phenomena in search of a neural foothold. *ASPR Newsletter*, 2, 13-14, 1976b.

Eilbert, L. & Schmeidler, G.R.: A study of certain psychological factors in relation to ESP performance. *JP*, 14, 53-74, 1950.

Eisenbud, J.: Telepathy and problems of psychoanalysis. *The Psychoanalytic Quarterly*, 15, 32-87, 1946.

Eisenbud, J.: *The World of Ted Serios: "Thoughtographic" Studies of an Extraordinary Mind*. New York: Paperback Library, 1969.

Eisenbud, J.: On Ted Serios' alleged "confession." *JASPR*, 69, 94-96, 1975.

Elgin, D.: Powers of mind: the promise and the threat. *New Realities*, 1, 1, 58-62, 1977.

Elguin, G.H. & Onetto, B.: *Acta psiquiat psicol Amer Lat*, 14, 47, 1968.

Eliade, M.: *Shamanism: Archaic Techniques of Ecstasy*. Princeton, N.J.: Princeton University Press, 1972.

Ellis, E.J.: Listening to the 'Raudive voices.' *JSPR*, 48, 31-42, 1975.

Ellison, A.J.: Some recent researches in psychic perceptivity. *JSPR*, 41, 355-364, 1962.

Estabrooks, G.H.: *Bulletin of the Boston Society for Psychic Research,* 5, 1927,

Evans, C.: Parapsychology—What the questionnaire revealed. *New Scientist,* 209, January 25, 1973.

Eysenck, H.J.: Personality and extrasensory perception. *JSPR,* 44, 55-70, 1967.

Fahler, J.: Exploratory "scaled" PK placement tests with nine college students with and without distance. *JASPR,* 53, 106-113, 1959.

Faraday, M.: Experimental investigation of table-moving. *The Athenaeum,* 801-803, 1853.

Feather, S.R.: A quantitative comparison of memory and psi. *JP,* 31, 93-98, 1967.

Feather, S.R. & Brier, R.: The possible effect of the checker in precognition tests. *JP,* 32, 167-175, 1968.

Feather, S.R. & Rhine, L.E.: PK experiments with same and different targets. *JP,* 33, 213-227, 1969.

Fechner, G.: *Memories of the Last Days of Odic Theory and Its Originator.* Leipzig: Breitkopf und Hartel, 1876.

Feinberg, G.: Precognition—a memory of things future. *Proceedings of an International Conference on Quantum Physics and Parapsychology.* New York: Parapsychology Foundation, Inc., 54-73, 1975.

Ferguson, M.: *The Brain Revolution.* New York: Taplinger, 1973.

Feynman, R.P.: The theory of positrons. *Physical Rev,* 76, 749-759, 1949.

Fielding, E., Baggaly, W.W., & Carrington, H.: Report on a series of sittings with Eusapia Palladino. *PSPR,* 58, 309-569, 1909.

Firsoff, V.A.: *Life, Mind and Galaxies.* Edinburgh & London: Oliver & Boyd, 1967.

Fisk, G.W. & Mitchell, A.M.J.: ESP experiments with clock cards: a new technique with differential scoring. *JSPR,* 37, 1-13, 1953.

Fisk, G.W. & West, D.J.: ESP tests with erotic symbols. *JSPR,* 38, 1-7, 1955.

Fisk, G.W. & West, D.J.: ESP and mood: report of a "mass" experiment. *JSPR,* 38, 320-328, 1956.

FitzHerbert, J.: The nature of hypnosis and paranormal healing. *JSPR,* 46, 1-14, 1971.

Flammarion, C.: *L'iconnu et les Problèmes Psychiques.* Paris, 1900.

Flournoy, T.: *From India to the Planet Mars: A Study of a Case of Somnambulism with Glossolalia.* New Hyde Park, N.Y.: University Books, 1963. Orig. publ. in French in 1900.

Fodor, N.: *Encyclopedia of Psychic Science.* New Hyde Park, N.Y.: University Books, 1966. Orig. publ. by Arthurs Press, 1933.

Forel, A.: *Jour für Psychol und Neurol,* 1918.

Forwald, H.: A continuation of the experiments in placement PK. *JP,* 16, 273-283, 1952.

Forwald, H.: An experimental study suggesting a relationship between psychokinesis and nuclear conditions of matter. *JP*, 23, 97-125, 1959.

Forwald, H.: A PK experiment with die faces as targets. *JP*, 25, 1-12, 1961.

Forwald, H.: Mind, matter, and gravitation. *Parapsychological Monographs*, No. 11. New York: Parapsychology Foundation, Inc., 1969.

Foster, A.A.: Is ESP diametric? *JP*, 4, 325-328, 1940.

Foster, E.B.: Multiple aspect targets in tests of ESP. *JP*, 16, 11-22, 1952.

Franklin, W.: Fracture surface physics indicating teleneural interaction. *New Horizons*, 2, 8-13, 1975.

Freeman, J.B.: Sex differences in ESP response as shown by the Freeman picture-figure test. *JP*, 34, 37-46, 1970.

French, P.J.: *John Dee*. London: Routledge & Kegan Paul, 1972.

Freud, S.: *The Interpretation of Dreams*. New York: Macmillan, 1913.

Freud, S.: Psycho-analytical notes upon an autobiographical account of a case of paranoia (dementia paranoides). *Collected Papers*, 3, 385-470, London: Hogarth, 1925.

Freud, S.: *New Introductory Lectures on Psychoanalysis*. New York: W. W. Norton, 1933.

Fukurai, T.: *Clairvoyance and Thoughtography*. New York: Arno Press, 1975. Orig. publ. London, 1931.

Fuller, J.G.: *Arigo: Surgeon of the Rusty Knife*. New York: Thomas Y. Crowell Co., 1974.

Gaddis, V.H.: *Mysterious Fires and Lights*. New York: David McKay, 1967.

Gatlin, L.L.: Meaningful information creation: an alternative interpretation of the psi phenomenon. *JASPR*, 71, 1-18, 1977.

Gauld, A.: The "super-ESP" hypothesis. *PSPR*, 53, 226-246, 1961.

Gauld, A.: *The Founders of Psychical Research*. New York: Schocken, 1968.

Gay, K., Salter, W. H., Thouless, R.H., Firebrace, R.H., Phillimore, M., & Sitwell, C.: Report on the Oliver Lodge posthumous test. *JSPR*, 121-133, 1955.

Geley, G.: *Clairvoyance and Materialization*. New York: Arno Press, 1975. Orig. publ. New York: George H. Doran, 1927.

Geller, U.: *Uri Geller: My Story*. New York: Praeger, 1975.

Gerber, R. & Schmeidler, G.R.: An investigation of relaxation and of acceptance of the experimental situation as related to ESP scores in maternity patients. *JP*, 21, 47-57, 1957.

Gibson, E.P. & Rhine, J.B.: The PK effect: III. Some introductory series. *JP*, 7, 118-134, 1943.

Giles, R.: A physical analysis of the psychic photography of Ted Serios. *Journal of Research in Psi Phenomena*, 1, no. 2, 56-69, 1977.

Good, I.J.: Quantum mechanics and yoga (In the symposium on Parapsychology and Yoga.) *Research Journal of Philosophy and Social Sciences*,

1, 84-91, 1963.

Goodfellow, L.D.: A psychological interpretation of the results of the Zenith radio experiments. *J Exp Psychol,* 23, 601-632, 1938.

Gorer, G.: *Africa Dances, a Book about West African Negroes.* New York: Knopf, 1935.

Gowan, J.C.: *Trance, Art and Creativity.* Buffalo, N.Y.: Creative Education Foundation, State University College, 1975.

Grad, B.: A telekinetic effect on plant growth. *International Journal of Parapsychology,* 4, 473-498, 1964.

Grad, B.: The "laying on of hands": implications for psychotherapy, gentling, and the placebo effect. *JASPR,* 61, 286-305, 1967.

Grad, B.: The biological effects of the "laying on of hands" on animals and plants: implications for biology. *Parapsychology: Its Relation to Physics, Biology, Psychology, and Psychiatry,* edited by G. R. Schmeidler. Metuchen, N.J.: Scarecrow Press, 1976.

Grad, B., Cadoret, R.J., & Paul, G.I.: An unorthodox method of treatment on wound healing in mice. *International Journal of Parapsychology,* 3, no. 2, 5-24, 1961.

Greeley, A.M.: *Sociology of the Paranormal: A Reconnaissance.* Beverly Hills/London: Sage Publications, 1975.

Green, C.: Out-of-the-body experiences. *Proceedings of the Institute of Psychophysical Research,* 2, 1968.

Green, C. & McCreery, C.: *Apparitions.* London: Hamish Hamilton, 1975.

Greenwood, J.A.: Analysis of a large chance control series of ESP data. *JP,* 2, 138-146, 1938.

Greenwood, J.A.: A preferential matching problem. *Psychometrika,* 8, 185-191, 1943.

Greenwood, J.A. & Stuart, C.E.: Mathematical techniques used in ESP research, *JP,* 1, 206-225, 1937.

Gurney, E., Myers, F.W.H., & Podmore, F.: *Phantasms of the Living.* Gainesville, Fla.: Scholars Facsimiles and Reprints, 1970. Orig. publ. by Trübner for the Society for Psychical Research, 1886.

Guthrie, M.: Further report on experiments in thought transference at Liverpool. *PSPR,* 3, 424-452, 1885.

Halifax-Grof, J.: Hex death. *Parapsychology Review,* 5, no. 5, 10, 1974.

Hall, T.H.: *The Spiritualists: The Story of Florence Cook and William Crookes.* London: Duckworth, 1962.

Hammond, A.L.: A note on telepathic communication. *Proceedings of the Institute of Radio Engineers (IRE),* 40, 605, 1952.

Hansel, C.E.M.: *ESP: A Scientific Evaluation.* New York: Scribner's, 1966.

Haraldsson, E.: Psychokinetic effects on yeast: an exploratory experiment. *RIP 1972,* 20-21, 1973.

Haraldsson, E.: National survey of psychical experiences and attitudes towards the paranormal in Iceland. *RIP 1976*, 182-186, 1977.

Hardy, A.: Telepathy and evolutionary theory. *JSPR*, 35, 225-237, 1950.

Hardy, A.: Anthropology, parapsychology and religion. *Proceedings of an International Conference on Parapsychology and Anthropology.* New York: Parapsychology Foundation, Inc., 136-149, 1974.

Hardy, A., Harvie, R., & Koestler, A.: *The Challenge of Chance.* London: Hutchinson, 1973.

Hare, R.: *Experimental Investigation of the Spirit Manifestations.* New York: Partridge & Brittan, 1855.

Hart, H.: Six theories about apparitions. *PSPR*, 50, 153-239, 1956.

Hart, H. & Hart, E.B.: Visions and apparitions collectively and reciprocally perceived. *PSPR*, 41, 205-249, 1932.

Hartmann, E. von: *Spiritismus.* London, 1885.

Hasted, J.B.: An experimental study of the validity of metal bending phenomena. *JSPR*, 48, 365-383, 1976.

Hasted, J.B., Bohn, D.J., Bastin, E.W., & O'Reagan, B.: Scientists confronting the paranormal. *Nature*, 254, 470-472, 1975.

Haynes, R.: *Philosopher King—the Humanist Pope Benedict XIV.* London: Weidenfeld & Nicolson, 1970.

Herbert, B.: Spring in Leningrad: Kulagina revisited. *Parapsychology Review*, 4, no. 4, 5-10, 1973.

Herbert, B.: The 'Padfield' effect. *Journal of Paraphysics*, 8, 137-150, 1974.

Herzberg, A.: Methods und ergebnisse des Berliner rundfunkversuchs. *Zeitschrift für angewandte Psychologies*, 31, 66-106, 1928.

Hettinger, J.: *The Ultra-Perceptive Faculty.* London: Rider, 1940.

Heymans, G., Brugmans, H.J.F.W., & Weinberg, A.A. Een experimental onderzoek betreffende telepathie. *Meededeelinger der S.P.R.*, no. 1, 3-7, 1921.

Hilton, H., Baer, G., & Rhine, J.B.: A comparison of three sizes of dice in PK tests. *JP*, 7, 172-190, 1943.

Hinton, C.H.: *The Fourth Dimension.* George Allen & Unwin, 1904.

Hodgson, R.: A further record of observations of certain phenomena of trance. *JSPR*, 13, 284-582, 1897.

Hollos, I.: Psychopathologie alltäglicher telepatischer erscheinungen. *Imago*, 19, 1933.

Honorton, C.: Objective determination of information rate in psi tasks with pictorial stimuli. *JASPR*, 69, 353-360, 1975a.

Honorton, C.: Receiver-optimization and information rate in ESP. Symposium at Annual Meeting of the AAAS, New York City, 1975b.

Honorton, C.: Has science developed the competence to confront claims of the paranormal? *RIP 1975*, 199-223, 1976.

Honorton, C. & Barksdale, W.: PK performance with waking suggestions for muscle tension versus relaxation. *JASPR*, 66, 208-214, 1972.

Honorton, C., Davidson, R., & Bindler, P.: Feedback-augmented EEG alpha, shift in subjective state, and ESP card-guessing performance. *JASPR*, 65, 308-323, 1971.

Honorton, C. & Harper, S.: Psi-mediated imagery and ideation in an experimental procedure for regulating perceptual input. *JASPR*, 68, 156-168, 1974.

Honorton, C. & Krippner, S.: Hypnosis and ESP: a review of the experimental literature. *JASPR*, 63, 214-252, 1969.

Honorton, C., Ramsey, M., & Cabibbo, C.: Experimenter effects in extrasensory perception. *JASPR*, 69, 135-150, 1975.

Honorton, C. & Stump, J.P.: A preliminary study of hypnotically-induced clairvoyant dreams. *JASPR*, 63, 175-184, 1969.

Honorton, C., Tierney, L., & Torres, D.: The role of mental imagery in psi-mediation. *JASPR*, 68, 385-394, 1974.

Hope, C., et al.: Report of a series of sittings with Rudi Schneider. *PSPR*, 41, 255-330, 1933.

Horowitz, K.A., Lewis, D.C., & Gasteiger, E.L.: Plant "primary perception": Electrophysiological unresponsiveness to brine shrimp killing. *Science*, 189, 478-480, 1975.

Huby, P.M. & Wilson, C.W.M.: The effects of drugs on ESP ability. *JSPR*, 41, 60-66, 1961.

Humphrey, B.M.: ESP and intelligence. *JP*, 9, 26-31, 1945.

Humphrey, B.M.: Success in ESP as related to forms of response drawings. I. Clairvoyance experiments. *JP*, 10, 78-106, 1946; II. GESP experiments, *JP*, 10, 181-196, 1946.

Humphrey, B.M.: Help-hinder comparison in PK tests. *JP*, 11, 4-13, 1947a.

Humphrey, B.M.: Simultaneous high and low aim in PK tests. *JP*, 11, 160-174, 1947b.

Humphrey, B.M.: Introversion-extraversion ratings in relation to scores in ESP tests. *JP*, 15, 252-262, 1951.

Humphrey, BM. & Nicol, J.F.: The feeling of success in ESP. *JASPR*, 49, 3-37, 1955.

Hyslop, J.H.: *Life after Death*. New York: E. P. Dutton, 1918.

Inyushin, V.M.: The biological plasma of human and animal organisms. *Proceedings of Symposium on Psychotronics*, Prague, 50-53, 1970.

Jaffé, A.: *Apparitions and Precognition*. New Hyde Park, N.Y.: University Books, 1963.

Janet, P.: Deuxième note sur le somneil provoqué à distance et la suggestion mentale pendant l'état somnambulique. *Revue Philosophique de la France et de l'Étranger*, 21 August, 212-224, 1886.

Jephson, I.: Evidence for clairvoyance in card-guessing. *PSPR*, 38, 223-271, 1928.

Johnson, M.: Relationship between dream recall and scoring direction. *JP*, 32, 56-57, 1968.

Johnson, M.: A new technique of testing ESP in a real-life, high-motivational context. *JP*, 37, 210-217, 1973.

Johnson, M. & Nordbeck, B.: Variation in the scoring behavior of a "psychic" subject. *JP*, 36, 122-132, 1972.

Joire, P.: *Traité de L'hypnotisme Experimental et Thérapeutique.* Paris: Vigot, 1908.

Jones, E.: *The Life and Work of Sigmund Freud.* Vol. 3, Chap. 14. New York: Basic Books, 1957.

Jung, C.G.: *Memories, Dreams, Reflections.* New York: Pantheon Books, 1963.

Jung, C.G. & Pauli, W.: *The Interpretation of Nature and the Psyche: Synchronicity; and the Influence of Archetypal Ideas on the Scientific Theories of Kepler.* New York: Pantheon, 1955.

Jürgenson, F.: *Hösterns fran Rymden.* Stockholm: Faxon & Lindstrom, 1964.

Kahn, S.D.: Studies in extra-sensory perception. Experiments utilizing an electronic scoring device. *JASPR*, 25, 1952.

Kanthamani, B.K.: A study of the differential response in language ESP tests. *JP*, 29, 27-34, 1965.

Kanthamani, B.K. & Rao, K.R.: Personality characteristics of ESP subjects: I. Primary personality characteristics and ESP. *JP*, 35, 189-207, 1971.

Kanthamani, H. & Kelly, E.F.: Awareness of success in an exceptional subject. *JP*, 38, 355-382, 1974.

Kanthamani, H. & Rao, H.H.: A study of memory—ESP relationships using linguistic forms. *JP*, 38, 286-300, 1974.

Keil, H.H.J.: "Mini-Geller" PK cases. *RIP 1974*, 69-71, 1975.

Kircher, A.: *The Magnet, or Concerning the Magnetic Art.* Rome, 1641.

Klein, J.: Lalsingh Harribance, medium in residence. *Theta* #31, spring, 1971.

Knight, D.C.: *The ESP Reader.* New York: Grosset & Dunlap, 1969.

Kogan, I.M.: Telepathy, hypotheses and observations. *Radio Eng*, 22, 141, 1967.

Kreitler, H. & Kreitler, S.: Does extrasensory perception affect psychological experiments? *JP*, 36, 1-45, 1972.

Kreitler, H. & Kreitler, S.: Subliminal perception and extrasensory perception. *JP*, 37, 163-188, 1973.

Krippner, S. & Zirinsky, K.: An experiment in dreams, clairvoyance, and telepathy. *A.R.E. Journal*, 6, 12-16, 1971.

Kulagin, I.V.: Nina S. Kulagina. *Journal of Paraphysics*, 5, 54-62, 1971.

Lambert, G.W.: Studies in the automatic writing of Mrs. Verrall. X. Concluding reflections. *JSPR*, 46, 207-222, 1971.

Laubscher, B.J.F.: *Sex, Custom and Psychopathology, A Study of South African Pagan Natives.* New York: R. McBride & Co., 1938.

Litvag, I.: *Singer in the Shadows: The Strange Story of Patience Worth.* New York: Macmillan, 1972.

Lloyd, D.H.: Objective events in the brain correlating with psychic phe-nomena. *New Horizons,* 1, 69-75, 1973.

Lustig, L.K.: Science and superstition: an age of unreason. *1976 Britan-nica Book of the Year,* 270-273. Chicago: Encyclopedia Britannica, Inc., 1976.

McConnell, R.A.: Wishing with dice. *J Exp Psychol,* 4, 245-269, 1955b.

McConnell, R.A.: Remote night tests for PK. *JASPR,* 49, 99-108, 1955a.

McCreery, C.: *Science, Philosophy and ESP.* London: Hamish Hamilton, 1969.

McDougall, W.: *The Group Mind.* Cambridge University Psychological Series, 1920.

McElroy, W.A. & Brown, W.R.K.: Electric shocks for errors in ESP card tests. *JP,* 14, 257-266, 1950.

MacFarland, J.D.: Discrimination shown between experimenters by sub-jects. *JP,* 2, 160-170, 1938.

MacFarland, J.D. & George, R.W.: Extra-sensory perception of normal and distorted symbols. *JP,* 1, 93-101, 1937.

MacKinnon, D.W.: The nature and nurture of creative talent. *Am Psychol,* 17, 1962.

McMahan, E.A.: An experiment in pure telepathy. *JP,* 10, 224-242, 1946.

McMahan, E.A.: A PK experiment under light and dark conditions. *JP,* 11, 46-54, 1947.

Mace, C.A.: Supernormal faculty and the structure of the mind. *PSPR,* 44, 279-302, 1937.

Maddock, D.P.: The parasciences, impact of science on society, UNESCO. *Parapsychology Review,* 6, no. 4, 15-19, 1975.

Maher, M. & Schmeidler, G.R.: Cerebral lateralization in ESP processing. *JASPR,* 71, 261-272, 1977.

Mangan, G.L.: An ESP experiment with dual-aspect targets involving one trial a day. *JP,* 21, 273-283, 1957.

Marino, S. & Benetti, G.: Esperiences psi con una bambina. *Metapsychica,* 31, 11-18, 1976.

Marshall, N.: ESP and memory: a physical theory. *Brit J Phil Sci,* 10, 265-285, 1960.

Matas, F. & Pantas, L.: A PK experiment comparing meditating versus non-meditating subjects. *Proceedings of the Parapsychological Association,* 8, 12-13, 1971.

Mattuck, R.D.: Random fluctuation ("noise") theory of psychokinesis. *RIP 1976,* 191-195, 1977.

Medhurst, R.G.: *Crookes and the Spirit World.* New York: Taplinger, 1972.

Medhurst, R.G. & Scott, C.: A reexamination of C.E.M. Hansel's criticism of the Pratt-Woodruff experiment. *JP,* 38, 163-184, 1974.

Melzack, R. & Wall, P.D.: Pain mechanisms: a new theory. *Science,* 150,

971-978, 1965.

Mercer, S.: Instrumental conditioning in a GESP experiment. *JP*, 31, 83-84, 1967.

Metta, L.: Psychokinesis on lepidopterous larvae. *JP*, 36, 213-221, 1972.

Millar, B.: Correspondence. *JSPR*, 47, 461-464, 1974.

Miller, R.N. & Reinhart, P.B.: Measuring psychic energy. *Psychic*, 46-47, June 1975.

Mishlove, J.: *The Roots of Consciousness*. New York: Random House, 1975.

Mitchell, E.D.: An ESP test from Apollo 14. *JP*, 35, 89-107, 1971.

Mitchell, E.D.: *Psychic Exploration: a Challenge for Science*. New York: G. P. Putnam's Sons, 1974.

Mitchell, J.: A psychic probe of the planet mercury. *Psychic*, 6, no. 2, 16-21, June 1975.

Moody, R.A.: *Life After Life*. Atlanta: Mockingbird Books, 1975.

Morris, R.L.: The use of detectors for out-of-body experiences. *RIP 1973*, 114-116, 1974.

Morton, R.C.: Record of a haunted house. *PSPR*, 8, 311-332, 1892.

Moss, T.: ESP effects in "artists" contrasted with "non-artists." *JP*, 33, 57-69, 1969.

Moss, T. & Gengerelli, J.A.: ESP effects generated by affective states. *JP*, 32, 90-100, 1968.

Mundle, C.W.K.: The experimental evidence for PK and precognition. *PSPR*, 49, 61-78, 1950.

Murphy, G.: Field theory and survival. *JASPR*, 39, 181-209, 1945.

Murphy, G.: Research in creativeness; what can it tell us about extrasensory perception? *JASPR*, 60, 8-22, 1966.

Murphy, G. & Ballou, R.O.: *William James on Psychical Research*. New York: Viking Press, 1960.

Murray, M.A.: *Witch-cult in Western Europe*. New York: Oxford University Press, 1921.

Mùses, C.: Trance states, precognition, and the nature of time. *Journal for the Study of Consciousness*, 5, no. 1, 1972.

Myers, F.W.H.: The subliminal consciousness. *PSPR*, 8, 436-536, 1892; 9, 2-128, 1893.

Myers, F.W.H.: *Human Personality and Its Survival of Bodily Death*. New York: Longmans, Green, 1954. Orig. publ. in 1903.

Nambu, Y.: The confinement of quarks. *Scientific American*, 235, no. 3, 48-60, 1977.

Nash, C.B.: Psychokinesis reconsidered. *JASPR*, 45, 62-68, 1951.

——: Psi and probability theory. *Science, 120*, 581-582, 1954.

——: The PK mechanism. *JSPR*, 38, 8-11, 1955.

——: Correlation between ESP and religious value. *JP*, 22, 204-209, 1958.

——: The Chesebrough-Pond's ESP television contest. *JASPR*, 53, 137-138, 1959.

——: Can precognition occur diametrically? *JP*, 24, 26-32, 1960a.

——: The effect of subject-experimenter attitudes on clairvoyance scores. *JP*, 24, 189-198, 1960b.

——: Retest of high scoring subjects in the Chesebrough-Pond's ESP television contest. *JASPR*, 57, 106-110, 1963a.

——: Physical and metaphysical parapsychology. *JP*, 27, 283-300, 1963b.

——: A television test on ESP. *International Journal of Parapsychology*, 6, 139-142, 1964.

——: Relation between ESP scoring level and the Minnesota Multiphasic Personality Inventory. *JASPR*, 60, 56-62, 1966.

——: Cutaneous perception of color with a head box. *JASPR*, 65, 83-87, 1971.

——: Intersubject effect and experimental autonomy. *JSPR*, 47, 341-342, 1974.

——: Note on precognition of the percipient's calls as an alternative hypothesis to telepathy. *JP*, 39, 21-23, 1975a.

——: Dominant participant effect. *JSPR*, 48, 56-58, 1975b.

——: Two orders of psi-missing, *JSPR*, 48, 125-126, 1975c.

——: Psi and the mind-body problem. *JSPR*, 48, 267-270, 1976a.

——: Group section of target painting. *European Journal of Parapsychology*, 1, 37-49, 1976b.

——: Correspondence. *JSPR*, 49, 563-564, 1977a.

——: Le psi masqué. *Psi*, 1, 1, 101, 1977b.

——: Effect of response bias on psi mediation. *JASPR*, 72, 1978a.

Nash, C.B. & Buzby, D.E.: Extrasensory perception of identical and fraternal twins. *J Hered*, 56, 53-54, 1965.

Nash, C.B. & Nash, C.S.: Checking success and the relationship of personality traits to ESP. *JASPR*, 52, 98-107, 1958.

——: An experiment with targets that differ in degree of similarity. *JASPR*, 55, 73-76, 1961.

——: Negative correlations between the scores of subjects in two contemporaneous ESP experiments. *JASPR*, 56, 80-83, 1962.

——: Comparison of responses to ESP and subliminal targets. *International Journal of Parapsychology*, 5, 293-307, 1963.

——: Relations between ESP scoring level and the personality traits of the Guilford-Zimmerman Temperament Survey. *JASPR*, 61, 64-71, 1967.

Nash, C.B. & Richards, A. Comparison of two distances in PK tests. *JP*, 11, 269-282, 1947.

Nelson, R.: From the Central Premonitions Registry. *Parapsychology Review*, 7, 3, 22-24, 1976.

Nicol, J.F. & Carington, W.W.: Some experiments in willed die-throwing. *PSPR*, 48, 164-175, 1947.

Nicol, J.F. & Humphrey, B.M.: The exploration of ESP and human personality. *JASPR,* 47, 133-178, 1953.

Nielsen, W.: Mental states associated with success in precognition. *JP,* 20, 96-109, 1956.

Novomeidkii, A.S.: The nature of the dermo-optic sense. *International Journal of Parapsychology,* 7, 341-367, 1965.

O'Brien, D.P.: Book review. *JP,* 40, 76-81, 1976.

Ochorowicz, J.: *De la Suggestion Mentale.* Paris, 1887.

Ochorowicz, J.: A new mediumistic phenomenon. *Annals of Psychical Science,* 7, 1909.

O'Donnell, S.: The theory of repressed pre-call: a new approach to personal time. *Parapsychology Review,* 5, no. 3, 5-8, 1974.

Omez, R.: *Psychical Phenomena.* Trans. by Renée Haynes. London: Burns & Oates, 1958.

Orme, J.E.: Precognition and time. *JSPR,* 47, 351-365, 1974.

Ornstein, R.E.: *The Nature of Human Consciousness.* San Francisco: Freeman, 1973.

Osis, K.: Deathbed observations by physicians and nurses. *Parapsychological Monographs,* No. 3, New York: Parapsychology Foundation, Inc., 1961.

Osis, K.: ESP over distance: a survey of experiments published in English. *JASPR,* 59, 22-42, 1965.

Osis, K.: Field research in India. *ASPR Newsletter,* no. 26, 6, 1975.

Osis, K. & Bokert, E.: ESP and changed states of consciousness induced by meditation. *JASPR,* 65, 17-65, 1971.

Osis, K. & Carlson, M.L.: The ESP channel—open or closed? *JASPR,* 66, 310-319, 1972.

Osis, K. & Foster, E.B.: A test of ESP in cats. *JP,* 17, 168-186, 1953.

Osis, K. & Turner, M.E.: Distance and ESP: a transcontinental experiment. *PASPR,* 27, 1-48, 1968.

Osis, K., Turner, M.E., & Carlson, M.L.: ESP over distance: research on the ESP channel. *JASPR,* 65, 245-288, 1971.

Ostrander, S. & Schroeder, L.: *Psychic Discoveries Behind the Iron Curtain.* Englewood Cliffs, N.J.: Prentice-Hall, 1970.

Osty, E.: *Supernormal Faculties in Man: An Experimental Study.* Trans. by Stanley de Brath. London: Methuen, 1923.

Osty, E.: *Une facilité de connaissance supranormale.* Paris, 1926.

Osty, E. *Revue Métapsychique,* 127, 1929.

Osty, E.: *Supernormal Aspects of Energy and Matter.* Frederic W. H. Myers Lecture, London: Society for Psychical Research, 1933.

Owen, A.R.G.: *Can We Explain the Poltergeist?* New York: Garret/Helix, 1964.

——: Generation of an "aura": a new parapsychological phenomenon. *New Horizons,* 1, 9-23, 1972a.

————: A demonstration of voluntary psychokinesis: report of a seminar. *New Horizons*, 1, 25-27, 1972b.

————: The evidence for psychokinesis. *New Horizons*, 1, 196-199, 1975.

Owen, I.M. & Sparrow, M.H.: Generation of paranormal physical phenomena in connection with an imaginary "communicator." *New Horizons*, 1, no. 3, 6-13, 1974.

Pagenstecher, G.: Past events seership: a study in psychometry. *PASPR*, 16, 1-136, 1922.

Palmer, J.: Scoring in ESP tests as a function of belief in ESP. Part I. The sheep-goat effect. *JASPR*, 65, 373-408, 1971.

Palmer, J. & Dennis, M.: A community mail survey of psychic experiences. *RIP 1974*, 130-133, 1975.

Palmer, J., Tart, C.T., & Redington, D.: A large-sample classroom ESP card-guessing experiment. *European Journal of Parapsychology*, 1, no. 3, 40-56, 1976.

Panati, C.: *The Geller Papers: Scientific Observations on the Paranormal Powers of Uri Geller*. Boston: Houghton Miflin, 1976.

Parker, A.: A pilot study of the influence of experimenter expectancy on ESP scores. *RIP 1974*, 42-44, 1975.

Parsons, D.: The black boxes of Mr. George de la Warr. *JSPR*, 41, 12-31, 1961.

Passidomo, L.: PK effects on the course direction of Eurycereus, Lamaellatus, Eurycerine. *New Realities*, 1, 1, 40-44, 1977.

Pehek, J.O., Kyler, H.J., & Faust, D.L.: Image modulation in corona discharge photography. *Science*, 194, 263-269, 1976.

Penwell, L.: Sensitive versus non-sensitive conditions on a general extrasensory perception test. Paper given at fourth annual convention of Southeastern Regional Parapsychological Association, 1977.

Persinger, M.A.: The Paranormal: Part I. *Patterns*. New York: MSS Information Corporation, 1974.

Persinger, M.: ELF waves and ESP. *New Horizons*, 1, 232-235, 1975.

Pfungst, O.: *Clever Hans*. (Ed. by Robert Rosenthal). New York: Holt, Rinehart and Winston, 1965. 1st Am. ed. trans. by C. L. Rahn. New York: Henry Holt, 1911.

Podmore, F.: *Mediums of the 19th Century*. New Hyde Park, N.Y.: University Books, 1963. Orig. publ. under title *Modern Spiritualism*. London: Methuen, 1902.

Pollack, J.H.: *Croiset the Clairvoyant*. Garden City, N.Y.: Doubleday & Co., Inc., 1964.

Pratt, J.G.: Clairvoyant blind matching. *JP*, 1, 10-17, 1937.

————: Trial-by-trial grouping of success and failure in psi tests. *JP*, 11, 254-268, 1947.

————: The meaning of performance curves in ESP and PK test data. *JP*, 13, 9-22, 1949.

———: On the question of control over ESP: the effect of environment on psi performance. *JASPR*, 55, 128-134, 1961.

———: On the Evaluation of Verbal Material in Parapsychology. *Parapsychological Monographs*, No. 10. New York: Parapsychology Foundation, Inc., 1969.

———: A decade of research with a selected ESP subject: an overview and reappraisal of the work with Pavel Stepanek. *PASPR*, 30, 1-78, 1973.

Pratt, J.G. & Birge, W.R.: Appraising verbal test material in parapsychology. *JP*, 12, 236-256, 1948.

Pratt, J.G. & Woodruff, J.L.: Size of stimulus symbols in extra-sensory perception. *JP*, 3, 121-158, 1939.

Price, A.D.: Subject's control of imagery, "agent's" mood, and position effects in a dual-target ESP experiment. *JP*, 37, 298-322, 1973.

Price, G.R.: Science and the supernatural. *Science*, 122, 359-367, 1955.

Price, H.: *Stella C.: An Account of Some Original Experiments in Psychical Research*. London: Hurst & Blackett, 1925.

Price, H.H.: Haunting and the "psychic ether" hypothesis; with some preliminary reflections on the present condition and possible future of psychical research. *PSPR*, 45, 307-343, 1939.

Price, M.M.: A comparison of blind and seeing subjects in ESP tests. *JP*, 2, 273-286, 1938.

Price, M.M. & Rhine, J.B.: The subject-experimenter relation in the PK test. *JP*, 8, 177-186, 1944.

Puharich, A.: Protocommunication. *Parapsychology Today: a Geographic View*. *Proceedings of an International Conference*. New York: Parapsychology Foundation, Inc., 224-249, 1973.

Puthoff, H. & Targ, R.: PK experiments with Uri Geller and Ingo Swann. *RIP 1973*, 125-128, 1974a.

Puthoff, H. & Targ, R.: Psychic research and modern physics. In *Psychic Exploration* by E. M. Mitchell, New York: G. P. Putnam, 1974b.

Puthoff, H. & Targ, R.: Physics, entropy, and psychokinesis. *Proceedings of an International Conference on Quantum Physics and Parapsychology*. New York: Parapsychology Foundation, Inc., 129-150, 1975.

Randall, J.L.: Experiments to detect a psi effect with small animals. *JSPR*, 46, 31-38, 1971.

Rao, K.R.: The preferential effect in ESP. *JP*, 26, 252-259, 1962.

Rao, K.R.: Studies in the preferential effect. II. A language ESP test involving precognition and "intervention." *JP*, 27, 147-160, 1963a.

Rao, K.R.: Studies in the preferential effect. III. The reversal effect in psi preference. *JP*, 27, 242-251, 1963b.

Rao, K.R.: ESP and the manifest anxiety scale. *JP*, 29, 12-18, 1965.

Rao, K.R. & Puri, I.: Subsensory perception (SSP), extrasensory perception (ESP), and meditation, *RIP 1976*, 77-79, 1977.

Raudive, K.: *Breakthrough*. New York: Taplinger, 1971.

Reeves, M.P. & Rhine, J.B.: Exceptional scores in ESP tests and the conditions: I. The case of Lillian. *JP,* 6, 164-173, 1942.

Reeves, M.P. & Rhine, J.B.: The PK effect: the first doubles experiment. *JP,* 9, 42-51, 1945.

Reichbart, R.: Group psi: comments on the recent Toronto PK experiment as recreated in Conjuring Philip. *JASPR,* 71, 201-212, 1977.

Reynolds, C. & Eisendrath, D.B.: An amazing weekend with the amazing Ted Serios. *Popular Photography,* 61, 81-87, 131-140, 158, 1967.

Rhine, J.B.: *Extrasensory Perception.* Boston: Branden, 1964. Orig. publ. by the Boston Society for Psychic Research in 1934.

———: ESP tests with enclosed cards. *JP,* 2, 199-216, 1938.

———: Terminal salience in ESP performance. *JP,* 5, 183-244, 1941.

———: Evidence of precognition in the covariation of salience ratios. *JP,* 6, 111-143, 1942.

———: Dice thrown by cup and machine in PK tests. *JP,* 7, 207-217, 1943.

———: Early PK tests: sevens and low-dice series. *JP,* 9, 106-115, 1945a.

———: Telepathy and clairvoyance reconsidered. *JP,* 9, 176-193, 1945b.

———: Precognition reconsidered. *JP,* 9, 264-277, 1945c.

———: Some exploratory tests in dowsing. *JP,* 14, 278-286, 1950.

———: The problem of psi-missing. *JP,* 16, 90-129, 1952.

———: Location of hidden objects by a man-dog team. *JP,* 35, 18-33, 1971a.

———: The importance of parapsychology to William McDougall. *JP,* 35, 169-188, 1971b.

———: Second report on a case of experimenter fraud. *JP,* 39, 306-325, 1975.

Rhine, J.B. & Feather, S.R.: The study of cases of "psi-trailing" in animals. *JP,* 26, 1-22, 1962.

Rhine, J.B. & Humphrey, B.M.: The PK effect: special evidence from hit patterns: I. Quarter distributions of the page. *JP,* 8, 18-60, 1944.

Rhine, J.B., Humphrey, B.M., & Averill, R.L.: An exploratory experiment on the effect of caffeine upon performance in PK tests. *JP,* 9, 80-91, 1945.

Rhine, J.B. & Pratt, J.G.: A review of the Pearce-Pratt distance series of ESP tests. *JP,* 18, 165-177, 1954.

Rhine, J.B. & Pratt, J.G.: *Parapsychology: Frontier Science of the Mind.* Springfield, Ill.: Thomas, 1962.

Rhine, J.B., Pratt, J.G., Smith, B.M., & Stuart, C.E.: *Extrasensory Perception After Sixty Years: A Critical Appraisal of the Research in Extrasensory Perception.* Boston: Branden, 1966. Orig. publ. New York: Henry Holt, 1940.

Rhine, J.B. & Rhine, L.E.: An investigation of a "mind-reading" horse. *J Abnorm Soc Psychol,* 23, 449-466, 1929.

Rhine, L.E.: Some stimulus variations in extra-sensory perception with child subjects. *JP,* 1, 102-113, 1937.

——: Placement PK tests with three types of objects. *JP*, 15, 132-138, 1951a.

——: Conviction and associated conditions in spontaneous cases. *JP*, 15, 164-191, 1951b.

——: The relation of experience to associated event in spontaneous ESP. *JP*, 17, 187-209, 1953.

——: Frequency of types of experience in spontaneous precognition. *JP*, 18, 93-123, 1954.

——: Precognition and intervention. *JP*, 19, 1-34, 1955.

——: The relationship of agent and percipient in spontaneous telepathy. *JP*, 20, 1-32, 1956a.

——: Hallucinatory psi experiences. I. An introductory survey. *JP*, 20, 233-256, 1956b.

——: Hallucinatory psi experiences. II. The initiative of the percipient in hallucinations of the living, the dying, and the dead. *JP*, 21, 13-46, 1957.

——: Psychological processes in ESP experiences: Part I. Waking experiences. *JP*, 26, 88-111, 1962a. Part II. Dreams. *JP*, 26, 172-199, 1962b.

——: Auditory psi experience: hallucinatory or physical? *JP*, 27, 182-198, 1963.

——: Research methods with spontaneous cases. In *Handbook of Parapsychology*, edited by B.B. Wolman. New York: Van Nostrand Reinhold, 1977.

Richet, C.: Somnambulisme a distance. *Revue Philosophique de la Pays et de l'Étranger*, 21, 199-200, 1886.

Richet, C.: Xénoglossie: l'écriture automatique en langues étrangères. *PSPR*, 19, 162-194, 1905.

Richet, C.: *Thirty Years of Psychical Research: Being a Treatise on Metapsychics*. New York: Arno Press, 1975. Orig. publ. in French in 1922.

Richmond, N.: Two series of PK tests on paramecia. *JSPR*, 36, 577-587, 1952.

Robertson, M.: The wreck of the Titan. *McClure's Magazine*, New York, 1898.

Rogers, D.P.: Negative and positive affect and ESP run-score variance. *JP*, 30, 151-159, 1966.

Rogers, D.P.: An analysis for internal cancellation effects on some low-variance ESP runs. *JP*, 31, 192-197, 1967.

Rogers, D.P. & Carpenter, J.C.: The decline of variance of ESP scores within a testing session. *JP*, 30, 141-150, 1966.

Rogo, D.S.: Psi and psychosis: a review of the experimental evidence. *JP*, 39, 120-128, 1975.

Rogo, D.S.: *The Haunted Universe*. New York: New American Library, 1977.

Roll, W.G.: The psi field. *Proceedings of the Parapsychological Association*,

1, 32-65, 1957-1964.

Roll, W.G.: ESP and memory. *International Journal of Neuropsychiatry*, 2, 505-521, 1966.

Roll, W.G.: *The Poltergeist*. New York: New American Library, Signet Books, 1974.

Roll, W.G.: Experimenting with poltergeists? *European Journal of Parapsychology*, 1, 47-71, 1977.

Romains, J.: *Eye-less Sight: A Study of Extra-retinal Vision and the Paroptic Sense*. Trans. by C. K. Ogden. New York: Putnam, 1924.

Rose, L.: Some aspects of paranormal healing. *JSPR*, 38, 105-120, 1955.

Russell, J.C.: Correspondence. *JP*, 37, 335-336, 1973.

Russell, W. & Rhine, J.B.: A single subject in a variety of ESP test conditions. *JP*, 6, 284-311, 1942.

Ryzl, M.: Training the psi faculty by hypnosis. *JSPR*, 41, 234-251, 1962.

Ryzl, M.: A model of parapsychological communication. *JP*, 30, 18-30, 1966.

Salter, W.H.: *The Society for Psychical Research: an Outline of its History*. London: S.P.R., 1948.

Salter, W.H.: 'An adventure': a note on the evidence. *JSPR*, 35, 178-186, 1950.

Salter, W.H.: F.W.H. Myers' posthumous message. *PSPR*, 52, 1-32, 1958.

Saltmarsh, H.F.: *Foreknowledge*. London: G. Bell, 1938.

Sannwald, G.: Beziehungen zwischen parapsychischen erlebnissen und Persönlichkeitsmerkmalen. *Zeitschrift für Parapsychologie und Grenzgebiete der Psychologie*, 5, 81-119, 1962.

Sargent, C.L.: Cortical arousal and psi: a pharmacological study. *European Journal of Parapsychology*, 1, 72-79, 1977.

Scherer, W.B.: Spontaneity as a factor in ESP. *JP*, 12, 126-147, 1948.

Schmeidler, G.R.: Position effects as psychological phenomena. *JP*, 8, 110-123, 1944.

——: Rorschach variables in relation to ESP scores. *JASPR*, 41, 35-64, 1947.

——: Rorschachs and ESP scores of patients suffering from cerebral concussion. *JP*, 16, 80-89, 1952.

——: Evidence for two kinds of telepathy. *International Journal of Parapsychology*, 3, no. 3, 5-48, 1961.

——: An experiment on precognitive clairvoyance. *JP*, 28, 93-107, 1964.

——: Quantitative investigation of a "haunted house." *JASPR*, 60, 137-149, 1966.

——: ESP breakthroughs: paranormal effects in real life. *JASPR*, 61, 306-326, 1967.

——: Respice, adspice, prospice. *Proceedings of the Parapsychological Association*, 8, 117-145, 1971.

———: PK effects upon continuously recorded temperature. *JASPR*, 67, 325-340, 1973.

———: The relation between psychology and parapsychology. *Parapsychology: Its Relation to Physics, Biology, Psychology, and Psychiatry*, edited by G.R. Schmeidler. Metuchen, N.J.: Scarecrow Press, 1976.

Schmeidler, G.R., & LeShan, L.: An aspect of body image related to ESP scores. *JASPR*, 64, 211-218, 1970.

Schmeidler, G.R. & McConnell, R.A.: *ESP and Personality Patterns*. New Haven: Yale University Press, 1958.

Schmidt, H.: A PK test with electronic equipment. *JP*, 34, 175-181, 1970a.

Schmidt, H.: PK experiments with animals as subjects. *JP*, 34, 255, 1970b.

Schmidt, H.: PK tests with a high-speed random number generator. *JP*, 37, 105-118, 1973.

Schmidt, H.: A new role of the experimenter in science suggested by parapsychology research. *Proceedings of an International Conference on Parapsychology and the Sciences*. New York: Parapsychology Foundation, Inc., 266-280, 1974a.

Schmidt, H.: Comparison of PK action on two different random number generators. *JP*, 38, 47-55, 1974b.

Schmidt, H.: Observation of subconscious PK effects with and without time displacement. *RIP 1974*, 116-121, 1975a.

Schmidt, H.: Toward a mathematical theory of psi. *JASPR*, 69, 301-320, 1975b.

Schouten, S.A.: Psi in mice: positive reinforcement. *JP*, 36, 261-282, 1972.

Schouten, S.A.: Autonomic psychophysiological reactions to sensory and emotive stimuli in a psi experiment. *European Journal of Parapsychology*, 1, 2, 57-71, 1976.

Schreiber, F.R.: *Sybil*. Chicago, Ill.: Henry Regnery Co., 1973.

Schrenck-Notzing, A. von: *Phenomena of Materialization: A Contribution to the Investigation of Mediumistic Teleplastics*. New York: Arno Press, 1975. Orig. publ. London & New York, 1920.

Schwarz, B.E.: Telepathic events in a child between 1 and 3½ years of age. *International Journal of Parapsychology*, 3, no. 4, 5-52, 1961.

Scott, C.: Experimental object-reading; a critical review of the work of Dr. J. Hettinger. *PSPR*, 49, 16-50, 1949.

Scott, C.: A discussion of Dr. Pratt's monogram on the evaluation of verbal material in parapsychology. *JSPR*, 46, 79-90, 1972.

Scott, C., Haskell, P., Goldney, K.M., Mundle, C.W.K., Thouless, R.H., Beloff, J., Pratt, J.G., Barrington, M.R., Stevenson, I., & Smythies, J.R.: The Soal-Goldney experiments with Basil Shackleton: a discussion. *PSPR*, 56, 41-131, 1974.

Sedlak, W.: The electromagnetic nature of life. *Proceedings of the Second International Congress on Psychotronic Research*. Paris: Saison, 1975.

Sergeyev, G.: *Invisible fire. Telepathy, Telegnosis, Dowsing, Psychokinesis.* Prague: Svoboda, 1970.

Shields, E.: Comparison of children's guessing ability (ESP) with personality characteristics. *JP*, 26, 200-210, 1962.

Shields, E.: Severely mentally retarded children's psi ability. *RIP 1975*, 135-139, 1976.

Shields, E. & Mulders, C.: Pleasant versus unpleasant targets on children's ESP tests and their relationship to personality tests. *JP*, 39, 165-166, 1975.

Sidgwick, H.: Report on the Census of Hallucinations. *PSPR*, 10, 25-422, 1894.

Sidgwick, Mrs. H.: On the evidence for clairvoyance. *PSPR*, 7, 30-99, 1891.

Sidgwick, Mrs. H.: An examination of book-tests obtained in sittings with Mrs. Leonard. *PSPR*, 31, 241-400, 1921.

Sinclair, U.: *Mental Radio.* Springfield, Ill.: Thomas, 1962. Orig. publ. by the author in 1930.

Smith, J.: Paranormal effects on enzyme activity. *JP*, 32, 281, 1968.

Soal, S.G.: A report on some communications received through Mrs. Blanche Cooper. *PSPR*, 35, 471-594, 1926.

Soal, S.G. & Bateman, F.: Agents in opposition and conjunction. *JP*, 14, 168-192, 1950.

Soal, S.G. & Bateman, F.: *Modern Experiments in Telepathy.* New Haven: Yale University Press, 1954.

Solfin, G.F. & Roll, W.G.: A case of RSPK with an epileptic agent. *Parapsychology Review*, 7, no. 2, 20-21, 1976.

Solfvin, G.F., Kelly, E.F., & Burdick, D.S.: Some new methods of analysis for preferential-ranking data. *JASPR, 72*, 93-110, 1978.

Spencer Brown, G.: *Probability and Scientific Inference.* New York: Longmans, Green, 1957.

Spinelli, E.: The inverse relation between chronological age and GESP acticity. *RIP 1976*, 122-125, 1977.

Spiransky, S.V.: Telepathy in mice. *International Journal of Paraphysics*, 9, 74-76, 1975.

Stanford, Ray.: Interview. *Psychic*, 7, April 1974.

Stanford, R.G.: A study of the cause of low run-score variance. *JP*, 30, 236-242, 1966.

Stanford, R.G.: Response bias and the correctness of ESP test responses. *JP*, 31, 280-289, 1967.

Stanford, R.G.: "Associative activation of the unconscious" and "visualization" as methods for influencing the PK target. *JASPR*, 63, 338-351, 1969.

Stanford, R.G.: Extrasensory effects upon associative processes in a directed free-response task. *JASPR, 67*, 147-190, 1973.

Stanford, R.G.: An experimentally testable model for spontaneous psi events. I. Extrasensory events.; II. Psychokinetic events. *JASPR*, 68, 34-57; 321-356, 1974.

Stanford, R.G.: The application of learning theory to ESP performance: a review of Dr. C. T. Tart's monograph. *JASPR*, 71, 55-80, 1977a.

Stanford, R.G.: Are parapsychologists paradigmless in psiland? *Proceedings of an International Conference on the Philosophy of Parapsychology.* New York: Parapsychology Foundation, Inc., 1-18, 1977b.

Stanford, R.G.: Conceptual frameworks of contemporary psi research. In *Handbook of Parapsychology*, edited by B.B. Wolman. New York: Van Nostrand Reinhold, 1977c.

Stanford, R. G. & Fox, C.: An effect of release of effort in a psychokinetic task. *RIP 1974*, 61-63, 1975.

Stanford, R.G. & Lovin, C.A.: EEG alpha activity and ESP performance. *JASPR*, 64, 375-384, 1970.

Stanford, R.G. & Stio, A.: A study of associative mediation in psi-mediated instrumental response. *JASPR*, 70, 55-64, 1976.

Steen, D.: Success with complex targets in a PK baseball game. *JP*, 21, 133-146, 1957.

Sterling, T.C.: Publication decisions and their possible effects on inferences drawn from tests of significance—or vice versa. *Journal of the American Statistical Association*, 54, 30-34, 1959.

Stevenson, I.: The evidence for survival from claimed memories of former incarnations, Part I. *JASPR*, 54, 51-71, 1960.

———: Twenty cases suggestive of reincarnation. *PASPR*, 26, 1-362, 1966.

———: Telepathic impressions: a review and report of thirty-five new cases. *PASPR*, 29, 1-198, 1970a.

———: A communicator unknown to medium and sitters. *JASPR*, 64, 53-65, 1970b.

———: Xenoglossy: a review and report of a case. *PASPR*, 31, 1-268, 1974.

Stewart, W.C.: Three new ESP test machines and some preliminary results. *JP*, 23, 44-48, 1959.

Strauch, I.: Medical aspects of "mental" healing. *International Journal of Parapsychology*, 5, 135-165, 1963.

Stuart, C.E.: The effect of rate of movement in card matching tests of extra-sensory perception. *JP*, 2, 172-183, 1938.

Stuart, C.E.: An ESP test with drawings. *JP*, 6, 20-43, 1942.

Stuart, C.E.: GESP experiments with the free response method. *JP*, 10, 21-35, 1946.

Sugrue, T.: *There Is a River.* New York: Holt, Rinehart & Winston, 1943.

Taddonio, J.L.: Attitudes and expectancies in ESP scoring. *JP*, 39, 289-298, 1975.

Tanagras, A.: The theory of psychobolic. *JASPR*, 43, 151-154, 1949.

Targ, R., Cole, P., & Puthoff, H.E.: *Techniques to Enhance Man/Machine Communication.* Stanford, California: Stanford Research Institute, July, 1974.

Targ, R. & Hurt, D.B.: Learning clairvoyance and perception with an extrasensory perception teaching machine. *Parapsychology Review, 3,* no. 4, 9-11, 1972.

Targ, R. & Puthoff, H.: Information transmission under conditions of sensory shielding. *Nature,* 251, 602-607, 1974.

Tart, C.T.: Physiological correlates of psi cognition. *International Journal of Parapsychology,* 5, 375-386, 1963.

——: A second psychophysiological study of out-of-the-body experiences in a gifted subject. *International Journal of Parapsychology,* 9, 251-258, 1967.

——: A psychophysiological study of out-of-the-body experiences in a selected subject. *JASPR,* 62, 3-27, 1968.

——: States of consciousness and state-specific sciences. *Science,* 176, 1203-1210, 1972a.

——: Concerning the scientific study of the human aura. *JSPR,* 46, 1-21, 1972b.

——: Parapsychology. *Science,* 182, 222, 1973.

——: The Application of Learning Theory to ESP Performance. *Parapsychological Monographs,* No. 15. New York: Parapsychology Foundation, Inc., 1975.

——: Space, time and mind. *RIP 1977,* 1978.

Taylor, J.: *Superminds: A Scientist Looks at the Paranormal.* New York: Viking Press, 1975.

Tenhaeff, W.H.C.: Psychoscopic experiments on behalf of the police. *Conference Report* No. 41, First International Conference of Parapsychological Studies, Utrecht, Holland, 1953.

Tenhaeff, W.H.C.: Seat experiments with Gerard Croiset. *Proceedings of the Parapsychological Institute,* State University of Utrecht, 1, 53-65, 1960.

Tenhaeff, W.H.C.: Summary of the results of a psychodiagnostic investigation of forty paragnosts. *Proceedings of the Parapsychological Institute,* State University of Utrecht, 2, 1962.

Tenhaeff, W.H.C.: *Telepathy and Clairvoyance: Views of Some Little Investigated Capabilities of Man.* Springfield, Ill.: Thomas, 1972.

Terry, J.C. & Harris, S.A.: Precognition in water-deprived rats. *RIP 1974,* 81, 1975.

Thomas, C.D.: *Life Beyond Death with Evidence.* London: Collins, 1928.

Thomas, C.D.: A proxy experiment of significant success. *PSPR,* 45, 257-306, 1939.

Thouless, R.H.: Some experiments on PK effects in coin spinning. *JP,* 9, 169-175, 1945.

Thouless, R.H.: A report on an experiment in psycho-kinesis with dice, and a discussion on psychological factors favouring success. *PSPR,* 49, 107-130, 1951.

Thouless, R.H.: *From Anecdote to Experiment in Psychical Research.* London: Routledge and Kegan Paul, 1972.

Thouless, R.H. & Wiesner, B.P.: On the nature of psi phenomena. *JP,* 10, 107-119, 1946.

Thouless, R.H. & Wiesner, B.P.: The psi process in normal and '"paranormal" psychology. *PSPR,* 48, 177-196, 1947.

Thurston, H.: *The Physical Phenomena of Mysticism.* London: Burns & Ostes, 1952.

Thy, M. de: Télépathie et déficience mentale. *Revue Métapsychique,* 2, no. 10, 4, 1959.

Tietze, T.R.: *Margery.* New York: Harper & Row, 1973.

Timm, U.: Mixing-up of symbols in ESP card experiments (so-called consistent missing) as a possible cause for psi-missing. *JP,* 33, 109-124, 1969.

Tischner, R.: *Telepathy and Clairvoyance.* 2d ed. Trans. by W. D. Hutchinson. New York: Harcourt, Brace, 1925.

Toksvig, S.: *Emanuel Swedenborg: Scientist and Mystic.* New Haven: Yale University Press, 1948.

Tornatore, N.V. : The paranormal event and psychotherapy as a psychotherapeutic tool: a survey of 609 psychiatrists. *RIP 1976,* 114-116, 1977.

Troland, L.T.: A Technique for the Experimental Study of Telepathy and other Alleged Clairvoyant Processes. *JP,* 40, 194-216, 1976. Orig. publ. as a monograph, Albany, N.Y., 1917.

Tromp, S.W.: Review of the possible physiological causes of dowsing. *International Journal of Parapsychology,* 10, 363-391, 1968.

Tyrrell, G.N.M.: Further research in extra-sensory preception. *PSPR,* 44, 99-167, 1936.

Tyrrell, G.N.M.: The "modus operandi" of paranormal cognition. *PSPR,* 48, 65-120, 1947.

Tyrrell, G.N.M.: *Apparitions.* London: Duckworth, 1953.

Ullman, M.: PK in the Soviet Union, *RIP 1973,* 121-125, 1974.

Uphoff, W. & Uphoff, M.J.: *New Psychic Frontiers.* Gerrards Cross, Bucks: Colin Smythe, 1975.

Usher, F.L. & Burt, F.P.: Thought transference. *Annals of Psychical Science* (London), 8, 561-600, 1909.

Van de Castle, R.L.: An exploratory study of some personality correlates associated with PK performance. *JASPR, 52,* 134-150, 1958.

Van de Castle, R.L.: Psi abilities in primitive groups. *Proceedings of the Parapsychological Association,* 7, 97-122, 1970.

Van de Castle, R.L.: An investigation of psi abilities among the Cuna Indians of Panama. *Proceedings of an International Conference on Para-*

psychology and Anthropology. New York: Parapsychology Foundation, Inc., 1974.

Van de Castle, R.L.: Sleep and dreams. In *Handbook of Parapsychology*, edited by B. B. Wolman. New York: Van Nostrand Reinhold, 1977.

Vasiliev, L.L.: *Experiments in Distant Influence*. New York: E. P. Dutton & Co., 1976. Orig. pub. as *Experiments in Mental Suggestion*. Church Crookham, Hampshire, England: Institute for the Study of Mental Images, 1963.

Vaughan, A.: Development of the psychic. *Psychic*, 40-46, August 1970.

Vaughan, A.: The phenomena of Uri Geller. *Psychic*, 13-18, June 1973.

Velissaris, C.N. & Velissaris, C.R.: Similar experience-memory factors and psi scoring. *New England Journal of Parapsychology*, 1, 1, 4-18, 1977.

Vogel, M.: Man-plant communication. In *Psychic Exploration* by E. M. Mitchell. New York: G. P. Putnam, 1974.

Vogt, E.Z. & Hyman, R.: *Water Witching U.S.A.* Chicago: University of Chicago Press, 1959.

Walker, E.H.: Foundations of paraphysical and parapsychological phenomena. *Proceedings of an International Conference on Quantum Physics and Parapsychology*. New York: Parapsychology Foundation, Inc., 1-53, 1975.

Wallace, A.R.: *Miracles and Modern Spiritualism*. New York: Arno Press, 1975. Orig. publ. London, 1896.

Wallace, R.K. & Benson, H.: The physiology of meditation. *Scientific American*, 226, 2, 84-90, 1972.

Warcollier, R.: *Experimental Telepathy*. New York: Arno Press, 1975. Orig. publ. by Boston Society for Psychic Research in 1938.

Warcollier, R.: *Mind to Mind*. New York: Creative Age Press, 1948.

Watkins, G.K. & Watkins, A.M.: Possible PK influence on the resuscitation of anesthetized mice. *JP*, 35, 257-272, 1971.

Watkins, G.K. & Watkins, A.M.: Apparent psychokinesis on static objects by a "gifted" subject. *RIP 1973*, 132-134, 1974.

Watson, L.: *The Romeo Error: A Matter of Life and Death*. Garden City, N.Y.: Anchor Press/Doubleday, 1974.

Wells, R. & Watkins, G.K.: Linger effects in several PK experiments. *RIP 1974*, 143-147, 1975.

West, D.J.: *Eleven Lourdes Miracles*. New York: Helix Press, 1957.

West, D.J.: Visionary and hallucinatory experiences: a comparative appraisal. *International Journal of Parapsychology*, 2, no. 1, 89-100, 1960.

West, D.J. & Fisk, G.W.: A dual ESP experiment with clock cards. *JSPR*, 37, 185-197, 1953.

White, R.A.: A comparison of old and new methods of response to targets in ESP experiments. *JASPR*, 58, 21-56, 1964.

White, R.A.: The influence of persons other than the experimenter on the subject's scores in psi experiments. *JASPR,* 70, 133-166, 1976.

White, R.A. & Angstadt, J.: Student preferences in a two classroom GESP experiment with student-agents acting simultaneously. *JASPR,* 57, 32-42, 1963.

Whiteman, J.H.M.: Parapsychology and physics. In *Handbook of Parapsychology,* edited by B.B. Wolman. New York: Van Nostrand Reinhold, 1977.

Whitton, J.L.: Qualitative time-domain analysis of acoustic envelopes of psychokinetic table rappings. *New Horizons,* 2, 20-24, 1975.

Wiesinger, A.: *Occult Phenomena.* London: Burns & Oates, 1957.

Winther, C.: Experimental inquiries into telekinesis. *JASPR,* 22, 1928.

Wolstenholme, G.E. & Millar, E.C.P.: *Extrasensory Perception: A Ciba Foundation Symposium.* New York: Citadel, 1956.

Wood, G.H. & Cadoret, R.J.: Tests of clairvoyance in a man-dog relationship. *JP,* 22, 29-39, 1958.

Woodruff, J.L. & Dale, L.A.: ESP function and the psychogalvanic response. *JASPR,* 46, 62-65, 1952.

Woodruff, J.L. & George, R.W.: Experiments in extrasensory perception. *JP,* 1, 18-30, 1937.

Woolley, V.J.: The broadcasting experiment in mass-telepathy. *PSPR,* 38, 1-9, 1928.

Worrall, A.: *The Gift of Healing.* New York: Harper & Row, 1965.

Zöllner, J.C.F.: *Transcendental Physics.* Boston: Colby & Rich, 1888.

Zorab, G.: Have we to reckon with a special phantom-forming predisposition? *JSPR,* 48, 19-30, 1975.

RECOMMENDED READING*

Books

Thirty Years of Psychical Research: Being a Treatise on Metapsychics, by C. Richet. New York: Arno Press, 1975. Orig. publ. in French in 1922. A summary of Richet's investigations and conclusions on various aspects of psychical research.

Extrasensory Perception, by J.B. Rhine. Boston: Branden, 1964. Orig. publ. by the Boston Society for Psychic Research in 1934. An account of the early ESP experiments at the Duke University Parapsychology Laboratory, including the psychological and physiological conditions favoring success.

Extrasensory Perception After Sixty Years: A Critical Appraisal of the Research in Extrasensory Perception, by J.B. Rhine, J.G. Pratt, B.M. Smith and C.E. Stuart. Boston: Branden, 1966. Orig. publ. New York: Henry Holt, 1940. A survey of the experimental research on ESP from 1882 to 1939, mathematical and experimental methods, and criticisms of the research with a rebuttal to them.

The Reach of the Mind, by J.B. Rhine. New York: Peter Smith, 1972. Orig. publ. by Sloane in 1947. Characteristics of ESP and PK determined by experiments at the Duke University Parapsychology Laboratory and elsewhere.

Modern Experiments in Telepathy, by S.G. Soal and F. Bateman. New Haven: Yale University Press, 1954. An account of the better experimental work in ESP from 1883 to 1953, and of Soal's experimental work with two highscoring ESP subjects.

Hidden Channels of the Mind, by L.E. Rhine. New York: Sloane, 1961. A description of spontaneous psi events.

Challenge of Psychical Research: A Primer of Parapsychology, by G. Murphy, with L.A. Dale. New York: Harper & Row, 1961. A collection of basic source materials on spontaneous cases, quantitative psi investigations, and the survival question.

Experimental Parapsychology: A Review and Interpretation With a Comprehensive Bibliography, by K.R. Rao. Springfield, Ill.: Thomas, 1966. Short, systematic reviews of all psi experiments published from 1940 through 1965, and a critical survey of several theories of psi.

---

*Listed in order of original publication.

From Anecdote to Experiment in Psychical Research, by R.H. Thouless. London and Boston: Routledge & Kegan Paul, 1972. An introduction to experimental parapsychology presenting the methodological advantages and disadvantages of the major approaches to the investigation of psi, and the basics of what has been learned about psi from empirical research.

Psychic Exploration: A Challenge for Science, by E.D. Mitchell and others. Edited by J. White. New York: Putnam, 1974. A large collection of papers on various aspects of parapsychology written for this volume.

Parapsychology: A Century of Inquiry, by D.S. Rogo. New York: Taplinger, 1975. An entertainingly presented and reasonably accurate account of the subject matter of parapsychology.

Handbook of Parapsychology, edited by B.B. Wolman. New York: Van Nostrand Reinhold, 1977. A large collection of papers on various aspects of parapsychology, each specially written for this volume.

Periodicals

Journal and *Proceedings of the Society for Psychical Research.* Society for Psychical Research, 1 Adam & Eve Mews, London, England W8 6UQ.

Journal and *Proceedings of the American Society for Psychical Research.* American Society for Psychical Research, 5 West 73rd St., New York, N.Y. 10023.

Journal of Parapsychology. Parapsychology Press, Box 6847, College Station, Durham, N.C. 27708.

Zeitschrift für Parapsychologie und Grenzgebiete der Psychologie. 78 Freiburg i. Br., Eichalde 12, Germany.

Parapsychology Review. Parapsychology Foundation, 29 West 57th St., New York, N.Y. 10019.

Research in Parapsychology. Scarecrow Press, Inc., 52 Liberty St., Metuchen, N.J. 08840.

New Horizons. New Horizons Research Foundation, P.O. Box 427, Station F, Toronto 5, Ontario, Canada.

European Journal of Parapsychology. Parapsychology Laboratory, University Utrecht, Varkenmarkt 2, Utrecht 2501, The Netherlands.

Psi News. Bulletin of the Parapsychological Association, 214 West 21st St., New York, N.Y. 10011.

PERSON INDEX

A

Agpaoa, Tony, 169
Albicerius, 13
Anderson, M., 90, 103, 105, 119, 250
Andrew, K., 195, 250
Angstadt, J., 119, 120, 277
Arigo, Jose, 169
Aristotle, 11
Artley, B., 142, 250
Assailly, A., 115, 250
Augustine, Saint, 13, 203-204
Averill, A. L., 93, 111, 112, 250, 268

B

Backster, C., 144, 212, 250
Bacon, Francis, 14
Baer, G., 93, 259
Baggaly, W. W., 22, 172, 256
Ballou, R. O., 210, 263
Barksdale, W., 108, 259
Barrett, W., 19-20, 149, 150-151, 250
Barrington, M. R., 271
Barry, J., 142, 168, 250
Bastin, E. W., 259
Batcheldor, K. J., 173, 250
Bateman, F., 27, 42, 44, 91, 98, 99, 103, 120, 181, 186, 188, 197, 272, 279
Bayless, R., 174, 250
Bechterev, W., 140, 250
Behrendt, T., 100, 255
Bell, L., 17
Bell, M., 14, 250
Beloff, J., 46, 187, 196, 251, 271
Bender, H., 25, 148, 171, 177, 251
Benedict XIV, Pope, 13-14, 203
Benetti, G., 185, 262
Benson, H., 97, 276
Beraud, Marthe, 22
Berger, H., 216, 251
Bergson, H., 199, 251
Berkeley, George, 203

Bernstein, M., 163, 251
Bertrand, A., 15-16
Bestall, C. M., 141, 251
Besterman, T., 151, 250
Billott, G. P., 16
Bindler, P., 110, 259
Birchall, J., 20
Birge, W. R., 39, 58, 267
Bleksley, A. E. H., 35, 251
Bloomfield, H., 97
Bohn, D. J., 259
Boirac, E., 148, 251
Bokert, E., 110, 113, 265
Bozarth, J. D., 79, 251
Braud, L. W., 107, 108, 195, 251
Braud, W. G., 64, 107, 108, 142, 184, 185, 195, 251
Brier, B., 252
Brier, B. M., 252
Brier, R. M., 101, 118, 144, 146, 252, 256
Broad, C. D., 205, 222, 252
Brookes-Smith, C., 65, 172, 252
Broughton, R. S., 195, 252
Brown, S. G., 17, 167, 252
Brown, W. R. K., 107, 262
Browning, N. L., 103, 153, 252
Brugmans, H. J. F. W., 259
Buchanan, J. R., 152, 252
Burdick, D. S., 58, 272
Burt, C., 215, 252
Burt, F. P., 26, 275
Buzby, D. E., 100, 105, 113, 252, 264

C

Cabibbo, C., 79, 119, 260
Cadoret, R. J., 89, 109, 140, 143, 151, 168, 188, 252, 258, 277
Caesar, Julius, 12
Cahagnet, L. A., 16, 252
Cain, M. P., 97
Calpurnia, 12

SUBJECT INDEX

A

AAAS (American Association for the Advancement of Science), 3, 31
Acausal theory of psi, 213
Acceptance of psi, 69, 80
Accidents, as origin of psychic ability, 103
 cerebral concussion, 103, 107-108
 train, 183
Activity of subject, 113
Actualization of potentialities, 214
Acupuncture, 146-148
Advanced wave, 221
Age of subject, 102, 177
Agents, 4, 117
 activity of, 82, 135-136, 139
 in conjunction *vs* in opposition, 120-121
 exposure to targets of, 118
 mood of, 119
 motivation of, 120
 multiple, 120-121
 number of, 47
 paranormal effects of, 117
 relationship with subjects of, 118-119, 136
 relaxation of, 120
 split, 120, 196-197
 stimulation of *(see* Stimulation of agent)
Akashic records, 210
Alchemy, 211
Alcohol, 111-112
Allport Study of Values, 110
Alpha waves, 36, 100, 108-109
Altered states of consciousness, 62, 211
 (see also Dreaming, Drugs, Hypnosis, Meditation, Mysticism, Shifts of consciousness, Trance, Transcendental meditation)
American Association for the Advance-

ment of Science (AAAS), 3, 31
American Institute of Mathematical Statistics, 70
American Society for Psychical Research (ASPR), 21, 31
Anesthesia, recovery from, 143-144, 186-187
Animals, psi in, 139-145 *(see also* Birds, Cats, Dogs, Rodents)
 seeing apparitions, 144
Animism, 8
Antimatter, 218-219
Anxiety, 114, 119 *(see also* Neuroticism)
Apparatus, for testing ESP, 26-27 *(see also* Machines, for testing ESP)
 for testing PK, 17-18, 63-66, 171
Apparitions, 16, 40, 129 *(see also* Haunting)
 characteristics of, 130-132
 collectively perceived, 132
 during OBE, 156-157
 near time of death, 130, 132
 of persons before arrival, 129
 seen by animals, 144
 theories of, 132-133, 215-216
Apports, 16, 18, 176
Archetypes, 24, 213
Around-the-die technique, 63, 86
Artists, 104, 113
Astral body, 133
Astral projection, 155
Astrology, 100-101, 150, 211
Attention seeking, 113
Attitude, of subject to experimenter, 105
 of experimenter to subject, 119-120
Augury, 149
Aura, 146-147
Automatic speaking, 25, 154
Automatic writing, 5, 21, 23, 25, 115, 133, 154, 205

289